FX
Option
Performance

FX
Option
Performance

An Analysis of the Value Delivered by FX Options Since the Start of the Market

JESSICA JAMES
JONATHAN FULLWOOD
PETER BILLINGTON

WILEY

Library of Congress Cataloging-in-Publication Data

James, Jessica, 1968–
    FX option performance : an analysis of the value delivered by FX options since the start of the market / Jessica James, Jonathan Fullwood, Peter Billington.
        pages cm. – (The wiley finance series)
    Includes index.
        ISBN 978-1-118-79328-2 (hardback)   1. Options (Finance)   I. Fullwood, Jonathan, 1976–
II. Billington, Peter, 1948–   III. Title.
    HG6024.A3J355 2015
    332.64′53–dc23

                                                                                    2015001988

A catalogue record for this book is available from the British Library.

ISBN 978-1-118-79328-2 (hbk) ISBN 978-1-118-79326-8 (ebk)
ISBN 978-1-118-79327-5 (ebk) ISBN 978-1-118-79325-1 (ebk)

Cover Design: Wiley
Top Image: ©iStock.com/Maxiphoto
Bottom Image: Gears ©iStock.com/Marilyn Nieves
Business Graph: ©iStock.com/kickimages

Certain figures and tables compiled from raw data sourced from Bloomberg

Set in 11/13pt Times by Aptara Inc., New Delhi, India
Printed in Great Britain by TJ International Ltd, Padstow, Cornwall, UK

Contents

About the Authors

Prof Jessica James

Jessica James is a Managing Director and Head of FX Quantitative Solutions at Commerzbank AG in London. She has previously held positions in foreign exchange at Citigroup and Bank One. Before her career in finance, James lectured in physics at Trinity College, Oxford. Her significant publications include the *Handbook of Foreign Exchange*, *Interest Rate Modelling* and *Currency Management*.

Jessica is a Managing Editor for the *Journal of Quantitative Finance*, and is a Visiting Professor both at UCL and at Cass Business School. She is a Fellow of the Institute of Physics and has been a member of their governing body and of their Industry and Business Board.

Dr Jonathan Fullwood

Jonathan Fullwood began his career in finance in 2002 and has since held positions in research, sales and trading at Commerzbank AG in London. He was awarded a CFA charter in 2007 and remains a member of the CFA Institute.

Before his career in finance he graduated with first class honours in physics from the University of Manchester, where he also worked as a mathematics tutor. Jonathan completed his particle physics doctoral thesis in 2001, on work carried out at the Stanford Linear Accelerator Centre.

Peter Billington

Peter Billington is Global Head of FX Exotic Options at UniCredit in London. Since 1993 he has worked in FX option trading roles for Standard Chartered Bank and BNP Paribas and has traded metals for Dresdner Kleinwort Wasserstein. He has also worked at Commerzbank AG in several positions, including that of Global Head of FX Trading.

Prior to his career in finance, Peter read mathematics and then mathematical modelling and numerical analysis at the University of Oxford.

CHAPTER 1

Introduction

1.1 WHY READ THIS BOOK?

Let's be honest, there is no shortage of books·on Foreign Exchange (FX) options. There are plenty of places, online and on paper, where you can read about how to value FX options and associated derivatives. You can learn about the history of the market and how different valuation models work. Regular surveys will inform you about the size and liquidity of this vast market, and who trades it.

This is not what this book is about. This is about what happens to an option once it is bought or sold. It is about whether the owner of an option had cause to be happy with their purchase. It is about whether FX options deliver value to their buyers.

In the financial markets, there is huge and detailed effort made to value contracts accurately at the start of their lives. Some decades ago this work was begun in earnest when Black and Scholes published their famous paper [1]. Perhaps indeed we could say it started in 1900 when Bachelier derived a very similar model [2] though this was not followed up on. But, in general, quantitative researchers in the markets and in universities spend long hours to devise ways of correctly valuing complex contingent deals under sets of assumptions which make the mathematics possible.

But are these assumptions right, i.e. over time, do they turn out to have been correct? Bizarrely, they do not have to have been 'correct' to continue to be used; later in the book we will give some detailed examples of assumptions that turn out to be manifestly incorrect. For an option, we can say that in an efficient ('correctly priced') market, on average, we would expect an option to pay back the money it cost in the first place – less costs, of course.[1] In this book we will use terms like 'mispriced' or 'misvalued' to indicate that the average payoff of the option is significantly different from the average premium paid to own the option.[2]

---

[1] See the Appendix for a discussion on the 'right' price for an option.
[2] It is worth noting that other common uses of these same terms indicate that a technical valuation error has been made, but we are not concerned with that usage here.

That this is not always the case may be surprising. But that options can be systematically 'cheap' or 'expensive' throughout the history of the market, depending on their precise nature, is even more surprising, and should be of significant interest to many different areas of the finance community.

Why is this not widely known? In part it is simply the focus of the market participants. Most trading desks will operate on a daily mark to market P/L with drawdown and stop-loss limits.[3] Another way of putting this is that they will want to make money all or most days, with limited risk. So the timescale and nature of a trading desk dictates that the price of a contract 'now' is the focus of the market. Further, depending on the hedging strategy and how the option is traded, different end results can be seen. So pricing the contract 'now' is in many ways simpler than trying to model an option's performance. Later, we will discuss in detail how a desk manages its portfolio of options to make money, but we may summarise it now by saying that, ideally, deals are done and hedged so that a small but almost riskless profit is locked in almost immediately. After that, the combination of the deal and its offsetting hedges should be almost immune to market movements – so a systematic tendency for deals to be cheap or expensive over time may well not be noticed on a trading desk, as long as they can be hedged at a profit. The situation is complicated by the fact that a perfect hedge is rarely available, combined with the fact that a trading desk may want to have a 'position' – a sensitivity to market movements – when they believe that certain moves are likely to occur.

But the other reason that the long-term mispricing of parts of the FX option markets is not well known is that FX options are a young market! Before one can say that a contract is generally cheap or expensive, one needs to observe it under a variety of circumstances. To say that 12M options bought in 2006, when market confidence was high and volatility low, were cheap because they paid out large sums in 2007, when confidence was greatly shaken and volatilities had begun a very sharp rise, would be to look at a particular case which does not represent the generality of market conditions. It is only really now, with widely available option data available going back to the 1990s, that we can say we have information available for a wide variety of market regimes, and importantly, the transitions between these regimes. We will discuss exactly what data are needed and available in the next chapter, but for now we may say that for most liquid currencies there will be perhaps 20 years of daily data available, with longer time series or higher frequencies available in some cases.

So, we are now in a position to say whether FX options have performed well or badly for their buyers and sellers. We can take a day in the past, collect all the data needed to calculate the cost of the option and look ahead to the payoff of the option at expiry to compare the two. We can tell, on average and for different time periods, whether the options have had the correct price.

If they have not had the correct price – and the fact that there is a book being written on the subject implies that this has been the case at least some of the time! – then the situation becomes much more interesting. Why did the market appear to be inefficient?

---

[3]For a definition of P/L and other terms, please see the Glossary.

Was there a good reason? Is it connected to the way options are used, the way they are hedged, differences in demand and supply? We will show that indeed, in different ways, the payoff and the cost of the options have differed significantly throughout the history of the market, and moreover these differences have been systematic, repeated in different currency pairs and market regimes.[4]

1.2 THIS BOOK

The book is laid out in increasing order of complexity. We give a brief history of the market and describe how options are valued – this will cover simple widely used valuation techniques; it is not our intention to go deeply into the details of exotic option pricing. Then we set the scene by introducing the available dataset and discussing the way that the market operates. We next introduce the first set of comparisons, looking at payoff vs cost or premium for options of different tenors.[5] We then move on to look at different types of option: puts, calls, options which pay out at different levels or strikes, and options on emerging market currencies, which present particular features and may have less data available. Finally we examine whether some of the anomalies we see are predictable and whether it is possible to use some market indicators to buy and sell options in a dynamic fashion to improve the protection they provide or to deliver value.

Perhaps we need to say at this point – before the reader gets too far – that there will be no magical profit-making trading strategy found in these pages. Though the market can consistently show features which seem to indicate that it lacks efficiency, inevitably they are not those which lead to a fast buck and early retirement for those who happen upon them. That is not to say that the information here may not be useful to those looking for trading strategies. At the very least it could prevent them from reinventing the wheel, show them where opportunity may lie and where they may be wasting their time. But the authors confess freely that they have not yet discovered the Holy Grail of risk-free yet profitable trading. And if they do, they may not be publishing it in a book…

1.3 WHAT IS AN FX OPTION?

Before we discuss which market participants can use this information, we should define more precisely what kind of contract we are talking about. Foreign Exchange (FX) options are contracts whose payoff depends upon the values of FX rates, and they are widely used financial instruments.

---

[4]Between the initial cost of an option and the final payout there is of course a continuous series of values of the contract, which converge to the final amount, be that positive or negative. Thus whether an option has been 'cheap' or 'expensive' can become apparent as the option nears expiry.

[5]The tenor of the option is the time between the start ('inception') and payoff date ('expiry').

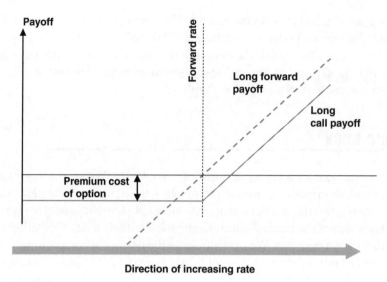

FIGURE 1.1   Payoff profile at expiry for a call option

Let's look at a definition from a popular website...[6]

A foreign-exchange option is a derivative financial instrument that gives the owner the right but not the obligation to exchange money denominated in one currency into another currency at a pre-agreed exchange rate on a specified future date.

The price or cost of this right is called the premium, by analogy with the insurance market, and it is usually (depending on the tenor and the market at the time) a few percent of the insured amount (notional amount). The specified future date is called the expiry or expiry date.[7] The payoff profile at expiry of the simplest type of option is shown schematically in Figure 1.1.

The figure shows the payoff received by the holder of an at-the-money-forward (ATMF) call option on an FX rate. This means that the strike of the option is the forward rate, and the option is the right to buy the base currency, or, in other words, an option to buy the FX rate.[8] In other markets such as commodities and equities it is obvious what the call or put is applied to but in FX more clarity is needed. For instance a call option associated with the currency pair USDJPY could be a call on USD (and thereby a put on JPY) or a call on JPY (and therefore a put on USD). As different currency pairs have different conventions it is always best to clarify the exact details

---

[6]Wikipedia – yes, even real researchers use it. Or for a more formal definition see http://assets.isda.org/media/e0f39375/1215b0eb.pdf/.
[7]The markets delight in detail; the expiry date will define the payoff of the option but settlement, when cash is transferred, will occur a day or so later, depending on the currency pair.
[8]It is worth noting that while we choose to refer to the two currencies in an FX quotation as base and quote, other alternatives are common. We discuss some of these alternatives and FX market conventions in general in the Appendix.

before trading. A put option would be the right to sell the base currency, or FX rate. We will discuss forward rates and their relationship with options more completely in later chapters but in essence the forward rate is the current FX rate adjusted for interest rate effects. If the interest rates for the period of the option were identical in both currencies involved in the FX rate, then the forward rate would be identical to today's FX rate. Because they usually are not the same, the rate which one may lock in an exchange without risk for a future date will be somewhat different from today's rate.

The figure shows the premium cost of the option. At all FX rates at expiry which are less than the forward rate, this will be what the option holder loses, meaning that he or she paid a premium to buy the option and will make no money from it. The net result is the loss of the premium. At the forward rate, the payoff begins to rise, at first reducing the overall cost and then taking the owner of the option into profitable territory for higher FX rates at expiry. We have also shown the payoff from a forward contract, which is simply when the owner of the contract locks in the forward rate at the expiry date. This will lose money when the rate at expiry is less than the forward, and make money when the rate is higher. The forward rate is costless to lock in other than bid-offer costs.

The essential thing to grasp about the payoff to an option contract is that it is asymmetric. There is limited loss (the owner of the option can only lose the premium) but in theory unlimited gain. Conversely, the seller of the option stands to make a limited gain but an unlimited loss. Thus the option payoff looks very much like that of an insurance contract: we expect to pay a fixed premium to cover a variety of different loss types, up to and including very large losses indeed.

The difference between FX options and the more familiar types of insurance such as for a house or car is that, with the latter, we are pretty sure that we are paying more than we really need to. After all, in addition to covering losses, the insurance companies are paying their staff salaries, taxes and business costs. With FX options, we would anticipate that the bid-offer costs or trading activity cover the desk and business costs as a market-making desk makes money from buying and selling options, unlike an insurance company, which can only sell. We would expect the premium to add relatively little to the costs of the option; that the average cost of an option is close to the average payoff for the same option. If it is not (and in many cases we can show that it is not, at least on a historical basis) then there will be a number of interested parties. See the Appendix for more detail on what an option 'should' cost.

1.4 MARKET PARTICIPANTS

This information has potential to be of use to a wide variety of market participants. One way of looking at it would be to think of option suppliers (sellers of risk) and option consumers (buyers of risk). The former might be balance sheet holders who can sell a 'covered option' – essentially, if they hold the underlying currency, they can make money by selling an option which pays out if the currency rises but not if it falls. If it rises, their holdings will increase in value so they can pay the option holder.

If it falls, they do not have to pay but they collect the premium. The option consumers have unwanted currency risk they need to reduce, like an investor with an international portfolio of bonds, or a corporation selling goods in another country. Additional to option suppliers, there are market makers like the option desks of larger banks, which both buy and sell options to make a profit from the bid-offer spread. Also there are purely profit-focused entities, like hedge funds, which take views on direction or inefficiencies in the market to make money. Finally the world's central banks can direct massive FX flow, sometimes using options, to execute policy aims like currency strength or weakness. And each of these has properties of the others; a portfolio manager may wish to protect against currency risk but derive some return, and even a central bank may maintain a trading arm to smooth volatility and influence currency levels.

The accounting and regulatory bodies additionally maintain a strong interest in the use of FX options, and could be interested to learn that in some circumstances simple options can be more useful than forward contracts. Thus a wide range of market participants from central banks to hedge funds, investment banks to insurance companies, corporations to pension funds could find much of interest in the data we present.

Perhaps the most useful division of FX option traders is into two broad categories: those who wish to protect against losses due to foreign exchange movements, and those who wish to make money from those same movements. We can call them the hedgers and the investors, while understanding that most trading entities contain both types to some extent.

1.4.1 How Hedgers Can Use This Information

A good example of a hedger would be a European corporate which sells cars to the United States (US). Assuming they have no manufacturing capacity in the US, then their expenses are largely in EUR while a large part of their income will be in USD.[9] If the value of the USD falls relative to that of the EUR, their income will drop but their expenses will remain fixed. Thus they would possibly like to insure themselves against this eventuality.

Such insurance will naturally be temporary in nature; one could insure for a period, but eventually it will expire and the company will be left with the new exchange rate to deal with. But what can be covered are sudden price jumps over the period, so that at the end of the year (if the period is a year) the company can take stock and plan the following year with some confidence.

So it will be useful to be able to protect against sudden damaging drops in the value of the USD. But it would be good for the company if sudden rises in the value of the USD, which would be beneficial, could nevertheless be taken advantage of. These two facts are important to the company's decision of whether to hedge the risk.

Clearly an option, with its asymmetric payoff, will be of interest in this situation. If the company could be reasonably confident that the option offered good value for

---

[9]When referring to currencies we will use the three-letter ISO codes, so EUR for the euro and USD for the US dollar. A table is given in the Appendix.

money, then it would be the obvious choice. However, in general, the company will simply not know whether the option is good value. It is often assumed that because options are more complex than forward hedges they must be much more expensive. So if we can show that under some circumstances options have historically not been expensive, the corporates which currently avoid them would be interested to take another look.

Of course payoff is not the only factor to consider when choosing a hedge strategy. A forward hedge will reduce overall volatility, as it is in some ways simply the opposite exposure to the hedged quantity. So if this is important, the forward rate will have an advantage.

Additionally, for a hedger the evolution of the underlying is critical. Many corporate hedgers already effectively have an FX position – our European car manufacturer mentioned above might buy a protective option and never need it, with the money spent on the premium being lost. But, if the USD has appreciated several percent in the period, they will have made money overall. Conversely, a sophisticated hedge programme might sell a few short dated call options on the EURUSD rate, reasoning that if it moves in their favour (decreasing rate in this example) then they will make money and can cover the option payoffs. Their reasoning may be that if the rate moves mildly against them then they will pick up some mitigating profit from the option premiums – but this will not help them much if the rate move is large.

Finally, accounting and tax treatments will play significant roles in the choice of hedge strategy and tend to favour forward contracts. Perhaps if the historical behaviour of options were more widely known it might have an effect in these very different circles.

1.4.2 How Investors Can Use This Information

The word 'investors' covers a wide variety of market participants; we list a few below:

- Insurance companies
- Hedge funds
- Pension funds
- Mutual funds
- High Net Worth individuals.

The investors will want to make money. They are motivated to use money to make more of it. Thus they will buy an option if they have reason to believe that the payoff will be larger than the premium, and sell it if the opposite is the case.

Short[10] dated option selling uses the fact that, in some markets, the investor believes that the premium is too large given the risks in the market (more of this

---

[10]Short dated contracts in FX usually refer to anything up to 3M tenor. Long dated would be 1–5 years.

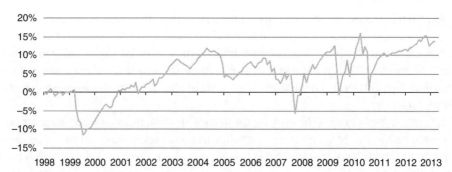

FIGURE 1.2   Cumulative returns in percent of notional to a 1W short put strategy in EURCHF

later…). A truly classic example of this would be in the aftermath of a high risk period. Shortly after the market shock caused by the Lehman bankruptcy in the autumn of 2008, FX option volatilities remained very high for some months. They were implying that markets in the future would be choppy and very active. Essentially, they were reflecting the views of nervous and shaken market participants that the market was in a state of high risk. In fact, the months following the 2008 crisis were consistently less volatile than implied by the option volatilities; selling options would have been very profitable. In Figure 1.2 we show the cumulative result of selling one-week EURCHF options each week between 1998–2013. We chose EURCHF as an example here to include a currency pair which had periods of very low and very high volatility. It is easily seen that the investor who correctly judged when the market was overestimating the future risks would have made strong returns – but it would have taken nerves of steel. A misjudgement could have seen sharp losses, which would have been almost impossible to avoid as liquidity was at times non-existent during this period.

Anecdotally, many hedge funds do make money by selling volatility in this way. ATMF options might not be the contracts of choice; they are liquid and have relatively large premiums, but the investor might want to collect a larger premium with a more complex structure, or might want to make a payoff less likely by choosing an out-of-the-money option – see Chapters 5 and 6 on these. But the principle is the same: selling volatility makes money when the market overestimates future risk. However, this route to profit is paved with disasters. Many a hedge fund has seen literally years of steadily accrued profits evaporate in a day or two of crisis-driven market action. We see this in Figure 1.2; though the option selling strategy ends up in profit, the losses or drawdowns can be huge and sudden.[11] The data set finishes in 2013, but one can imagine the effect of 2015 events when the currency peg was removed by the central bank.

---

[11]It is worth a quick note on returns and leverage. The graph gives returns in percent of notional amount. However, this is not the same as capital invested, as no more than a few percent of the notional amount is ever needed or risked. So to make a comparison with this and an equity investment, it is common to specify capital 'at risk', which, looking at the graph, might be considered to be 20–30% of the notional amount. Thus the returns would be multiplied by a factor between 5 and 3 in this case.

The other way that investors in general trade option markets is to buy options which they believe are undervalued – the idea behind Naseem Taleb's famous 'Black Swan' fund [3]. This type of strategy seeks out markets where risks seem to be underestimated and buys options which will pay out handsomely if this is true. Consider a longer dated option, say for 12M, bought in the spring of 2008 on USDJPY. The investor might have reasoned that problems surfacing in the US housing market would sooner or later cause a sharp depreciation of the USD – and they would have been right. Buying an option with a longer tenor allowed them to make money even though they were uncertain of the precise timescale.

So clearly there is much of interest in systematic differences between premium and payoff for the investor community. However, we said that there is no magical formula for trading strategies within these pages. Why not?

Once one considers how trading strategies would be executed, it becomes possible to understand how inefficiencies are not necessarily pots of gold at the end of financial rainbows. Imagine we identified a strategy which said that selling options of a certain type could result over time in a profit. We know, however, that sold options have unlimited loss potential, so even if the result after a few years was likely to be profitable, the risks in between could be enormous. The investor might have to tolerate a loss of 20% in one year to average a 5% return over several. That's not a very good risk/reward ratio on your investment. Or perhaps one might identify an opportunity to buy options and make money. In this case the risks would at least be limited, but what if the options were long term and only made money near the end of their lives? The investor would have to fund a loss for some time before it was likely he would see profit. Given that the strategies would only be expected to make money over a number of years, with profit and loss in between, there would always be a risk that in any one year they would be unlucky. In short, while we hope this book will inform investors about likely areas for further investigation, as we said before, there is no magical recipe within these pages.

Finally, investors often buy overseas assets which have good return potential. In this case they may wish only to have exposure to the asset itself, and not to accept the FX risk. In this case they turn back into hedgers and may find utility in this book as previously discussed.

1.5 HISTORY AND SIZE OF THE FX OPTION MARKET

During the mid-1980s a confluence of events gave birth to the FX option market as we know it today, namely: a demand for the product, the ability to price the product, a market place to trade and, with the advent of computer power, the ability to manage risk.

To have an option market, first it is necessary to have a liquid market in the underlying rate (usually called just the underlying) upon which the options are based. Before the 1970s, when exchange rates were in general fixed to specific values and adjusted at intervals, there was no possibility of an option in the market. But as different countries gradually abandoned the increasingly unworkable fixed FX rate regime which had been implemented after the post-war Bretton–Woods agreement, risk appeared, and the first to take note and act upon this risk were the corporations of the world. As has been described earlier, companies with income and liabilities in other countries are highly sensitive to exchange rate fluctuations and seek ways to minimise them. Corporate treasurers initially used forward FX contracts to lock in rates but then realised they could sell them if the contracts entered very negative territory, assuming a trending market, and replace them if they became close to positive once more. This crudely replicates the protective properties of an option, though it was a cumbersome and imprecise process. The idea of a product where another company took over this adjustment process was attractive. The very early currency overlay companies did exactly this, calling it option replication. As the markets started to swing wildly during the 1980s the demand for this increased. True options in FX began to be bought and sold, though the correct price for an option was hotly debated.

Equity option traders began to use the Black-Scholes-Merton model shortly after its publication in 1973 [1] but there was at that time little thought of using it for FX contracts. In 1983 Garman and Kohlhagen published the extension to the Black-Scholes-Merton model which enabled FX options to be clearly and simply valued for the first time, as it included dual interest rates [4].

With the demand for the product, and the ability to price it, came the distribution. The first FX option was dealt on the Philadelphia Stock Exchange in November 1982 [5]. At that time they were a small futures exchange who courageously introduced the new instrument when there was no OTC[12] market at all, and virtually no other instruments available to use as pricing references. These options, consistent with similar equity products at the time, were, American-style, exercisable by the option purchaser any time up to expiry, which would have made them even more challenging to value. But clearly they showed promise; by the mid-1980s the exchange in Chicago was also actively trading contracts on FX options, and the number of boutique option houses grew.

However, the growth didn't stop there. The contracts offered on the exchanges were well defined in terms of contract size, a list of available strikes and set maturity dates offered throughout the year. But this was too limiting for most FX users, who wanted to tailor-make the option to match their exact risk profile, and to have the ability to combine options in different strategies. Hence, the OTC market was born. Investment banks bought boutique option houses for their knowledge and with the increased access to corporate hedging activity option trade flow increased tremendously. Since 1995 the Bank of International Settlements has conducted a survey every three years to ascertain the size and nature of the FX market [6]. It breaks down flow by currency pair and contract type, among other ways. The data show

---

[12]OTC means Over The Counter, a reference to a liquid secondary market where many market users are willing to trade with each other off-exchange. Because the trades are bilateral, contracts are not limited to standard formats as is the case for exchange-traded products.

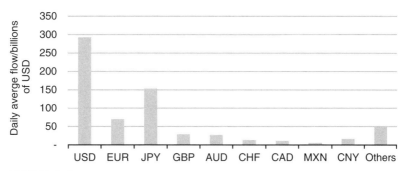

FIGURE 1.3 Daily FX option flow (notional) from 2013 BIS triennial survey

an apparently inexorable rise in daily average traded amounts for FX options over time, with a daily average flow of 337 billion USD in 2013, up from 21 billion USD in 1995.

In Figure 1.3 we show the 2013 results broken out by currency. By the nature of currency pairs this graph double counts as every option involves two currencies, so the sum of the amounts in the graph will add up to twice the total of the final bar in Figure 1.3. Options on USD currency crosses alone had global flows of over 300 billion USD per trading day. This is a similar order of magnitude to equity flows on exchanges, which was 49 trillion USD annually, according to the World Federation of Exchanges in 2012 [7], or about 200 billion USD per trading day.

As might be expected, the USD dominates the market, but JPY volumes are also considerable, at about half of those of the USD. As this volume is hardly caused by global trade with Japan, it is likely that much of it is due to speculative currency trading. The JPY's long history of low interest rates makes it a popular choice as a trading tool; it is the funding currency to many structured trades.

Despite the size and liquidity of the FX option market, it is dwarfed by the underlying FX spot and forward market. In Table 1.1 we show the data table for 2013 from the BIS Triennial Survey [6] which shows the flow for other FX deal types. The spot and forward daily flows are both greater than 2 trillion USD each, making the 300-odd billion of the FX option market look relatively modest. However, it is worth noting that the hedging of FX option positions can generate considerable flow in the spot market, so the option flow itself is not the only contribution that FX options make to overall FX market flow.

At the top left of the table is the overall daily FX flow in 2013. It is a remarkable 5.3 trillion USD, a considerable increase on its 2010 value of 4.0 trillion USD. Increases are likely to be driven by the recent swift growth in electronic trading; as can be seen in the table, it has overtaken other trading methods by a large margin. Interestingly, London still remains the dominant trading zone for the market, probably due to its central position in the time zones. Note that the BIS quotes all numbers in millions not billions.

TABLE 1.1 OTC foreign exchange turnover by instrument, currency counterparty, execution method and country in April 2013

OTC foreign exchange turnover by instrument, currency, counterparty, execution method and country in April 2013
Summary table
Daily averages, in millions of USD

	Total	Spot transactions	Outright forwards	Foreign exchange swaps	Currency swaps	FX options
Total, 'net-net' basis[1]	**5,344,549**	**2,046,158**	**679,994**	**2,227,629**	**54,023**	**336,745**
by currency						
USD	4,652,192	1,691,238	587,706	2,029,559	50,262	293,427
EUR	1,785,720	754,276	177,772	765,505	17,858	70,308
JPY	1,231,249	612,341	122,686	331,876	11,002	153,344
GBP	631,173	226,741	69,347	301,418	4,707	28,960
AUD	461,689	195,977	49,642	182,599	6,014	27,457
CHF	275,472	84,369	26,952	149,139	1,419	13,594
CAD	244,089	93,488	36,096	100,712	2,188	11,606
MXN	135,280	56,751	13,844	57,849	794	6,041
CNY	119,563	33,950	28,104	39,923	510	17,077
Others	1,152,670	343,186	247,839	496,676	13,293	51,677
by counterparty						
with reporting dealers	2,069,970	675,359	181,549	1,085,194	29,026	98,841
local	743,073	262,395	45,736	381,880	14,755	38,308
cross-border	1,326,897	412,965	135,813	703,314	14,271	60,534
with other financial institutions	2,809,435	1,182,690	402,051	999,391	18,740	206,564
local	1,242,103	550,905	178,337	404,634	5,340	102,888
cross-border	1,567,332	631,785	223,715	594,757	13,400	103,676
non-reporting banks	1,277,822	505,547	95,361	606,211	7,983	62,721
institutional investors	602,689	267,054	126,783	152,914	1,665	54,273
hedge funds and PTFs	575,645	282,484	115,410	104,312	4,019	69,421

official sector	53,008	11,705	7,633	31,415	656	1,600
other	243,682	84,539	40,958	95,876	4,404	17,905
undistributed	56,588	31,362	15,906	8,662	14	645
with non-financial customers	465,143	188,109	96,394	143,044	6,257	31,339
local	273,570	120,263	57,896	77,489	4,008	13,914
cross-border	191,573	67,846	38,498	65,555	2,249	17,425
Of which: prime brokered	*873,857*	*598,252*	*115,917*	*104,185*	*955*	*54,548*
Of which: retail-driven	*185,306*	*78,406*	*24,086*	*74,153*	*1,393*	*7,268*
by execution method						
Voice direct	1,474,884	517,563	214,864	578,190	17,555	146,712
Voice indirect	785,134	187,665	91,434	435,357	8,607	62,070
Electronic direct	1,589,849	763,421	214,073	527,515	13,546	71,294
Electronic indirect	1,369,488	542,861	138,334	628,725	10,501	49,068
Undistributed	125,192	34,648	21,289	57,841	3,813	7,601
Total, 'net-gross' basis[2]	**6,671,446**	**2,459,123**	**815,807**	**2,930,943**	**68,294**	**397,278**
by country						
United Kingdom	2,725,993	1,031,908	308,808	1,126,586	32,167	226,524
United States	1,262,799	619,357	227,281	340,991	4,397	70,773
Singapore	383,075	103,295	61,703	172,787	1,843	43,447
Japan	374,215	156,630	35,220	169,558	6,388	6,419
Hong Kong SAR	274,605	51,172	37,305	174,130	2,528	9,469
Switzerland	216,394	62,768	13,844	131,535	169	8,078
France	189,878	37,213	8,999	134,921	3,357	5,388
Australia	181,709	47,754	11,615	115,243	4,466	2,630
Netherlands	112,268	54,623	12,435	43,254	938	1,018
Other countries	950,511	294,403	98,598	521,938	12,041	23,531

[1] Adjusted for local and cross-border inter-dealer double-counting.
[2] Adjusted for local inter-dealer double-counting.
This corresponds to the total on a 'net-net' basis plus local reporting dealers.

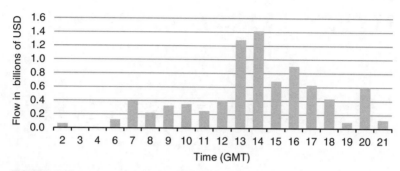

FIGURE 1.4   Hourly flow for EURUSD options, for 7 July 2014, from
Commerzbank AG

1.6   THE FX OPTION TRADING DAY

The flow reported is not constant through the day. The FX market is almost 24-hour.
Beginning in Asia, the markets start to trade. Europe enters as the Asian markets slow
down, smoothly taking over. When the US markets join in the European afternoon,
peak flow conditions prevail. As Europe closes the USA maintains trading for several
more hours, with San Francisco finally pulling the curtains closed for a few moments
until Asia awakes. All regions will maintain at least a skeleton overnight coverage so
even these few minutes are not so much closed as quiet.

To give a picture of flow through the day, we have taken data for 7 July 2014
from the internal flow database of Commerzbank AG, reproduced with permission in
Figure 1.4. Though this is only a fraction of the global flow, it serves to give a good
picture of the peak times and slower times over a typical 24-hour period.

1.7   SUMMARY

We have stated our aims for this book and why we feel they are important. The FX
option market is huge, and used by a large variety of market participants. But, there
is little information available about the historical relationship between payoff and
premium – in other words, have these contracts actually been value for money? The
rest of the book will attempt to answer this question.

REFERENCES

[1] Black, F. and Scholes, M. (1973) The pricing of options and corporate liabilities. *Journal
of Political Economy* 81(3), 637–654.
[2] Bachelier, L. (1900) Théorie de la spéculation. *Annales Scientifiques de l'Ecole Normale
Supérieure* 3(17), 21–86, English translation Cootner, P. H. (ed.), *The Random Character
of Stock Market Prices* (Cambridge, MA: MIT Press, 1964).

[3] Universa fund, founded in 2007 by Mark Spitznagel, to which Nassim Taleb is a principal advisor, http://universa.net/.

[4] Garman, M. B. and Kohlhagen, S. W. (1983) Foreign currency option values. *Journal of International Money and Finance* 2, 231–237.

[5] Conversations with Neil Record, CEO of Record Currency Overlay.

[6] Bank of International Settlements Triennial Surveys, https://www.bis.org/about/index.htm and https://www.bis.org/publ/rpfx.htm.

[7] World Federation of Exchanges, 2009 annual report and statistics, http://www.world-exchanges.org/insight/reports/2009-wfe-annual-report.

The FX Option Market: How Options Are Traded and What That Implies for Option Value

2.1 INTRODUCTION

There is a school of thought that says 10,000 hours of practice are required in order to become expert in a specific field. For an aspiring FX option dealer this equates to around five years of hard work on a trading desk – a figure that empirically at least appears to be reasonable.[1]

If this is true, it is fair to assume that the 20 minutes it takes to read this chapter will not be sufficient to transform the reader into an expert option trader. The good news, however, is that one does not need to spend half a decade gaining experience in option markets in order to have an insight into how trading activity can impact option relative value.

In the following sections we will expand on the introductory comments of Chapter 1, going into more detail about how option markets developed and what their current state of evolution implies for option valuation. As we will see, the way in which most option trading desks operate does not rule out long-term relative value opportunities in currency options.

---

[1]Malcom Gladwell in his 2008 book *Outliers* gives numerous examples of successful people, generally thought simply to be more talented than others, who practised for at least 10,000 hours before they became leaders in their chosen field. Scientific evidence appears to support the theory, showing that, in some cases, characteristics once believed to reflect innate talent are more likely to be the result of deliberate, well-structured practice over a period of many years [1].

2.2   THE BASICS OF OPTION PRICING

The details of an FX financial engineer's toolbox of models could on their own quite easily fill a whole book. Indeed, there are many excellent works that describe in great detail how foreign exchange options are priced. As we have made clear, we do not wish to add a further volume to the already large catalogue of option-pricing literature.

However, while this book is not about option pricing, a section on the fundamental principles of the subject is in our view essential. If we are to understand how option pricing can present relative value opportunities, we at least need to understand the factors that set the price of an FX derivative. To give an example, we will see that expectations regarding the volatility of the underlying exchange rate over the lifetime of an option play an important role in determining how much a buyer is willing to pay for the derivative contract. Since the expected volatility of an exchange rate over various future periods is closely related to the perception of risk over those different time horizons, we can immediately see a way in which behavioural finance may play a part in the way in which options are priced. We will explore this theme in more detail in Chapter 5, but first we dive straight into some theory with a discussion of the Black-Scholes-Merton model.

2.2.1   The Black-Scholes-Merton Model

If we are to say something about the price of an FX option, then we must in some way decide on the probability that it will retain some value on the date for which exercise is possible. Put another way, how likely is it that a European option will expire in-the-money? To answer this question we require some insight into the possible evolution of the option-underlying, i.e. the currency exchange rate.[2]

At this point it is insightful to consider the way in which option market participants tend to describe developments in spot prices for the purpose of FX derivative pricing. The treatment here is deliberately concise; for a rigorous description of the way in which option pricing formulae are derived, including the assumptions made along the way, please refer to an appropriate text.[3]

If we make some assumptions, then we can model FX spot rates as evolving according to geometric Brownian motion.[4] That is, we assume that spot prices change

---

[2]If we are to discuss how option traders think, a little bit of terminology will be necessary. In the simplest terms, a European-style option may be exercised only at expiry.

[3]For example, Iain J. Clark, *Foreign Exchange Option Pricing: A Practitioner's Guide* (John Wiley & Sons, 2010).

[4]There are other possible choices of process. Bachelier derived closed form solutions for European option prices based on arithmetic Brownian motion at the turn of the 20th century, for example [2].

according to a stochastic process given by:

$$dS_t = \mu S_t dt + \sigma S_t dW_t$$

where S_t is the spot price at time t, μ gives the strength of any drift, σ is the volatility of returns of the underlying asset and W_t is a Wiener process (commonly known as Brownian motion).

By imposing risk-neutral pricing so that all risk-free investments earn the same rate of return, this price process, along with a little algebra, leads us to the Black-Scholes-Merton equation:

$$\frac{\partial V}{\partial t} + \frac{1}{2}\sigma^2 S^2 \frac{\partial^2 V}{\partial S^2} + (r - r_b)S\frac{\partial V}{\partial S} - rV = 0$$

where V is the price of the derivative, σ is the volatility of returns of the underlying asset, S is the spot price and r and r_b the interest rates on the quote and base currencies respectively. The Black-Scholes-Merton partial differential equation (PDE) describes how the price of an option varies with the price of the underlying, the expected volatility of the underlying and risk-free interest rates for the two currencies in the exchange rate.[5]

Solving the Black-Scholes-Merton PDE for known final conditions allows us to write down analytical solutions for the theoretical prices of European put and call options:

$$c = S_0 e^{-r_b T} N(d_1) - K e^{-rT} N(d_2)$$
$$p = K e^{-rT} N(-d_2) - S_0 e^{-r_b T} N(-d_1)$$

with:

$$d_1 = \frac{\ln(S_0/K) + (r - r_b + \sigma^2/2)T}{\sigma\sqrt{T}}$$

$$d_2 = \frac{\ln(S_0/K) + (r - r_b - \sigma^2/2)T}{\sigma\sqrt{T}}$$

$$= d_1 - \sigma\sqrt{T}$$

---

[5]Those having taken a finance course are most likely to have come across the Black-Scholes-Merton model as applied to equity derivative pricing where only a single risk-free rate applies. For FX option pricing the underlying principles are the same, though the application of risk-free pricing during the derivation of the equation is slightly different, leading to minor differences in resulting PDEs. Garman and Kolhagen adapted the Black-Scholes-Merton equation to incorporate the dual interest rates involved in an FX option [3].

and:

S_0 = FX rate at inception,
K = strike rate,
r = interest rate for tenor of the option in the quote currency,
r_b = interest rate for the tenor of the option in the base currency,
T = tenor of the option, and
σ = implied volatility of the option.
$N(.)$ denotes the standard normal cumulative distribution function.

We say 'theoretical' prices because the solutions do not account for either the term structure of implied volatility or the term structure of interest rates – these theoretical values act only as a starting point for option traders.[6] Nonetheless, for our purposes these expressions for European put and call option prices will be adequate to allow us to identify the main drivers of option premiums. For the non-mathematically inclined reader it is only important to see that option pricing is heavily dependent on volatility and interest rates.

2.2.2 The Impact of Volatility

Volatility can mean many things depending on context, but in this instance we are concerned with a specific type of volatility, namely the standard deviation of log returns. Even once we have settled on this definition, we still need to be more specific as there are broadly speaking two main classes of volatility that may be of interest to those active in FX markets.

Realised (or historical) volatility, as the name suggests, is the volatility that has actually been seen in the market on the underlying. It is a known, calculated, backward-looking value. As the FX market is dominated by spot transactions the realised volatility is usually based on the underlying spot rate. Depending on when the data point is collected (in the middle of the day or at the market close, for example) or which data point is taken (the mid-point of the price, the bid or the offer), daily realised volatility can vary slightly. Either way, the measure gives an indication of the day-to-day variability in an exchange rate over a recent period of time. For gamma traders (see Section 2.3), high frequency realised volatility may be of greater interest. For example, data points may be taken once an hour rather than once a day.

Implied volatility on the other hand is a forward-looking number. It is the expected volatility of (usually) daily changes in an exchange rate over a quoted period. Because the level is forward looking, nobody knows for certain at the point of dealing if it is an accurate or fair value. It is the market's best estimation based on past performance and expected events. Hence, as a baseline, implied volatility will normally be relatively close to realised volatility. If a currency pair moved at 1% a day over the last month and

---

[6]Term structure refers to the way in which a quantity, in this case an implied volatility or interest rate, varies with tenor or maturity.

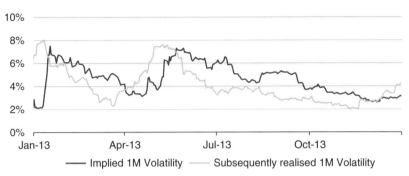

FIGURE 2.1 Annualised daily 1M EURCHF implied volatility and subsequent 1M realised volatility

has done so over the last year it would be reasonable to assume it would move at 1% a day over the next month. But, there is always the financial cliché: past performance is no guide to future returns. As shown in Figure 2.1, while the series are similar it is obvious that forward-looking implied volatility rarely provides an accurate forecast of spot rate volatility for the subsequent month.[7] Future volatility is impacted by events such as elections and data releases (higher volatility) or holidays (lower volatility).

In general when option traders discuss volatility they are likely talking about implied volatility measured on an annualised basis. This is what is of most interest since, as we have already seen, the value of an option is closely related to the expected volatility of the exchange rate underlying over the lifetime of the contract. In short, higher implied volatility leads to higher option prices. We can immediately see that human nature comes into play at this point. For traders to price options of differing tenors accurately, they must be able to evaluate risks rationally over wildly different periods of time. We all know, however, that in financial markets it is immediate risks that tend to dominate the newswires. Combined with a human bias in risk evaluation over different periods of time, we have a mechanism by which long-running relative value opportunities in FX option markets may persist.

2.2.3 The Impact of Rate Differentials

During our discussion of the Black-Scholes-Merton model we referred in passing to risk-free pricing. In fact interest rates play an important role in determining the relative value of FX options versus alternative hedging products such as currency forward contracts. We continue by considering a simple but effective example of how interest rates come to play a role in option pricing.

---

[7]While the realised volatility of changes in an exchange rate over a one-month period will appear to lag 1M implied volatility, this is a consequence of the backward looking calculation of historical volatility. In reality, it is implied volatility that lags market developments as traders react to changes in the dynamics of the spot FX rate.

It is well known that the forward rate for a currency pair is the current spot FX rate adjusted for interest rate effects. It is the only future rate which may be locked in at zero cost, apart from the bid-offer spread, and is calculated as:

$$F = S\frac{(1 + i_q)}{(1 + i_b)}$$

where F is the forward exchange rate, S the current spot rate and i_b and i_q the interest rates for the base and quote currencies respectively. We can see how this relationship arises by considering that investing N units of base currency at i_b and then exchanging at the forward rate should be equivalent to exchanging the base currency at the current spot rate and then depositing the quote currency holding at i_q.

If these two alternatives are not equivalent it becomes possible to create 'free money' by offsetting one against the other. Thus, if the two alternatives are not quite equal due to some anomaly, they will converge quickly as the market takes advantage of any discrepancy. This type of pricing is known as 'no-arbitrage' pricing; it works on the simple principle that any opportunities for free money or arbitrage will be quickly eliminated by market action. This is the same concept of 'no-arbitrage' pricing that was used in the derivation of the Black-Scholes-Merton formula where a certain amount of money at the start (the premium) will accrue interest and must be worth the same at maturity as the value of the option at the end.

From these arguments it is interesting to note that option pricing inherently relies on the forward rate. Market participants are obliged to use it, but this does not guarantee that it is correct or even that it is a good estimate. We will discuss this in detail in Chapter 7 when we cover the FX carry trade; historically the forward rate has not been a good estimator of future spot rates. As we will see in later chapters, assuming that we acknowledge that the FX carry trade exists and that option traders build forward rates into their pricing, there are implications for option relative value.

2.3 HOW OPTIONS ARE TRADED

In Chapter 1 we touched briefly on the history of option trading. In this section we expand somewhat on the evolution of the market and discuss how different participants can have very different outlooks. In particular, we discuss ways in which distortions in the pricing of options can persist.

Early option trading was dominated by prices given in premium terms. This was perfect for an occasional hedger wanting to buy or sell an option to cover a risk and know the exact cost. Indeed, for a hedger implementing static option positions there is little need to understand much more. However, market makers wanting to cover their 'options' exposure wanted to find the contract offering the best value. As the underlying was constantly moving it was a cumbersome task to feed the price into a formula in order to calculate an implied volatility for each contract. Each time spot moved you needed to start the calculation again. However, if the market makers started with the implied volatility then they had a standardised way of comparing contracts with different strikes and different maturities. Traders understood that as volatility was directly related to premium this was a more efficient way to deal. After agreeing the volatility all the underlying parameters would be set at the prevailing market conditions to determine the premium. Hence, for dynamic traders the market evolved to implied volatility quoting and trading to identify the relative cost of different options. This still holds true for the over-the-counter options market where the majority of the volume is transacted in the form of vanilla options.[8] A useful guide to quoting conventions can be found in the Appendix.

This simple example of how the option market developed gives us a first indication that there are two fundamental approaches to trading options. On the one hand the static trader has a long-term view and, as described in more detail below, will tend to think in terms of matching an option with an underlying view or exposure over a relatively long horizon. An option dealer on the other hand is far more likely to act in the much shorter term to continually hedge risk exposure.

One of the beautiful things about options is that both the buyer and seller can make money from the same trade. Conversely they can both lose! This is all down to risk management of the option, the skill of the trader and sometimes luck. We will explore in more detail how the buyer and seller can both make money as we consider different types of trading style.

2.3.1 Two Views of Volatility

Depending on the market participant and the reason for trading an option, volatility can be viewed differently. A corporate hedger wishing to protect a risk may enquire about the price of an option. From this the breakeven of the contract at maturity can be determined – how far will the spot rate have to move before the payoff from the option covers the premium? The hedger will have an appreciation of whether in his mind the price is too high or too low. In essence he is judging how far from the current expectation the underlying will finish. As such, the corporate treasurer may rely on intuition, economic research or forecasts to determine whether the implied volatility is too high or too low and if the contract offers good value.

For a dynamic trader volatility means something rather different. It is how volatile the underlying is during the journey to maturity of the contract and how much value can be extracted from this movement. An underlying could start and finish at the same level, but if it is extremely volatile in the intervening period the dynamic trader can make money.

Hence there is a different concept of 'good value', which is one of the reasons there is such an active market in FX options. We describe the two strongly diverging outlooks in greater detail when we consider static and dynamic trading approaches below.

---

[8] See the Glossary for an explanation of the term 'vanilla' and other option market terminology.

2.3.2 Static Trading

A static trader or hedger will usually not be interested in a lot of option market jargon. A typical static trader might be a corporate treasurer. They could have a predefined currency exposure in a 'risk currency' which they want to hedge back into a base currency. Purchasing an option with a strike rate based on the worst exchange rate they can tolerate can be used as an insurance policy. A premium is paid upfront and if the market moves against the hedger the option is exercised.

For such applications, a relatively small amount of terminology is required, specifically relating to the setting of the option strike rate. The alternatives are listed below.

ATMF: At-the-money forward
> ATMF options are the simplest options to understand and to value of all the FX option contracts. The strike of the option is determined by the forward rate at the time the option is purchased. A person who buys an ATMF call option on an FX rate will receive a payoff if the FX rate is above the strike rate on the expiry date; if instead they have bought a put option then they will receive a payoff if the FX rate is below the strike rate. The forward rate at inception is the critical point at which the option holder begins to make some return. The breakeven is the point where the option value overtakes the premium.

OTM: Out-of-the-money
> Where the strike is unfavourable compared to the forward.

ITM: In-the-money
> Where the strike is favourable compared to the forward.

Given the nature of FX markets, with spot and forward rates constantly moving, options starting out ATMF will soon be either OTM or ITM. What is more, the status of an option's strike rate can oscillate during the life of the contract.

At this point we need to mention a piece of jargon that can often be heard when discussing FX option strike prices. The delta of an option gives the rate of change in the derivative's price for moves in the price of the underlying. We discuss delta in more detail in the following pages but we note that the delta of an option is sometimes used to describe how likely it is to be exercised. A 50-delta option will be an ATMF option where the underlying has an equal chance to move up or down and so broadly speaking has a 50% chance of exercise. An option with a delta of 85% or more may be described as deeply ITM and a delta of 15% or lower may be associated with deeply OTM options. We note that this is just a rule of thumb and that one must be careful when using deltas in this fashion – for exotic options delta can easily be $\pm 200\%$, but this does not imply that the probability of exercise can reach 200%!

2.3.3 Dynamic Trading

If we choose to describe a corporate treasurer as a static trader, then an FX option dealer working for a bank might be labelled a dynamic trader. Compared to the static trader, who is most interested in the option premium versus the expected size and probability of the payoff, the dynamic trader is far more interested in volatility. In the notation of Chapter 1, our dynamic trader would fall into the class of 'investors', though as a special case, usually focusing on the shorter term.

A dynamic trader will typically have many option positions and may trade day-to-day if not intraday in order to maximise the returns on a portfolio. We can see immediately that, unlike for the static trader, the size of daily changes in the underlying are very important for the dynamic trader. To help us understand how an active option dealer goes about making money we can consider a crude example.

Let's imagine a market where the only parameter to vary is the underlying spot rate. Let's also assume that a trader that buys a one-week ATMF EUR call USD put option for 10 million EUR notional. He thinks there will be a lot of volatility, but he is not sure of the direction of moves in the spot rate.

To protect against the case of EURUSD moving lower and the premium being paid for no return, the trader sells EURUSD in the spot market. Given that the spot rate could equally well move higher or lower, the trader sells 5 million EUR – half of the option notional. During the day the spot rate does indeed move lower and the trader buys back the 5 million EURUSD position at a profit and is left with just the option. If the spot rate retraces back to the original level, this process can be repeated. This is the essence of delta hedging. On each trading day to maturity of the option the trader buys and sells currencies in the spot market, hopefully making a profit. A dynamic trader will judge the cost of an option with reference to its implied volatility and whether they can cover the premium of the option through this delta hedging process. This is clearly a different measure of value than that utilised by the static trader.

It is worth mentioning at this point why it is that most dynamic traders will not be too concerned about the specific characteristics of an option and will instead concentrate on the risk-reward and the payoff. This is specifically due to put-call parity.

In simple terms, the profile of an ATMF call option that has been bought can be turned into the profile of an ATMF put option that has been bought if the full notional amount of the forward contract is sold. Similarly, the profile of an ATMF put option that has been bought can be turned into the profile of an ATMF call option that has been bought if the full notional amount of the forward contract is bought. This would also hold true if the options had been sold as opposed to bought.[9]

Hence, a dynamic trader will care more about the volatility and the strike rather than whether the option is a put or a call. Naturally whether an option is deep ITM or deep OTM will have credit implications and there has been a lot more focus on this from market makers in the post-2008 environment.[10]

---

[9]Put-call parity also holds more generally as long as the option strikes and forward rate are equal. A long call, short put combination gives a synthetic long FX position.

[10]Credit is another subject which has its own shelf of books which we will only skim over. Deep OTM or ITM options mean that even at the start of a deal one party owes the other a substantial amount of money, so creditworthiness becomes important.

2.4 A MORE DETAILED DISCUSSION OF OPTION TRADING

In the previous section we highlighted two very different approaches to option trading. We suggested how static and dynamic traders, broadly corresponding to corporate hedgers and option dealers respectively, tend to judge option value. Our aim in doing so was to attempt to explain why relative value 'features' in option markets may persist for long periods of time.

For the purposes of our argument, the details presented in the previous sections are probably sufficient; it is hopefully clear now that market participants have very different ways of judging value. However, by taking our arguments a step further we will be able to demonstrate how it is that both sides of an option trade can profit. This will help us to explain why market makers historically have not paid particular attention to payoff-to-premium ratios for options.

In order to get a better insight into the option traders' world we will need to discuss the sensitivity of option prices to various factors. The market uses Greek letters to describe these sensitivities, but this should not deter non-mathematical readers. Since this book is at least in some respects about demystifying the option market for non-experts, we will keep the explanations formulae-free.

2.4.1 The Greeks

Anybody having investigated the pricing and trading of options is bound to have come across a plethora of Greek letters. For persistent readers, it is possible to come to terms with the quantities represented by these letters, and for those so inclined, mathematical definitions can be found. What is likely to be hard to find is an explanation of how this theory is applied in a practical situation. In the following sections we address this issue and attempt to provide a trader's view.

For vanilla options in general it is simplest to stick to a few well-defined sensitivities. A more extensive list of option Greeks can be found in any option pricing textbook or on one of the many financial education websites.[11]

Delta measures the rate of change of option value with respect to changes in the underlying asset's price. More formally, delta is the first derivative of the value of the option with respect to the underlying instrument's price, but what does this mean in practice? To understand better, let us imagine an option with five days to maturity and an implied volatility of 10%.

1. Trading from the long side (the desk has bought the option)
   A customer sells an option to a market-making volatility desk and collects the premium. The desk has no view on the direction of spot, but just believes

---

[11]The higher order Greeks are more relevant to exotic option risk management. Even then it is important to know that for exotic options near barriers Greeks can become unstable and the numbers involved huge or meaningless.

that buying the option at that level of volatility provides good value. Hence, the exact delta of the option will be calculated and the underlying traded in the open market.

As spot moves up and down, the desk trades the delta back and forth. It is easy to imagine a market where spot is volatile but mean-reverting and finishes each day where it started. In this environment the purchaser of the option will be adjusting furiously throughout the day and will make more money on the spot deals than they have spent on the premium. At the same instance, the seller of the option waits and collects the premium. Both buyer and seller of the option can make money from the same deal.

2. Trading from the short side (the desk has sold the option)

A customer buys an option from a market-making trading desk to hedge an exposure. The desk has no view on the direction of spot, only that selling the option at that level of volatility is an attractive trade. Hence, the exact delta of the option will be calculated and the underlying traded in the open market. The desk will now try to adjust the delta as little as possible, knowing that each time they incur trading costs they will eat into the premium they have received.

Whether you are long or short an option the burning questions are how do you know exactly when to time adjustments and how often to do so? As no-one can foresee market moves this is all down to interpretation of what will happen. But gamma can give a guide to the level of delta hedging required.

Gamma measures the rate of change in delta with respect to changes in the underlying's price. Gamma is the second derivative of the value function with respect to the underlying price. There is not much to understand about gamma, it's just a number that helps traders evaluate an option and how much delta hedging they should be doing. A simplified guide to interpreting gamma is shown in Table 2.1.

Delta hedging an option is also sometimes called 'trading the gamma' and trades can be entered manually or automatically. In an automated approach, as the delta is a calculated quantity it is possible to leave buy and sell orders in the market at

TABLE 2.1   Different regimes, implications for gamma and likely trading strategies

Regime	Likely gamma	Likely trading strategy for LONG option position
High volatility	Low gamma	Wait for the larger swings to develop to trade the delta as the high volatility makes the option expensive and therefore the premium paid large.
Low volatility	High gamma	You haven't paid much for the option. If you see a chance, take it.
Long maturity	Low gamma	Relax. You have plenty of time to see how the underlying develops.
Short maturity	High gamma	Trade as much as you can, you are running out of time.

pre-defined levels based on the implied volatility. This is more prevalent now with electronic platforms and loop orders.[12]

Most trading desks, however, prefer to have some manual input based on experience and/or ego. Because long and short positions in a vanilla option have equal and opposite gamma, sometimes the decision of whether or not to trade boils down to who blinks first: the traders who are long options or those who are short. If the market is quiet and range-bound, the short option holders are in control and the longs need to actively trade to cover the premium they have paid. Conversely, if the market is breaking out of a trading range, moves can be accelerated by short gamma players all rushing to cover their positions at the same time.

The potential rush to cover positions by those who are short gamma is the reason the market has a fascination with, and a desire to find out, where the strikes with big notional value are, i.e. are there large trades done which are waiting for the strike rate to be reached? If an underlying starts to trade near a strike close to expiry then even people who are not connected with the option will start to trade around that level, buying the underlying below and selling above. This can help concertina the movements of the underlying so much that at exercise time the underlying is right at the strike level. This phenomenon is known to traders as 'pinning the strike'.

DELTA HEDGING: CURRENCY CORRELATION

Delta hedging is all very well for liquid markets where the portfolio of options is restricted to one currency pair. But a market-making desk will have a variety of customers interested in different exchange rates, perhaps including non-standard crosses. Supply and demand as well as liquidity will have some influence on the initial quoted price of an option, but these factors also play a part in determining how the option is hedged.

For less liquid crosses where there is limited supply and demand, currency correlations can help a trader manage risk. For example, a trader may be paid by an oil company for NOKJPY options and the resulting risk may be offset by a combination of more liquid option markets such as EURNOK and EURJPY. However, this would not be a perfect hedge and would require the trader to judge and monitor correlation risk.

If we look at a simple example of delta hedging we can see explicitly how it is that both the option buyer and seller can make money (Figure 2.2). At inception of

---

[12]A loop order may be created when a cyclical movement in the market is expected. Two orders may be placed with each triggered in turn as specific conditions occur. The process is repeated until the order is cancelled by the trader.

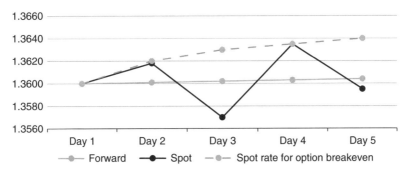

FIGURE 2.2 A simple example of delta hedging. With the spot rate finishing below the option breakeven rate the seller makes a profit. Spot rate volatility means that the option buyer could have realised a profit too

the trade the spot rate is at 1.3600 and the forward points are slightly positive.[13] The option seller sells a call option for 1.3640 – the breakeven on the premium is mapped out for each day in the figure. As spot finishes below the breakeven the seller collects the premium and does not have to make any payments to the buyer. Thus, the seller ends in profit, but what about the other side of the trade? While the trader who bought the option will have initially been out of pocket due to paying the option premium, by actively 'trading the gamma' this premium could have been covered and a small profit generated. Both sides of the trade can win!

DELTA HEDGING: G10 VS EMERGING MARKET CURRENCIES

Currencies of developed countries usually have comparatively stable interest rates; the volatility of associated forward rates is predominantly due to changes in the spot market. Emerging market currencies meanwhile tend to have higher volatility in both spot and interest rates, leading to larger fluctuations in outright forward prices. For the small portion of the world's currencies that are currently pegged, volatility still exists as the forward is able to fluctuate and in exceptional circumstances the peg may break leading to elevated levels of volatility.

For delta hedging purposes G10 currency pairs will be hedged via spot and emerging currencies using the outright forward. This is not just to do with crossing the bid-offer spread; higher trading costs in emerging currencies are already incorporated by wider option bid-offer prices. In emerging currencies the correlation between spot moves and interest rates is strong so that normally the spot movement is amplified in the forward price, allowing the trader to capture more gamma.

---

[13]See the Glossary for a definition of forward points.

Theta measures the sensitivity of option value to the passage of time.

An initial estimate of theta can be calculated by valuing the option and then revaluing the option with all the parameters the same but with one trading day less. This gives the value attached to the next trading day or the 'time decay' of an option. The target for most active gamma traders is to 'beat the theta' every day and thereby lock in a profit as time passes. This again highlights bank trading desks' focus on short-term trading, spot (rather than interest rate) moves and daily mark-to-market profits.

When valuing different options, traders will often compare the gamma-to-theta ratio to determine the most attractive option to buy. In other words, they ask which option has the best potential to allow money to be made from gamma adjustments, but will cost the least each day in time decay. Options with shorter maturities will have higher gamma *and* theta numbers. Hence, these Greeks are most relevant for vanilla options that have a maturity of less than one month. The grey box 'Intraday Options' describes the special case of options very near expiry.

INTRADAY OPTIONS

While discussing the Greeks it is interesting to consider what happens as options near the end of their lives. In particular, what happens on the day that an option expires? When an option reaches this point it is known as an intraday option. Daily volatility is a meaningless measure at this point as the option only has hours to live. Instead the market reverts back to basics and discusses premium.

In reality very few intraday options are traded. Given that a large number of contracts remain open this requires risk management of many options right until exercise. Since there is no volatility assigned to the option it is hard to assign a gamma number. Close to expiry the market reverts back to the layman's view where an option is either ITM (100-delta) at the strike (50-delta) or OTM (zero-delta).

The best case scenario for a dynamic trader is not only that the option ends in-the-money, but that the spot rate gyrates across the strike several times during the day, allowing profitable delta adjustments.

Vega is another important Greek for option traders. It gives the sensitivity of an option to changes in implied volatility. More formally, vega is the derivative of option value with respect to the volatility of the underlying asset. Whereas for shorter dated options, traders are most concerned about the gamma-to-theta ratio, for longer dated options vega has a much greater impact.

Finally, **rho** measures sensitivity to rates. Specifically, it is the derivative of the option value with respect to the interest rate. For currency trading there are two exposures, relating to the rates for the base and quote currencies.

For observers of the option trading world it is surprising how fixated the FX market is with spot. Most traders will actively adjust their gamma via spot hedges with the interest rate risk considered only as an afterthought – something to clean up at the end of the day. Given the losses that have arisen over the years due to negligence of currency balances or interest rate exposure, it is in fact amazing how little attention is paid to these factors. The findings of this book echo this sentiment.

2.5 SUMMARY

This chapter discussed the FX option market, how it is traded and what that implies for FX option performance. Our goal was to convince the reader that participants in the option market can have very different outlooks and also different ways of determining the fair value of a contract.

Beginning by discussing the fundamentals of option pricing, we went on to explain how implied volatility and interest rates are important in determining the price of options – something that is often presented even in introductory finance courses. However, this chapter was about more than the theory behind the valuation of options.

We described how corporates hedging FX risk can usually be thought of as 'static traders'. This type of trader tends to think in terms of the protection afforded by an option and may want to know how far the underlying rate will need to move before the contract breaks even. Depending on the hedger's outlook for financial markets, the option may be judged to be too expensive or to offer good value. 'Dynamic' traders, however, have a totally different way of looking at things. They are far more active in their trading and tend to think in terms of how much can be made from the risk management of an option – the resulting payoff-to-premium ratio for a contract is not of interest.

Perhaps the most important point to come out of this chapter is the way in which both sides of an option trade can make a profit. Driven by very diverse goals, successful dynamic and static traders can in theory at least both achieve their goals even in the presence of long-term relative value 'features' in the FX option market.

REFERENCES

[1] Ericsson, K., Anders, K., Ralf, T. and Tesch-Römer, C. (1993) The role of deliberate practice in the acquisition of expert performance. *Psychological Review* 100(3), 363–406.
[2] Bachelier, L. (1900) Théorie de la spéculation. *Annales Scientifiques de l'Ecole Normale Supérieure* 3(17), 21–86.
[3] Garman, M. B. and Kohlhagen, S. W. (1983) Foreign currency option values. *Journal of International Money and Finance* 2, 231–237.
[4] Wystup, U. and Reiswich, D. (2012) A guide to FX options quoting conventions. *Wilmott*, 60, 58–69.

It Is All About the Data

3.1 INTRODUCTION

In the course of the earlier chapters of this book we hope to have tempted the reader with two main assertions:

1. FX options do not have to be the expensive and unfathomable instruments that some in the business of hedging currency exposure believe they are. In fact, we suggest that in many cases options offer better value than a simple FX forward hedge, as well as providing further attractive features.
2. Evidence relating to the relative value of different tenor and strike options can be surprising even to those market participants who are long since convinced of the potential benefits of currency options. In some cases, the information is surprising even to those who make a living from dealing in FX derivatives markets.

Having stuck with us this far, the reader is justified in asking for some proof that these statements stand up to rigorous testing. This chapter bridges the gap between our claims and the solid proof that any successful corporate treasurer or option trader will rightly demand.

One cannot simply quote results based on experience and hope that they are accepted. This is even truer when the ideas are in some way counter-intuitive to many people. At the same time, however, there are certain practical difficulties in performing the type of calculation necessary to identify relative value in derivatives markets. In these pages we identify these difficulties and explain how they can be addressed by the practitioner. This chapter is about getting down to brass tacks.[1]

---

[1] Although the source of this phrase is uncertain, it may come from the cloth trade. Brass tacks were often driven into a shop's counter to provide an accurate means of measuring a yard of cloth (rather than the more rough-and-ready method of holding one end to the nose and outstretching the arm).

3.2   THE GOAL: TO PRICE LOTS OF OPTIONS!

If we are to show how FX options have performed over the history of the market then we cannot hide from the fact that a certain amount of data juggling will be required. This is especially true if we adopt a brute force approach, i.e. price lots and lots of options spanning several decades and identify the eventual payoff in each case. If we wish to compare the relative performance of some of the main tenors (say 1W, 1M, 3M, 6M, 12M, 2Y and 3Y) for the main G10 and emerging market currencies, then it is clear that the task at hand is not a trivial one. Assuming seven tenors for 34 exchange rates over an average historical period in the region of 10 to 15 years, the scale of the challenge becomes clear. If we wish to compare forwards with at-the-money and out-of-the-money options, for puts, calls and straddles and long and short positions, then we will increase the required number of calculations many times over. We estimate that somewhere in excess of two million payoff calculations were required to construct our dataset.

Bearing all of this in mind we can begin to see why systematic studies of option relative value are not commonplace. In order to carry out the types of back-test that we are interested in, one requires a number of capabilities and resources, and certainly the will to overcome practical difficulties. A further complication arises from the fact that the results of an analysis may not be particularly useful in their raw form. The findings may be best put into context by somebody with first-hand experience of the diverse trading environments and conditions that have occurred as the option market developed from a standing start to a $300bn-per-day business. In the following sections we detail the necessary requirements, from the sourcing of high quality historical data, to the construction of option valuation models that take into account the correct market conventions.

Finally we note that even if the planets align perfectly, allowing one to assemble the correct resources, capabilities and expertise to perform a thorough analysis, limitations will remain. Data quality issues may arise, for example, or historical time series may be shorter than one might desire. This chapter also discusses the main limitations faced when attempting to back-test FX option strategies.

3.3   DEFINING A UNIVERSE OF CURRENCIES

The first decision to be made when sourcing the data for our analysis regarded the exchange rates to be studied. We decided on the currency pairs shown in Table 3.1 for a number of reasons. First, they cover most of the exchange rates that corporate treasurers and large investors are likely to be concerned with, while still all being liquid enough to allow a meaningful historical study. Second, they cover a wide range of currency types. We would like to know how the nature of a currency (EM or G10, commodity or funding currency, high interest rate or low interest rate) influences the relative value of options on that currency. By including a good selection of currencies

TABLE 3.1   Our universe of currencies – exchange rate versus the euro or US dollar

Exchange rate		Exchange rate	
AUDUSD	Australian Dollar	USDARS	Argentine Peso
EURAUD	Australian Dollar	USDBRL	Brazilian Real
EURCHF	Swiss Franc	USDCLP	Chilean Peso
EURGBP	British Pound	USDCOP	Colombian Peso
EURJPY	Japanese Yen	USDCZK	Czech Koruna
EURNOK	Norwegian Krone	USDHKD	Hong Kong Dollar
EURUSD	Euro	USDIDR	Indonesian Rupiah
GBPUSD	British Pound	USDILS	Israeli New Shekel
USDCAD	Canadian Dollar	USDINR	Indian Rupee
USDCHF	Swiss Franc	USDKRW	South Korean Won
USDDKK	Danish Krone	USDMXN	Mexican Peso
USDJPY	Japanese Yen	USDPHP	Philippine Peso
USDNOK	Norwegian Krone	USDPLN	Polish Zloty
USDSEK	Swedish Krona	USDSGD	Singapore Dollar
EURCZK	Czech Koruna	USDTRY	Turkish Lira
EURHUF	Hungarian Forint	USDTWD	Taiwanese Dollar
EURPLN	Polish Zloty	USDZAR	South African Rand

in our dataset we will be able to identify whether findings hold generally, or only in specific cases.

In Table 3.2 we divide the currency pairs into G10 and emerging market classifications and include start dates in order to show the periods for which the exchange rate was part of the dataset.[2] We must be careful to define clearly what we mean by 'start date' in this context – the dates shown in the table do not simply refer to the dates from which historical data are available. As we will discuss in Section 3.5, the start date refers to the point at which responsive pricing commences rather than the date at which the first price of any form was available. The end date in all cases was 31 December 2013.

On examining Table 3.2 the experienced reader may note that some of our selected currencies are not freely convertible. That is, there are foreign exchange controls for offshore market participants in some cases that mean the currency cannot be delivered as part of a transaction: there is no offshore spot market. Hence, trading these currencies offshore takes place on a non-deliverable basis in the form of a non-deliverable forward (NDF).

---

[2]We could enter into a long debate about which of the countries considered should actually be classified as emerging markets and we revisit this discussion in Chapter 5. For the sake of our study we consider all non-G10 markets as falling within the EM space, though we could of course have labelled this category 'other countries' or 'non-G10 countries'.

TABLE 3.2 G10 and EM exchange rates included in the analysis and start dates for the 3M tenor

G10		Emerging Markets	
Exchange rate	Start date for 3M tenor	Exchange rate	Start date for 3M tenor
AUDUSD	31/01/1996	EURCZK	30/06/1999
EURAUD	02/03/2005	EURHUF	01/10/2003
EURCHF	03/03/1999	EURPLN	02/01/2002
EURGBP	03/03/1999	USDARS	31/01/2007
EURJPY	03/02/1999	USDBRL	31/01/2003
EURNOK	03/02/1999	USDCLP	02/08/2000
EURUSD	06/01/1999	USDCOP	04/10/2006
GBPUSD	05/06/1996	USDCZK	06/04/2005
USDCAD	03/03/1999	USDHKD	03/03/1999
USDCHF	05/06/1996	USDIDR	04/07/2007
USDDKK	30/03/2005	USDILS	05/06/2002
USDJPY	31/01/1996	USDINR	04/02/2004
USDNOK	10/02/1999	USDKRW	31/03/1999
USDSEK	26/08/1998	USDMXN	01/12/1999
		USDPHP	31/03/1999
		USDPLN	02/05/2001
		USDSGD	03/01/2001
		USDTRY	31/12/2003
		USDTWD	05/05/1999
		USDZAR	03/03/1999

Usually for such currencies two markets exist in parallel for the same contract, an onshore deliverable market and an offshore non-deliverable market. Offshore instruments form a completely separate market from that in onshore instruments. There is no direct arbitrage opportunity. The onshore rate will be driven by trade agreements and the necessity of currency transactions, while the offshore rate is freely determined by the broader market, including speculators worldwide. It is worth noting that, although speculators may actually prefer to have foreign currency forward positions settled in, say, US dollars, this may not be a desired solution for corporate hedgers. It may be the case that the delivery or receipt of local currency plays a role in the cash flow position of the business. For this reason, corporations may attempt to manage the hedging of these currencies through local offices whenever possible.

NDFs are settled against a fixing rate with the payoff denominated in a deliverable currency such as US dollars – they are in effect a contract for difference. The fixing for each NDF market is set at the same pre-determined time each day by the market rate at that time. An option on the NDF is known as an NDO (non-deliverable option) and similarly to the associated underlying NDF market, NDOs are settled in alternative currencies, such as US dollars, and form a completely separate market from that in

TABLE 3.3 Currency pairs for which we consider offshore (non-deliverable) markets

Exchange rate	Currency
USDARS	Argentine Peso
USDBRL	Brazilian Real
USDCLP	Chilean Peso
USDCOP	Colombian Peso
USDIDR	Indonesian Rupiah
USDINR	Indian Rupee
USDKRW	South Korean Won
USDPHP	Philippine Peso
USDTWD	New Taiwan Dollar

onshore instruments. Despite the clear separation, onshore and offshore markets tend to be highly correlated during typical trading conditions.

Offshore markets can be very liquid and widely traded. The Korean won, for example, was the 17th most traded currency in the world during 2013, according to the BIS [1]. Data show that over a third of transactions in this market during 2010 involved an offshore party [2].

Table 3.3 lists the currencies for which we considered non-deliverable markets. We took non-deliverable forward rates for cases when an offshore market tended to dominate in terms of ease of trading and liquidity so that our findings were relevant to offshore market participants.

3.4 THE DATA

Chapter 2 provided an introduction to currency options, describing amongst other things the fundamentals of FX option pricing. By considering the Black-Scholes-Merton pricing model presented in the earlier chapter we can begin to appreciate the information needed in order to price the contracts necessary for a study of option relative value.

First, since an FX option is a derivative instrument it is clear that we will need access to underlying prices, i.e. currency exchange rates. The sourcing of FX spot rates does not pose too many problems, though one must accept that there are some decisions to be made about the source of the data and exactly which price is to be selected.[3]

---

[3]The FX market operates around the clock, from the time trading begins in Asia on Monday morning until the time US West Coast markets close on Friday evening. As one region's markets reach the end of their trading day another region's markets are already open. One must therefore decide at which point of the day (or for which region) daily closing prices are to be taken.

3.4.1 Pricing Model Data Requirements

Beyond spot prices, additional data are less simple to source since derivative markets necessarily see major development later than spot markets. Referring back to the discussion of pricing models in Chapter 2 we can see that to price an FX option we must take a view on the future volatility of the underlying currency exchange rate. The price of an option will be linked to the likelihood of it expiring in profit, which in turn depends upon the nature of moves in the underlying rate. Since we wish to back-test a wide range of option strategies our pricing models require implied volatility data for out-of-the-money strikes as well as at-the-money strikes.[4]

While some option studies may be able to use a crude estimate of historical implied option volatility based on realised volatility levels, in this case that very rough approximation may not be made. Over the longer term, differences in volatility can lead to large differences in payoff and price – the very things that we wish to determine accurately. In a similar vein, it is no secret that when back-testing financial market strategies the incorporation of an allowance for trading costs is essential; many a potentially successful money-making scheme falls flat on its face when realistic transaction costs are applied. In order to ensure that our results were representative of actual transactions we included costs based on historical bid-ask spreads. The median bid-ask spreads in quoted 3M implied volatilities can be found in Table 3.4.

Further to building a model for the implied volatility skew, the pricing of our options depends on a simple interest rate model; in order to price at-the-money-forward options, for example, we first need to know the forward rate. Discount factors for the period of an option contract are also important if one wishes to identify whether any discrepancies between payoff and premium exist on average.

The premium of an option is calculated at the inception of a trade. The payoff of a vanilla option meanwhile will not be known with certainty until the expiry date. Thus, the premium and payoff, the two quantities we are interested in comparing, are calculated at points in time that may be separated by several years in the cases of the longer tenors.[5] When comparing option payoffs and premiums in a systematic back-test, the period of time separating the two cash flows must be taken into consideration; as every student of finance knows, the time value of money must not be neglected! It is necessary to take into account the rate of interest over the life of the option in order to compare premium and payoff in consistent accounting units – in other words, the present value of a dollar in one year's time is slightly less than one dollar today (if the interest rate is positive, which it usually is).

---

[4]Implied volatilities for out-of-the-money strike prices tend to be quoted for several key structures. A detailed description of the meaning of these important reference points can be found in Chapter 5, but for now we simply state that 10- and 25-delta risk reversal and butterfly volatilities provided the skew structure information in our pricing models.

[5]While it is possible to arrange for the option premium to be rolled into the settlement amount so that no payment is required upfront, the discounting of cash flows must still be considered.

TABLE 3.4 Median implied volatility bid-ask spreads for the 3M tenor

G10		Emerging Markets	
Exchange rate	Bid-ask spread (volatility points)	Exchange rate	Bid-ask spread (volatility points)
AUDUSD	0.40	EURCZK	0.90
EURAUD	0.65	EURHUF	1.00
EURCHF	0.35	EURPLN	0.95
EURGBP	0.40	USDARS	4.00
EURJPY	0.40	USDBRL	0.85
EURNOK	0.60	USDCLP	1.25
EURUSD	0.28	USDCOP	2.00
GBPUSD	0.35	USDCZK	1.75
USDCAD	0.30	USDHKD	0.30
USDCHF	0.40	USDIDR	2.42
USDDKK	0.59	USDILS	0.70
USDJPY	0.30	USDINR	0.80
USDNOK	0.56	USDKRW	0.80
USDSEK	0.60	USDMXN	0.89
		USDPHP	2.00
		USDPLN	1.01
		USDSGD	0.55
		USDTRY	0.71
		USDTWD	0.60
		USDZAR	1.03

3.4.2 Sourcing the Data

We can now see that for each option pricing point we will need a full dataset consisting of:

- The underlying exchange rate
- Option implied volatility information
- Then two out of three of:
  - forward rate,
  - quote currency deposit rate, and
  - base currency deposit rate.

In addition, the spot rate at expiry is required in order to determine the payoff of the option. This, along with all other data mentioned, was downloaded from the market-data provider Bloomberg.

For those less familiar with FX market quotations, we note that care must be taken when sourcing implied volatility data; it is necessary to ensure that the correct conventions are built into one's pricing models as what are assumed by many to be at-the-money implied volatilities often aren't. For USDJPY, for example, Bloomberg by default quotes delta-neutral straddle volatilities, which under most circumstances will be close to, but different from, at-the-money volatilities. An option pricing model must be constructed in such a way that these subtleties are recognised – in practical terms, configuration data containing market conventions must be included for all currency pairs. These conventions were initially dominated by premiums paid in a way analogous to spot market transactions: generally settled after two business days. This all changed with the financial crisis of 2008.

As we have seen, an option price depends on a number of parameters, with volatility usually deemed to be the most important input. However, during the financial crisis in 2008 funding and liquidity became an issue and different banks were charged different interbank deposit rates depending on their perceived credit quality. There were material advantages, whether buying or selling an option, in where the deposit rate was set, and in many cases 'fast markets' meant that no market consensus could be reached on the correct rate to be applied.[6] In the face of such difficulties, option markets were unable to function smoothly. Markets, however, tend to be efficient; the situation lasted only a relatively short time before the traders moved to a forward premium model to ease friction.

Forward premium is where the option is paid for at maturity and is now the standard used in the professional market. Although a neat solution in terms of option risk, it increases credit exposure and makes collateral management more difficult. Hence, most corporate entities still prefer to trade options with premiums exchanged at the beginning of the trade.

We have used the current conventions right back to the start of the back-test. With forward premium, the dominating market factor is volatility. During the crisis the volatility spreads (bid-offer) were naturally large, so volatility was still the dominating input to any option price and no arbitrage existed between forward and spot premium. Before the crisis, volatility was the dominant input as spreads in deposit and forward rates were tight.

3.4.3 Calculation Frequency

The selection of the option pricing points used for the analysis is an important consideration. Since we have access to daily data, we could calculate the premium and payoff for option trades commencing on each and every trading day. However, because tests showed no significant difference between results based on daily and weekly data, to

---

[6]A 'fast market', as the name suggests, is where the movement of the underlying, index or volatility etc. is so fast that several different rates may appear (there may even be arbitrage). With the advent of computer-based trading systems this would seem less likely, but such events were seen as recently as October 2014 in US Treasuries, one of the most liquid markets in the world.

reduce the computational requirements and to make the resulting dataset more manageable we elected to perform calculations on a weekly basis. Weekly trades mean that the calculation frequency is aligned with the shortest tenor under consideration. To minimise the effects of local holidays on our weekly valuation points we chose Wednesday as the default trade initiation day.

3.4.4 Currency of Option Notional Amount

It is no surprise that the countries with the biggest economies dominated the list of actively traded currencies presented in Chapter 1, Figure 1.3. In particular, the US dollar takes top spot with its reputation as the world's reserve currency and the fact that many commodities are quoted in USD. With FX option contracts first appearing on the US exchanges, it was natural that for the currency pairs involving the US dollar the premium would be paid in USD. This theme continued as the market expanded to the different currency pairs traded. From a practical point, if an American company wants to hedge an exposure in Turkey, there is little point in paying the premium in TRY and then having to hedge that exposure or swap the TRY premium back in to USD.

For the crosses (i.e. exchange rates not including USD) the decision is a little less obvious, but the convention for payment generally follows the quotation for spot. Namely where spot is stated in units of quote currency per unit of base currency, the option premium will be payable in percent of the base. As an example, for market makers in EURNOK, where the currency rate is, say, 8.34 NOK per EUR, the options will be traded in percent of EUR. Corporate hedgers will, however, tend to trade in their own base currency. A Norwegian-based company will buy an option in percent of NOK (or in NOK pips when hedging a EUR notional amount).

Bearing all of this in mind, we would very much like the results presented in this book to be of practical value. Of course the conclusions of our analysis may be interesting at the theoretical level, but so much the better if the findings can be applied by corporate treasurers and portfolio managers to improve their companies' hedging policies. This ambition drove our choice of the currency in which we specified the notional amounts for the options in our study.

For emerging market exchange rates in particular, it is most likely that a hedger will be concerned about the prospect of a sudden depreciation of the quote currency. That is, for EURBRL it is our view that the most probable hedging application will be the protection of the future value of BRL receivables or assets by EUR-based companies. For this reason our analysis is based on option notional amounts specified in the base currency – EUR in the above example.[7]

---

[7] The findings presented in the following chapters also hold for notional amounts specified in the quote currency and in many cases the features that emerge are in fact more extreme than is the case for base currency notional amounts.

3.4.5　Spot Market Value

As we mentioned at the start of Section 3.4, the choice of dataset for spot prices is a significant one; it is important that all of the points in the dataset are coincident if accurate premiums are to be calculated. Data vendors often offer a choice of closing prices corresponding to the end of day in different regions and we studied the differences between these datasets as a starting point.[8]

OPTION MATURITY TIMES

Option maturities occur at different times depending on the currency pair and the region. So EURPLN options expire at 10am London time but EURHUF options at 11am. It would have been painful but why didn't we choose spot prices for the relevant times rather than closing prices? First, intraday pricing data are not always available on a historical basis – clearly a limiting factor. Second, taking spot rates for different times would have caused mass confusion when pricing, say, a EURKRW option. Invariably USDKRW is taken from a KRW fixing and EURUSD from, say, the ECB fixing several hours later, so the crossed rate EURKRW may never have even appeared in the market. Traders with trading books that contain lots of NDF trades face the issue of carrying fixing exposure every day.

Empirically, we concluded that New York closing prices were preferable to London Europe closes for the purpose of a systematic study of the nature described here. Since the final results were very similar for both London Europe and New York closes, this decision was primarily based on the frequency with which bad data points occurred for each closing time. We found that in the wings of the volatility skew in particular the London Europe closing data were subject to unexplained spikes far more often than the New York closes were.

We do not have a definitive explanation for this. However, one possible reason is that Europe covers two time zones with many financial centres. To run risk reports across many assets, banks need to take a data snapshot. But the timestamp for this is not universally set. Hence one dataset may be saved at 3pm London for option expiry and another at 4pm London (a 5pm Frankfurt close). A 5pm London time snapshot is also possible, or even a mixture of all three possibilities. This introduces an element of noise and disruption into a Europe close dataset. The close for the data in New York

---

[8]The selection of closing time is something of a pitfall for aspiring analysts. As the setting is often hidden away, it is not always obvious why the same spreadsheet produces different results for different users. For Bloomberg subscribers, the differences can often be resolved by comparing settings under XDF.

is much more clearly defined as 5pm NY. So despite trading being continuous and the market following the sun to Auckland and Sydney, the dataset is more uniform.

3.5 LIMITATIONS

When building an analytical model, the phrase 'rubbish in, rubbish out' should be at the front of one's mind. A model can be developed with great attention to detail in order to be extremely accurate, but if the quality of the data inputs is poor, one cannot expect to obtain meaningful results. To put it slightly differently in pre-FX option market terms: you can't make a silk purse out of a sow's ear.

Our most significant limitation in performing a meaningful long-term analysis of FX option performance is the sourcing of long time series of option data. Given the cyclical nature of financial markets, we should perform any analysis for a period that spans all of the phases of a market cycle, and preferably several cycles. We may then choose to split the dataset into smaller samples to evaluate whether structural developments have occurred over time, but this type of analysis is only possible if we have sufficient data to begin with.

The most fundamental limitation in relation to the availability of option data arises because, in the grand scheme of things, modern option markets are a recent development. However, on top of this insurmountable constraint there were further impediments to us sourcing the necessary data.

In today's world of 'big data' every minor detail of our lives appears to be preserved (whether we like it or not!) but early option trades were undertaken in different times. We cannot do much about periods for which no prices were recorded – we can simply begin the analysis at the start of the period for which we have high quality data. As we have already explained, this date may not be the date at which the data series commences.

As shown in Figure 3.1, we can download a historical series for USDMYR 1M implied volatility from Bloomberg that, according to the start date field associated

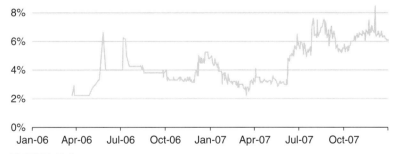

FIGURE 3.1   Downloaded series USDMYR 1M implied volatility.
Pricing was unresponsive in the early years, making the first part of the
history unsuitable for inclusion in the analysis

with the ticker, begins in March 2006. As we can clearly see, however, the data prior to October 2006 look suspicious. While there may have been quotes for USDMYR implied volatility prior to October 2006, we can guess that pricing contributions to the data vendor were few and far between, or at least the volatilities were updated by the contributing trading desk(s) only occasionally during these early months. Such data probably do not represent an accurate expectation of the volatility for the exchange rate over the subsequent one-month period and should therefore be excluded from any analysis. Indeed this and other data issues eventually led to us omit USDMYR from our dataset.

We can of course address the issues of poor quality data for earlier times, sometimes by deciding that nothing is to be done but perform the analysis with a later start date. This is how, for example, we handled long periods of unresponsive implied volatility data at the start of a time series – if options on a currency pair were not liquid at that time so that prices were not regularly refreshed, there is little to be done.

Sometimes, however, suspicious data points can be investigated further and any issues resolved. First, it is possible that a suspicious data point accurately reflects a blip in the market due to short-term squeeze effects meaning that no action is required. If this is not the case, we may be able to replace the erroneous point from other sources. For example, it may be that we have good deposit rate data for a period during which the forward point history is unreliable (see Figure 3.2, for example). In this case we could calculate forward points based on an interest rate differential in order to narrow down where the problem lies.

Because of the variety of possible errors in the downloaded data series, the cleaning of our dataset was a largely manual process – hardly the most glamorous of jobs but an essential part of the analysis nonetheless.

Earlier in this section we discussed the problem of data being unavailable at the start of our back-test period, but this is not the only fundamental limitation we must consider; we must also accept a constraint relating to the most recent period of our dataset. For longer dated options the outcome for recent contracts is unknown. For example, the payoff of a three-year option bought one year ago will not be known

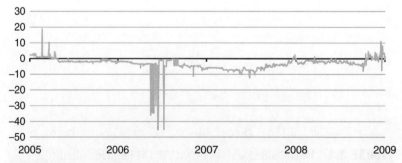

FIGURE 3.2   Downloaded series for EURCZK 1W forward points shows bad data points for 2006

with certainty for another two years. This unavoidable limitation must be handled with care; we should not compare the performance of strategies based on shorter dated options with longer tenor option histories without accounting for what may be considerable differences in the end dates.

3.6 SUMMARY

This chapter has dealt with the practicalities of analysing FX option markets. We have shed some light on the possible reasons that books on the theory of option pricing greatly outnumber those that describe the observed performance of options over the history of the market – despite the fact that for most of those involved in business the latter subject is more important.

We have listed the components required in order to perform a quantitative analysis of option relative value and detailed the data requirements for the necessary pricing models. We have described how allowances for costs can be included and have discussed the issues related to non-deliverable currencies. Finally, we have described some important limitations of historical studies and the precautions one must take.

While the discussion of a dataset may not be the most exciting of topics, it is certainly one of the most important. Data provide the foundation on which all subsequent analysis is built; without a robust dataset, one cannot have faith in the results of any study.

REFERENCES

[1] Bank of International Settlements Triennial Survey: Global foreign exchange market turnover in 2013.
[2] McCauley, R. and Scatigna, M. (2011) Foreign exchange trading in emerging currencies: More financial, more offshore. *BIS Quarterly Review* 72 (March), 67–75.

CHAPTER 4

At-the-Money-Forward (ATMF) Options

4.1   WHAT ARE ATMF OPTIONS?

ATMF options are the most liquid of the FX options, and also have the longest trading history. They are the simplest to value of all the FX option contracts. A person who buys an ATMF call option on an FX rate will receive a payoff if the FX rate is above the forward rate on the expiry date; if instead they have bought a put option then they will receive a payoff if the FX rate is below the forward rate. Hence the name: the strike of the option is the forward rate.

4.1.1   How Are ATMF Options Used and Traded?

ATMF options are used both for speculative and protective purposes. Their advantages are:

- They are highly liquid.
- They are simple to value.
- They have a lot of associated historical data which is easily accessed.

However, they are not always the instrument of choice. Disadvantages include:

- Upfront premium to pay (if it is not paid upfront then it is still usually accounted for as if it is[1]).
- Lack of specific risk or event targeting.
- Unfavourable regulatory treatment.

---

[1]In practice some option contracts will net both premium and payoff as a single cash flow on the expiry date, which simplifies credit calculations. Adjustments are made to account for interest rate effects.

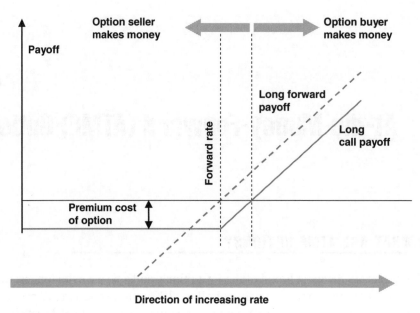

FIGURE 4.1   Payoff profile for call option

For speculators, liquidity and ease of valuation are very useful, as is the long history of volatility. However, both their upside and downside are somewhat limited. There are no highly levered returns available. So a speculator who has a specific view on a market event which he or she wants to monetise may prefer a less liquid but more precise instrument. A corporation may not want to pay the premium upfront, regarding it as a sunk cost (which is not entirely true, as the payoff, if any, will only act to reduce the net cost). And additionally, many regulations regard the premium as the 'cost' of the option – despite the fact that if the market were efficient, the payoff would be on average the same after costs.[2] So they are widely traded but do not meet everybody's needs.

4.1.2 What Is the 'Fair' Price for an ATMF Option?

In Figure 4.1 we show the payoff profile for a call option. It is worth pointing out that this is the payoff at expiry of the option, so we are currently neglecting the path that the value of the option may take before this date. This is also important but for now we will consider only what happens at the expiry point.

Who will make money with this contract? At the end, if we disregard trades that may be executed in order to manage risk, depending where the spot rate ends up one of the buyer and seller will win and one will lose. One will receive money that the other owes. What might we expect to happen on average?

---

[2]See the Appendix Chapter 1 for a discussion of what an option 'should' cost.

If the premium of the option is 'fair' we would expect that neither of the buyer and seller consistently makes or loses money. There will of course be a small effect due to bid-offer costs, but beyond this we would expect some kind of equality of outcome on each side. Of course, the distributions of returns which each side sees are by definition different. The seller has unlimited risk and limited gain, and the buyer has limited risk (worst case is that the option expires with no payoff so the buyer just loses the premium) but unlimited gain. That is why options were originally sold – to transform the risk profile of the option owner, to insure the owner against risk for a fixed price.

But we can say that we would expect, on average, that the seller and the buyer both end up with no profit or loss beyond costs. In any single case the situation can vary, but overall we would anticipate that there is no systematic bias.

How would this play out? It will happen if the premium is on average the right amount. Over the course of several years, we would expect that the average premium amount equals the average payoff amount, though, as stated before, the payoff will have a much wider possible set of values. This could happen, however, in various different ways. In Figure 4.2 we illustrate some of them. Let us assume that we are tracking the difference between premium and payoff over time, and that in all cases this difference averages to zero over the period.

1. We know that market conditions vary widely, so one possibility is that the premium changes in response to these conditions, being higher in more volatile, risky periods. Thus the premium and payoff would track each other fairly well. This would correspond to the Low Volatility case in Figure 4.2.
2. On the other hand, the market changes might be more rapid and unexpected, and the premium would track them less closely. This is represented by the High Volatility case in Figure 4.2.
3. Another way to arrive at the same average value would be to have two or more periods with larger mismatches, illustrated with the Large Swing case in Figure 4.2. An example of this would be a calm and confident market, where premia and payoffs are both low, which is followed by an unexpected surge in risk. The

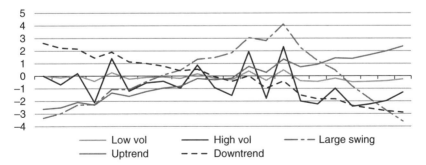

FIGURE 4.2 Difference between premium and payoff over time (% notional). Different series, same average value

initial period will greatly increase payoffs as spot rates make large moves. Premia will rise in response and stay high for some time even after the risk event is over. So while we might expect to see premia and payoffs approach each other in value when averaged over time, it would be quite possible to see them out of line for some time within the dataset. One might legitimately wonder how long they could stay out of line while preserving overall equality within a reasonable market time frame; there is no definitive answer to this but certainly if an unequal condition persists for some years, most market participants will start calling it an opportunity or a mispricing rather than a temporary misalignment.

4. Finally, perhaps more dangerously, we can see that the Uptrend and Downtrend cases will also give the same 'average' value, but here one might reasonably anticipate that relying on this value in the future would be foolish. In this case the average is concealing a changing situation.

4.2 HOW MIGHT MISPRICINGS ARISE?

Let us look at the calculation for the premium of an ATMF call option.

$$c = S_0 e^{-r_b T} N(d_1) - K^{-rT} N(d_2)$$

where:

c = premium of a call option on the base currency,

$$d_1 = \frac{\ln(S_0/K) + (r - r_b + \sigma^2/2)T}{\sigma\sqrt{T}}$$

$d_2 = d_1 - \sigma\sqrt{T}$

S_0 = FX rate at inception (value of one unit of base currency in quote currency),

K = strike rate,

r = interest rate for the tenor of the deal in the quote currency,

r_b = interest rate for the tenor of the deal in the base currency,

T = tenor of the deal, and

σ = implied volatility of the option (as explained in Chapter 2).

Of these parameters, both interest rates and implied volatility have the potential to have a systematic effect on the payoff/premium ratio. Essentially, an option is valued by making assumptions about the future distribution of market rates. The forward rate is taken to be the mean of this future distribution, and σ is taken to be a measure of the standard deviation. Though the Black-Scholes-Merton model assumes that rates are log-normally distributed, in practice this is untrue; modern pricing models will take a set of implied volatilities at different strikes to imply a future distribution which can be significantly non-normal. But that is more relevant for our future discussions on out-of-the-money (OTM) options in Chapter 5; for now, the precise shape of the distribution is less relevant than whether the standard deviation is correct or not.

Bluntly speaking, there are two ways that the ATMF option premium can be systematically out of line with the payoff: either the forward rate is not in general the mean of the future distribution, or the implied volatility is a biased estimate of the standard deviation. We can consider both of these in turn.

4.2.1 Can the Forward Rate Be on Average Wrong?

As was discussed previously, the forward rate is simply the current spot FX rate adjusted for interest rate effects, and it is the only future rate which may be locked in at zero cost, apart from bid-offer. To attempt to guarantee any other rate on the same future date would result in arbitrage opportunities, as discussed in Chapter 2, which would very quickly move the rate back to the forward. So it is unavoidable that it is used as the mean of the future distribution of spot rates. But the fact that market participants are obliged to use it does not, perhaps strangely, guarantee that it is correct or even that it is a good estimate. In fact, it is not on average correct. Multiple studies [1], [2], [3], [4] beginning in the 1980s have found that it is a biased indicator, and that the spot rate at the inception of the deal is a better predictor of the spot rate at the end than is the forward rate.

This fact is often still a surprise, even to experienced market participants. Many option traders might agree that spot is unlikely to go all the way to the forward rate, but are still surprised that the forward rate really contains no predictive power. They do appear to be somewhat aware that spot rates will not move as predicted; for example, the implied volatility which is quoted or calculated for ATMS (at-the-money-spot) options is often somewhat lower than the ATMF volatility, indicating that traders 'feel' that the spot is a more likely point for the market to end the deal on than the forward. Thus, without perhaps completely realising the full implications of the data, the market is to some degree 'aware' of what is going on. This is often most apparent in pegged currency pairs. Spot is pegged, but the forward moves. Where the forward is positive, the value of the put in premium terms is often the difference in value between spot and the outright forward rate.

An interesting example to take is the EURCHF currency pair between 2011 and Jan 2015. In 2011, the Swiss National Bank (SNB) announced that it would defend the level of 1.20 CHF per EUR by buying EUR as needed to keep the spot rate above that point. It did this because the CHF had become perceived as a safe-haven currency and in high-risk times investors aggressively bought the CHF. However, this strengthened the currency to the point where exports and tourism began to suffer, hence the SNB deemed intervention a good idea. In January 2015 the SNB abandoned this policy. However, during the period that the exchange rate floor was in place, the one year forward price was below 1.20 on many occasions. The low implied volatility environment in EURCHF showed that the market expected the floor to hold, but the forward market clearly showed a pricing anomaly. A trader might have been willing to buy a 1Y vanilla EUR put, predicting that he could make a profit through the delta hedging of the position even though the option had virtually no chance of ending in the money. However, as soon as the trader was asked about a more exotic option, whose payoff was spot path dependent, he would switch mode and start talking about how the option would never end in the money, or hit a barrier since the spot would not go below the intervention targeted rate. So in this extreme example traders knew that the forward was not a good measure of spot. What market participants often fail to do is to adopt this attitude for more general situations. Partly this is because, as stated before, long-term trends are less important to them than short-term evolution. Some traders in high carry currency pairs will position themselves against the carry, but it is largely instinctive and not a rigorous risk management technique.

The obvious question to ask then is can money be made from this mispricing? Indeed it can – the carry trade in FX is one of the more famous examples of markets systematically providing profit opportunities. It is not without risk; we will discuss it in detail in Chapter 7, but over the years since FX became a liquid floating market, it has on average delivered good returns. So the forward rate can indeed on average be wrong, which could easily provide a mechanism for systematic option mispricing.

4.2.2 Can the Implied Volatility Be on Average Wrong?

If market rates obligingly moved according to log-normal distributions, whose characteristics remained fixed, then one could simply measure the volatility in the past and apply it to the future to generate the correct price of the option.

If only it were so! We know, of course, that FX rates are better modelled by changing distributions; the moves of the autumn of 1998 or 2008 were far larger than could have been predicted by observations of the previous few years' rates. So implied volatility and option prices vary with market activity; they rise in times of higher risk and are lower in generally calmer markets.

Is the implied volatility on average correct? As with the forward rate, the fact that it is widely used and quoted does not actually mean that it has to be right. If it is too low, then it is implying a less active market than will be the case, and so options are too cheap. In this case the premium will be on average less than the payoff of the option, meaning that it will be a good idea to buy the options. If it is too high, then the premium will be too high and the options will be good value to sell. A final possibility exists: that it may be a reasonable estimate of the standard deviation but that the actual distribution of future moves will not be log-normal, though this will be most relevant to far out-of-the-money options.

Like the forward rate, then, the implied volatility certainly can be out of line with reality, though a large and very consistent difference would probably be arbitraged away. A final interesting thought is that the two factors can possibly act together to either eliminate or exacerbate mispricings. We might anticipate that a systematic difference between forward and spot at expiry is partially compensated for by the implied volatility implying a slightly broader distribution of rates than in fact is the case. But let us see what actually happens.

TABLE 4.1 Premium and payoff for USDJPY straddles

USDJPY	Premium	Payoff	Ratio
1W	1.31%	1.09%	82.7%
1M	2.57%	2.40%	93.4%
3M	4.47%	4.39%	98.2%
6M	6.30%	6.33%	100.6%
12M	8.77%	8.72%	99.4%
2Y	11.94%	12.37%	103.7%
3Y	13.41%	13.18%	98.3%

4.2.3 Simple Example with USDJPY

As will be the case throughout this book, we begin by considering the most basic definition of value – what the option costs in terms of the premium, and what it pays out (payoff) at the end of its life. In all cases we include the bid-offer costs as it would be unrealistic not to. Let us look at USDJPY, one of the best and cleanest data series, and see on average what each option cost, and what it paid out. The tenors which have reasonable data series are all tabulated and graphed in Table 4.1 and Figure 4.3, but it is worth noting that the longer tenors (2Y and 3Y) suffer from the dual disadvantage that first of all there are fewer data per se, and then that the first payoff occurs two or three years after the first deal date, so effectively we have fewer data to analyse. In all cases we have held the options to expiry and done no intermediate hedging trades.

The options we have used here are straddles. A straddle is usually a combination of an ATMF put and an ATMF call; we initially analyse these contracts as they will be relatively immune to directional drift in the spot market.

This is interesting. We see that, on average, it looks as if one could have made money by selling short dated options, and buying long dated ones. Even if we could accept that the 'correct' payoff/premium ratio need not be exactly 100%, for hedging or insurance reasons, then the longer dated options seem much too cheap relative to

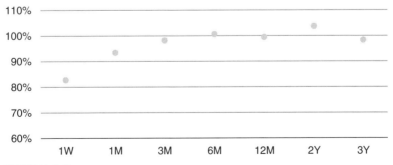

FIGURE 4.3 Payoff/premium ratio for USDJPY straddles

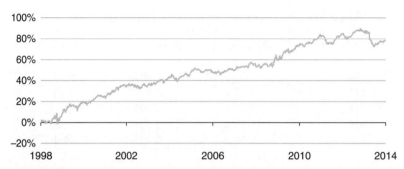

FIGURE 4.4 Result of continuously selling USDJPY 1W straddles

the shorter dated ones. But this is not the whole story, by a long way. Let's take the short dated options and look at the way in which the profit was accrued – the daily P/L (profit and loss) chart. After all, it's no good saying that a strategy is on average profitable over ten years if it makes a loss in nine of them.

As we see here, overall it looks really quite consistent. But once more, this is not the whole story. The data in Figure 4.4 give only the premium and payoff information. If this were a real trading book, we would be valuing the deals every day of their life, which would add considerable volatility to the result. So perhaps this is not a get-rich-quick strategy. But what can be seen is that something strange has been going on: in one of the most liquid instruments available there has been a systematic error in its valuation over time. Because it is not as simple as an arbitrage to take advantage of, there is no reason to think that it will disappear quickly. It seems to be persistent over time; we will shortly see whether the effect is duplicated in other currency pairs.

As an aside, selling short dated options can attract other problems than simply the inherent risk of large losses. Most traders operate under risk limits, and selling options uses these up very quickly, so short option positions have other associated 'costs' to the trader.

Another way in which one could consider whether there is an opportunity for a trading strategy is to examine the result of buying longer dated options. Below in Figure 4.5 we show the result for continuously buying 2Y straddles in USDJPY. We

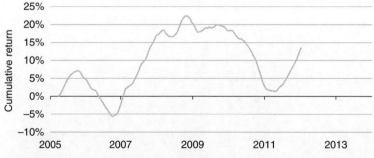

FIGURE 4.5 Result of continuously buying USDJPY 2Y straddles

have shown 2Y rather than 3Y as there are a few more useful data available. As can be seen, overall there is a profit, but it is not very consistent, being dominated by the crisis period in 2007 and 2008 where options bought cheaply before the crisis paid off significantly once volatilities rose. And in addition, the investor in this strategy would have to wait two years before seeing any return. So again, while it looks interesting, it is not necessarily a successful trading strategy. However, it does highlight that options bought for protective purposes would have been highly effective during the crisis period.

4.3 RESULTS FOR STRADDLES FOR ALL CURRENCY PAIRS

In Figures 4.6 and 4.7 and Tables 4.2, 4.3 and 4.4 we have graphed and tabulated the payoff/premium results for all the currency pairs in our sample. The results are interesting and bear some discussion. First of all, it should be noted that different amounts of data are available for the various tenors and pairs. The 1M–12M tenors have the longest and most complete datasets; the shortest and longest tenors are less well supplied, though the 1W set is quite well populated. So the interpretation of any results should bear in mind that the poorer datasets have a greater margin of error. However, even with this caveat, a few very clear patterns emerge.

1. Short dated options are too expensive, when averaged over the whole period. On average the payoff is just 83% of the premium. It is not only USDJPY which shows this feature; it appears to be universal. Moreover, though we do not graph them all here, the series of returns obtained from systematic option selling for the various pairs are in the majority similar to the fairly smooth returns shown in Figure 4.5 for USDJPY – the effect does not seem to be dominated by a single

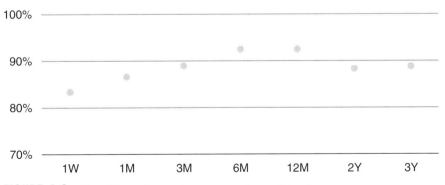

FIGURE 4.6   Payoff/premium ratio – averaged over 34 pairs

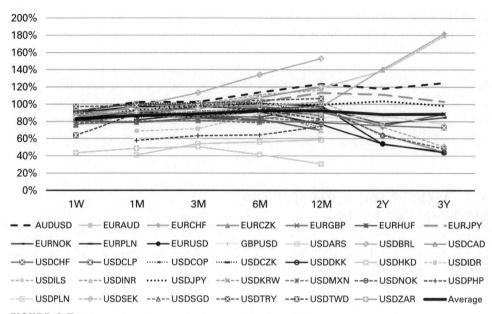

FIGURE 4.7   Payoff/premium ratio for straddles for different currency pairs

anomalous period.[3] This yields insight into the anecdotal evidence that many hedge funds generate returns by selling short-dated options. On average it has indeed been worth it.

2. There is a clear trend for longer dated options to become closer to fair value, culminating in some suggestions that for 12M and longer tenors the payoffs have been on average approximately equal to or sometimes greater than the premia. However, the different currency pairs show more noise for the longer tenors, consistent with both systematic effects and poorer data quality.

3. The results for the longest tenors, 2Y and 3Y, are quite noisy and show considerable disagreement. They tend to be dominated by the most recent data period as they have much less data than shorter tenors. Thus results obtained for these pairs should be treated with caution; nevertheless, the fact that they continue with trends observed for the better quality datasets is interesting. Note that for these longer tenors the effect of discounting becomes significant. As discussed in Chapter 3, we do include the effect of discounting the premia and, though small up to and including the 12M tenor, the 3Y average is brought down by about 10% by the discounting effect.

---

[3]However, as mentioned previously, these results do not include interim marked to market values, which would increase volatility and drawdowns, especially around risk episodes like 2008.

TABLE 4.2 Premium and payoff for ATMF straddles (1W–3M tenors)

	1W			1M			3M		
	Premium	**Payoff**	**Ratio**	**Premium**	**Payoff**	**Ratio**	**Premium**	**Payoff**	**Ratio**
AUDUSD	1.43%	1.30%	91.4%	2.66%	2.73%	102.5%	4.60%	4.72%	102.7%
EURAUD	1.28%	1.15%	89.5%	2.42%	2.35%	97.4%	4.27%	4.19%	98.1%
EURCHF	0.64%	0.52%	82.0%	1.20%	1.07%	89.4%	2.07%	1.73%	83.5%
EURCZK	0.87%	0.67%	77.2%	1.67%	1.32%	79.0%	2.87%	2.32%	80.9%
EURGBP	0.95%	0.83%	87.2%	1.85%	1.62%	87.4%	3.30%	2.77%	84.1%
EURHUF	1.28%	1.04%	80.9%	2.51%	1.98%	79.0%	4.42%	3.71%	84.0%
EURJPY	1.43%	1.31%	91.2%	2.84%	2.68%	94.3%	4.95%	4.84%	97.9%
EURNOK	0.88%	0.71%	80.9%	1.68%	1.45%	86.1%	2.91%	2.47%	84.9%
EURPLN				2.49%	2.04%	81.7%	4.30%	3.81%	88.6%
EURUSD	1.21%	1.09%	90.5%	2.42%	2.35%	97.2%	4.31%	4.19%	97.2%
GBPUSD	1.06%	0.94%	88.7%	2.08%	1.93%	93.1%	3.71%	3.22%	87.0%
USDARS				2.69%	1.10%	40.9%	5.90%	3.19%	53.9%
USDBRL	1.77%	1.50%	85.2%	3.42%	3.34%	97.8%	5.98%	6.76%	113.1%
USDCAD	1.04%	0.94%	91.2%	2.07%	1.80%	86.9%	3.57%	3.08%	86.5%
USDCHF	1.25%	1.16%	92.3%	2.47%	2.48%	100.4%	4.38%	4.30%	98.1%
USDCLP				2.78%	2.42%	87.2%	4.96%	4.81%	96.9%
USDCOP				3.42%	2.88%	84.2%	5.94%	5.46%	92.0%
USDCZK	1.61%	1.47%	91.6%	3.13%	3.15%	100.9%	5.44%	5.52%	101.5%
USDDKK	1.28%	1.05%	82.3%	2.50%	2.30%	92.1%	4.41%	3.76%	85.4%
USDHKD	0.11%	0.05%	43.5%	0.19%	0.09%	48.6%	0.36%	0.18%	50.5%
USDIDR				2.93%	2.01%	68.7%	5.56%	3.98%	71.6%
USDILS				1.98%	1.88%	94.9%	3.36%	3.34%	99.4%
USDINR				1.98%	1.82%	92.0%	3.61%	3.50%	97.0%
USDJPY	1.31%	1.09%	82.7%	2.57%	2.40%	93.4%	4.47%	4.39%	98.2%
USDKRW	1.31%	1.02%	77.7%	2.39%	2.08%	87.2%	4.25%	3.60%	84.8%
USDMXN	1.35%	1.06%	78.4%	2.58%	2.07%	80.4%	4.65%	3.79%	81.4%
USDNOK	1.43%	1.28%	89.6%	2.79%	2.48%	88.7%	4.90%	4.48%	91.3%
USDPHP				2.46%	1.42%	57.8%	4.62%	2.92%	63.2%
USDPLN				3.40%	3.21%	94.3%	5.98%	5.83%	97.6%
USDSEK	1.44%	1.26%	87.7%	2.83%	2.59%	91.5%	4.96%	4.48%	90.3%
USDSGD	0.73%	0.55%	75.9%	1.34%	1.20%	89.5%	2.43%	2.13%	87.6%
USDTRY	1.45%	1.41%	97.2%	3.13%	3.08%	98.4%	5.65%	5.70%	100.9%
USDTWD	0.66%	0.42%	63.8%	1.15%	1.02%	89.4%	2.13%	2.09%	98.0%
USDZAR	2.03%	1.73%	85.3%	3.96%	3.62%	91.4%	6.81%	6.44%	94.6%

4.3.1 Discussion of Results for Straddles

At this stage it is worth discussing the drivers of option value, particularly for the shorter dated contracts. While at this stage we cannot explain the tendency for longer dated options to become steadily better value, there are a number of different effects which influence the value of shorter dated options in a trading environment, and we detail them below.

TABLE 4.3 Premium and payoff for ATMF straddles (6M–3Y tenors)

	6M			12M			2Y			3Y		
	Premium	Payoff	Ratio	Premium	Payoff	Ratio	Premium	Payoff	Ratio	Premium	Payoff	Ratio
AUDUSD	6.39%	7.26%	113.7%	8.88%	10.97%	123.5%	12.43%	14.66%	118.0%	13.76%	17.17%	124.8%
EURAUD	6.12%	6.64%	108.6%	8.75%	10.42%	119.1%	12.18%	16.90%	138.7%	13.26%	23.78%	179.3%
EURCHF	2.94%	2.51%	85.3%	4.14%	4.02%	96.9%	6.46%	9.08%	140.6%	6.23%	11.33%	181.8%
EURCZK	4.03%	3.33%	82.7%	5.63%	5.15%	91.5%						
EURGBP	4.74%	3.81%	80.6%	6.73%	5.32%	79.0%	10.05%	7.55%	75.1%	11.66%	10.33%	88.6%
EURHUF	6.30%	5.20%	82.5%	8.89%	6.21%	69.8%						
EURJPY	7.02%	7.23%	102.9%	9.79%	11.09%	113.2%	14.34%	15.93%	111.1%	17.97%	18.50%	102.9%
EURNOK	4.06%	3.47%	85.4%	5.66%	5.41%	95.6%	8.34%	6.46%	77.4%	9.64%	8.15%	84.6%
EURPLN	6.04%	5.63%	93.2%	8.51%	8.43%	99.0%						
EURUSD	6.16%	6.19%	100.4%	8.75%	8.60%	98.3%	12.18%	6.50%	53.4%	13.50%	6.06%	44.9%
GBPUSD	5.30%	4.81%	90.6%	7.50%	6.34%	84.5%	11.71%	10.13%	86.5%	13.62%	10.47%	76.9%
USDARS	9.63%	5.41%	56.2%	16.00%	9.39%	58.7%						
USDBRL	8.59%	11.52%	134.1%	12.65%	19.38%	153.2%						
USDCAD	5.05%	4.67%	92.4%	7.20%	6.83%	94.9%	11.93%	7.74%	64.8%	14.53%	6.44%	44.3%
USDCHF	6.21%	6.04%	97.3%	8.72%	7.91%	90.8%	11.83%	8.90%	75.2%	12.93%	9.44%	73.0%
USDCLP	7.14%	6.78%	95.0%	10.29%	8.93%	86.8%						

(continued)

TABLE 4.3 *(Continued)*

	6M			12M			2Y			3Y		
	Premium	Payoff	Ratio	Premium	Payoff	Ratio	Premium	Payoff	Ratio	Premium	Payoff	Ratio
USDCOP	8.48%	7.98%	94.1%	12.89%	9.42%	73.1%						
USDCZK	7.69%	7.83%	101.9%	10.85%	9.80%	90.3%						
USDDKK	6.35%	5.80%	91.4%	9.09%	6.98%	76.8%	12.35%	6.66%	53.9%	13.54%	5.95%	44.0%
USDHKD	0.63%	0.26%	41.4%	1.26%	0.39%	30.8%						
USDIDR	8.31%	7.36%	88.5%	12.79%	11.30%	88.4%						
USDILS	4.70%	5.22%	111.1%	6.57%	7.65%	116.4%						
USDINR	5.23%	5.05%	96.5%	10.29%	7.16%	69.6%						
USDJPY	6.30%	6.33%	100.6%	8.77%	8.72%	99.4%	11.94%	12.37%	103.7%	13.41%	13.18%	98.3%
USDKRW	6.01%	5.54%	92.2%	8.50%	8.38%	98.7%						
USDMXN	6.73%	5.28%	78.5%	9.82%	7.97%	81.1%						
USDNOK	6.93%	6.59%	95.1%	9.76%	9.51%	97.5%	14.36%	9.14%	63.7%	16.15%	7.80%	48.3%
USDPHP	6.97%	4.47%	64.2%	10.25%	7.64%	74.5%						
USDPLN	8.43%	8.36%	99.2%	11.89%	12.06%	101.4%						
USDSEK	6.99%	6.82%	97.6%	9.81%	10.07%	102.7%	14.55%	10.71%	73.6%	16.72%	8.46%	50.6%
USDSGD	3.54%	3.00%	84.6%	5.13%	4.05%	79.0%						
USDTRY	8.37%	8.74%	104.5%	12.58%	13.42%	106.7%						
USDTWD	3.20%	3.00%	93.7%	4.83%	3.99%	82.6%						
USDZAR	9.61%	10.34%	107.5%	13.58%	16.32%	120.2%						

TABLE 4.4 Payoff/premium ratio for
straddles, averaged over all currency pairs

Average	Ratio
1W	83.4%
1M	86.6%
3M	88.9%
6M	92.5%
12M	92.5%
2Y	88.3%
3Y	88.7%

(i) Efficient, liquid trading   Where options and the underlying FX rate are liquid
and easily traded, the market is ruthlessly efficient. For short dated options, there is a
strong degree of consensus in the data that their payoff is about 80% of the premium –
this is shown in Figure 4.7, where almost all the currency pairs give similar results
for the 1W tenor. For an option sold by a trading desk, one can perhaps understand
that this ratio would be 'desirable' – they sell it, hope that the market does not move
too much and collect a profit at the end. It's not that simple of course – a lot of active
management is involved – but the principle is clear. However, we saw in Chapter 2
that in fact a bought option, where the ratio is the wrong way round for the desk,
can be traded dynamically with some positive gamma hedging as long as the spot FX
rate stays within a range. Thus it is conceivable that any shortfall in the payoff could
be made up in this way and the desk can still make a profit. It's not guaranteed, and
depends upon the market and the skill and experience of the trader. But essentially,
for a liquid option and spot market, a payoff/premium ratio of 80–100% could be
sustainable for a trading desk in a market regime which allows this kind of profitable
active hedging – though it does not allow it all the time by any means.

Can the desk really hope to make money under most circumstances? Probably
it can. If the traders were not good, they wouldn't last long – and they have a
lot of help. A huge amount of work goes into understanding the dynamics of the
markets. Examples include the different influences that stocks and interest rates have
on exchange rates. Hence, most banks have an FX forecast that is not necessarily
in line with the forward market, but will give a base guide as to how much drift of
volatility can be expected. Overlaying this most traders will have plenty of experience
about the effect of economic data releases that are due over the near future and have
an understanding of how much intraday volatility these will cause. Indeed, now spot
moves over various economic data releases are back-tested for a more precise estimate.
Further, as a lot of markets are built on confidence and no one likes surprises, the
market listens carefully to Central Bank guidance. This dampens high volatility jump
risk. All this means that the markets are generally liquid and have achieved a high
degree of commoditisation.

But apart from knowledge and experience, the general activities of trading desks around the world will tend to encourage these profitable range-trading conditions. Once the market has established a trading range for an implied volatility or spot rate, it can be difficult for it to break out. Essentially, once a range is in place then the trading activity by the option desk will tend to maintain it via gamma hedging. Dynamic traders who are positive gamma will set adjustment levels in keeping with the volatility that has been traded in order to recoup their theta, as explained in Chapter 2. The buying and selling will cause some volatility, but also a degree of mean-reversion in the underlying and so excessive moves will be curtailed. Dynamic traders who are negative gamma will be happy for the underlying to move around within a range and collect daily theta until any new impetus is found. So they too will not cause excessive volatility.

Does this mean that the value of about 80% for the payoff/premium ratio for 1W options is 'fair' or 'correct'? It just means that it is sustainable. Those who buy a 1W or 1M option to cover a risk are still paying more than, on average, they will get back, and they should be aware of it. But in a sense we would not have been surprised – and not written this book – if, overall, all FX options had a similar 80% payoff/premium ratio. The fact that they do not, which comes out strongly in the longer tenor data, is due to very different effects.

What does this 80% value indicate about implied versus historical volatility? For short dated options, the premium cost is dominated by the implied volatility, as the forward rate is very close to the spot rate for these tenors. Thus we are drawn to the conclusion that as far as the markets can be modelled by a log-normal distribution the implied volatility on average overestimates realised historical volatility by a noticeable amount. This could not become an extremely large overestimate, however, or arbitrage opportunities would arise.

(ii) Inefficient markets/illiquidity   For illiquid markets economic fundamentals can have a discrete impact on the currency. Specifically to FX this is normally in the form of a currency revaluation and is surprisingly common. Perhaps the most high profile example in recent times has been in Ukraine in 2014. In other cases the markets are very illiquid and the data are of poor quality with several gaps, which might explain the fact that the ratios are low, such as for the Argentine peso (ARS). The dramatic results in both directions for the 2Y and 3Y tenors in many pairs are in general a result of small datasets.

(iii) Carry in pegged currencies   Currencies which are to a greater or lesser extent controlled often still have higher interest rates than G10 currencies. These carry currencies in general have a higher level of volatility in the forward rates than their G10 counterparts. Some of these pegged currencies can have virtually no spot movement, but wild swings in the forward prices. As an example the Hong Kong dollar (HKD) has not been a free-floating currency for much of its life; it tends to be locked to the USD, so the currency pair displays little spot volatility. Consequently options rarely pay out so the premium tends to be more than the payoff. But there is still a demand to hedge the interest rate exposure, and by trading the forward gamma, buying options can still be profitable. We will look at carry currencies in more detail in Chapter 6.

(iv) Supply and demand, or positioning   Although the FX market is vast and there is usually enough liquidity, there are some examples of where constant supply and demand have affected the pricing. The most commonly cited example is for the USDJPY risk reversal during the 1990s when Japanese corporate hedgers dominated the market with a voracious appetite for USD puts. This was exacerbated by hedging of interest rate structures to the extent that banks struggled to find counterparties to offset the risk and the prices remained distorted for some time. Furthermore, JPY was used as a funding currency by most hedge funds and sometimes protection was bought on these positions. The extent of such positioning was apparent when they were unwound during the LTCM (Long-Term Capital Management) crisis at the end of the 1990s.

(v) Opportunity/mispricing   The biggest opportunities in the market generally come from a long held belief that breaks down. This can come in many forms and can be sudden or prolonged. Two powerful examples of this are EURCHF and EURAUD. In the case of EURCHF this centres on the external factor of the SNB (Swiss National Bank) and how much sway it has over the market; a sudden decision by the SNB to limit the rise of the CHF versus the EUR took everyone by surprise in 2011. Equally surprising was the abandonment of the policy in early 2015, and the subsequent violent market moves. In the case of EURAUD the belief in the market was that the main driver of the market would be the US dollar. Hence the two main currencies EURUSD and AUDUSD would move in tandem and have a strong correlation responding to economic events. So partly due to the underestimated volatility in the AUD in general and partly due to the breakdown of the correlation, EURAUD options have paid out more than their premiums.

4.3.2 A Breakdown of the Results by Currency Pair

From Figure 4.7 and Table 4.2 to Table 4.4 we can see that there is great variation among the various currency pairs. Some of this is clearly due to the effects discussed above – for example, the HKD is a classic pegged carry currency, and bought options return only a fraction of their value to the holder if statically hedged. To understand more of how value varies with tenor, however, will require analysis not just of straddles, as below, but of their constituents, puts and calls. This will shortly be discussed.

4.3.3 Drilling Down to Different Time Periods

The natural question to ask at this point would be: is this effect due to one or two extreme regimes? As most of the currency pair datasets include 2008, perhaps it has biased the results? Thus we repeat the analysis for several sub-periods of data. It would

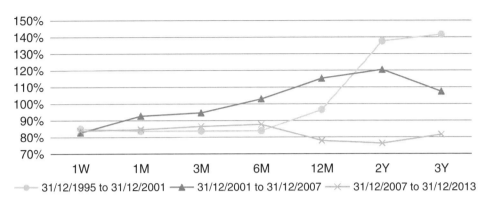

FIGURE 4.8 Payoff/premium ratio – averaged over 34 currency pairs for separate time periods

be tedious to put all of the tables in this chapter, so the equivalents of Figure 4.7 and Tables 4.2 and 4.3 for the different sub-periods are relegated to the Appendix, but in Figure 4.8 and Table 4.5 we show the different overall results for the sub-periods by analogy with Figure 4.6.

We can see that though there is significant variation, especially with the data-sparse longer tenors, on the whole the pattern holds. Longer dated options tend to offer much better value than shorter dated ones. If one drills down to much shorter periods there is more significant variation, and interestingly, the most recent years do show a change. The period from 2011 to 2013 shows a reversal of the pattern, though this is also found in some individual years from earlier periods. There is a strong tendency for the pattern to be preserved by spikes in volatility following long low 'fallow' periods. It is worth noting that the final period ends in Dec 2013; had it been continued to include the higher volatility periods at the end of 2014 and into 2015, then that line would have been very much in line with the two previous periods.

TABLE 4.5 Payoff/premium ratio, averaged over 34 currency pairs for separate time periods

Tenor	31/12/1995 to 31/12/2001	31/12/2001 to 31/12/2007	31/12/2007 to 31/12/2013
1W	85.1%	82.8%	83.9%
1M	83.7%	92.7%	84.7%
3M	83.8%	94.7%	86.5%
6M	83.9%	102.9%	87.7%
12M	96.5%	115.2%	77.9%
2Y	137.6%	120.4%	76.2%
3Y	141.6%	107.3%	81.5%

4.3.4   Comparison of Put and Call Options

So far we have dealt with at-the-money-forward straddles, which are in effect just a put plus a call. A put option gives the right to sell an asset at a future date, while a call option confers the right to buy. When the asset is something tangible like a share index, there is little ambiguity in these definitions. In foreign exchange, we need to clearly state whether we are talking about an option on the base currency, the quote currency or the rate itself. In all cases, we will refer to options on the rate, so a call option will pay out when the rate rises. In the case of EURUSD, for example, this is when the EUR appreciates relative to the USD.

At this point we are presenting raw data, and not taking account of any consistent interest rate differentials between the two currencies in the pair.

We repeat our analysis on ATMF puts and calls, graphing and tabulating the results.

This is really remarkable. Consider that the results shown in Figure 4.6, which are for ATMF straddles, show a strong tendency for longer dated options to be better value, though with noise for the very long tenors. We now see in more detail how these results originate. A straddle is just a put and a call added together, so the upwards tendency of the data in Figure 4.6 is coming from the average of the data in Figures 4.9 and 4.10. But in fact, all of the tendency to better value in longer tenors is coming from the puts! The calls show a strong tendency in the opposite direction, for longer dated options to be much worse value. The results for straddles were surprising enough but they come from even more unusual underlying data.

How should we interpret this? Calls, which pay out for depreciation of the quote currency, are poor value for longer tenors, while puts, which pay out for appreciation of the quote currency, are very good value indeed, with the payoff/premium ratio reaching 130% for the 3Y tenor. We might take the 2Y and 3Y tenor results as coming from inferior data but even the 12M tenor has a payoff/premium ratio of 120% for the puts. However, looking at the currency-by-currency results in Figures 4.11 and 4.12, which are tabulated in Tables 4.6 to 4.11, gives us a clue as to the cause.

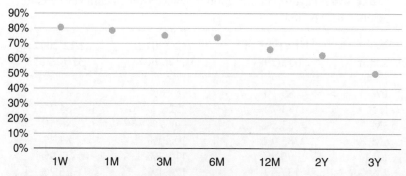

FIGURE 4.9   Payoff/premium ratio for ATMF calls – averaged over 34 pairs

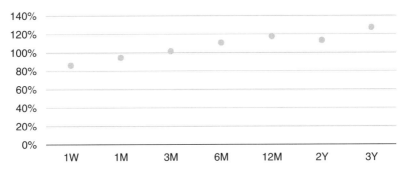

FIGURE 4.10 Payoff/premium ratio for ATMF puts – averaged over 34 pairs

One glaring outlier, particularly for the calls, is the AUDUSD currency pair. Where the average payoff/premium ratio for all the calls for the 3Y tenor is 41%, the AUDUSD pair comes in at 180%, by far the highest. The EURJPY and USDJPY results for the 12M tenor show a similar effect – they do not have much data in the 2Y and 3Y tenors. For the puts, the 3Y tenor for the AUD is 12%, in complete contrast to the average of 127%. This leads us in the direction of the answer. The AUD currency on average has had much higher interest rates, over time, than the USD. Most of the currency pairs in the sample are the other way round – in general, the USD or the EUR is the base currency, and in general they have lower interest rates than the other

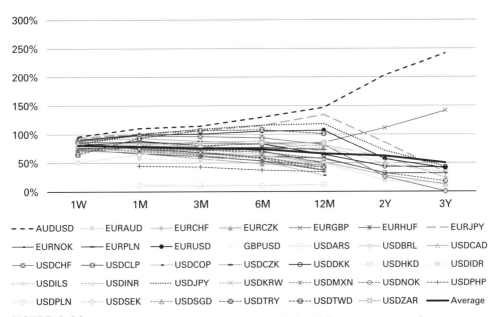

FIGURE 4.11 Payoff/premium ratio for ATMF calls for different currency pairs

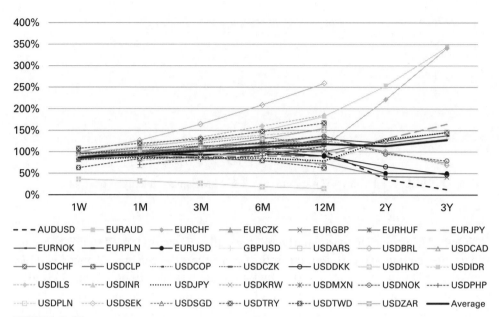

FIGURE 4.12　Payoff/premium ratio for ATMF puts for different currency pairs

currency in the pair. But AUD is the notable exception; other pairs where a similar effect has occurred would be those like USDJPY or EURJPY, as the JPY has had a very low interest rate regime for many years – and these pairs too show unusual behaviour.

To understand what is going on, we need to go back to the FX carry trade, which we mentioned at the beginning of the chapter. Harking back to our discussion on the forward rate and the fact that, historically, it has tended to be a biased indicator, we can consider what effect this systematic bias might have. Let us consider the distribution of spot rates as they evolve after the start of a contract.

Figure 4.13 demonstrates what history has shown to be the case, where the base currency has the lower interest rate. After the start of a contract, the spot rate at the inception of the deal is the best estimate of the spot rate at the end of the deal. The forward rate lies off to the side to the direction of depreciation of the (usually) higher yielding currency and is a biased predictor. The shaded area represents, schematically, the area where the spot rate is most likely to be – i.e. very large moves are unlikely.

Now in Figure 4.14 we have inserted a distribution around the forward rate, which represents the implied distribution derived from the option volatility. The forward rate and the implied distributions are assumed to be the best estimates of the future evolution of the deal when the premium of an option is calculated – but as we know, this is demonstrably not the case.

TABLE 4.6 Payoff/premium ratio for ATMF calls (1W–3M tenors)

	1W			1M			3M		
	Premium	**Payoff**	**Ratio**	**Premium**	**Payoff**	**Ratio**	**Premium**	**Payoff**	**Ratio**
AUDUSD	0.71%	0.69%	96.1%	1.33%	1.47%	110.6%	2.3%	2.6%	114.7%
EURAUD	0.64%	0.53%	82.7%	1.21%	1.01%	83.6%	2.1%	1.4%	66.2%
EURCHF	0.32%	0.25%	80.0%	0.60%	0.52%	86.5%	1.0%	0.8%	77.2%
EURCZK	0.43%	0.31%	72.2%	0.84%	0.56%	67.0%	1.4%	0.8%	57.6%
EURGBP	0.47%	0.41%	87.3%	0.93%	0.80%	86.1%	1.7%	1.4%	84.5%
EURHUF	0.64%	0.48%	74.6%	1.26%	0.83%	66.4%	2.2%	1.4%	61.3%
EURJPY	0.72%	0.68%	94.3%	1.42%	1.44%	101.2%	2.5%	2.7%	107.0%
EURNOK	0.44%	0.34%	76.5%	0.84%	0.64%	76.1%	1.5%	1.0%	68.0%
EURPLN				1.25%	0.95%	76.3%	2.2%	1.7%	77.1%
EURUSD	0.60%	0.55%	91.0%	1.21%	1.21%	99.5%	2.2%	2.2%	100.7%
GBPUSD	0.53%	0.47%	89.2%	1.04%	1.02%	98.1%	1.9%	1.7%	92.2%
USDARS				1.34%	0.15%	11.1%	2.9%	0.3%	10.1%
USDBRL	0.88%	0.63%	71.5%	1.71%	1.19%	69.5%	3.0%	1.8%	60.9%
USDCAD	0.52%	0.45%	85.9%	1.04%	0.76%	73.3%	1.8%	1.2%	65.2%
USDCHF	0.63%	0.56%	89.1%	1.24%	1.21%	97.9%	2.2%	2.1%	96.3%
USDCLP				1.39%	1.08%	77.9%	2.5%	2.0%	78.8%
USDCOP				1.72%	1.14%	66.1%	3.0%	1.8%	61.7%
USDCZK	0.80%	0.71%	88.9%	1.57%	1.46%	93.3%	2.7%	2.4%	88.2%
USDDKK	0.64%	0.52%	80.9%	1.25%	1.11%	88.5%	2.2%	1.8%	80.6%
USDHKD	0.06%	0.03%	51.2%	0.09%	0.06%	64.8%	0.2%	0.1%	74.5%
USDIDR				1.46%	0.84%	57.9%	2.8%	1.5%	53.3%
USDILS				0.99%	0.74%	74.9%	1.7%	1.1%	66.2%
USDINR				0.99%	0.81%	82.0%	1.8%	1.6%	86.9%
USDJPY	0.66%	0.55%	83.6%	1.29%	1.29%	100.6%	2.2%	2.4%	109.2%
USDKRW	0.65%	0.47%	72.2%	1.20%	0.92%	76.7%	2.1%	1.5%	71.1%
USDMXN	0.67%	0.51%	75.8%	1.29%	0.92%	71.2%	2.3%	1.5%	63.3%
USDNOK	0.72%	0.61%	84.8%	1.40%	1.08%	77.4%	2.5%	1.8%	72.5%
USDPHP				1.23%	0.55%	44.8%	2.3%	1.0%	43.1%
USDPLN				1.70%	1.28%	75.2%	3.0%	2.1%	70.6%
USDSEK	0.72%	0.61%	84.6%	1.42%	1.21%	85.3%	2.5%	2.0%	80.5%
USDSGD	0.36%	0.25%	69.6%	0.67%	0.52%	77.8%	1.2%	0.8%	67.8%
USDTRY	0.72%	0.63%	86.5%	1.57%	1.17%	74.6%	2.8%	1.9%	68.4%
USDTWD	0.33%	0.22%	64.9%	0.57%	0.54%	93.7%	1.1%	1.1%	106.7%
USDZAR	1.01%	0.82%	81.2%	1.98%	1.60%	80.8%	3.4%	2.7%	78.0%

Now in Figure 4.15 we have layered on the payoffs to a put and a call option, and suddenly all becomes clear. If we assume that the most likely scenario is that the spot rate at expiry lands in the shaded area, then it's very clear that the put option has a good chance of making money while the call option is much more likely to lose its premium. The results in Figures 4.9 and 4.10 arise automatically!

As an encore, we can now add the forward contract payoffs to the already rather complicated diagram, and we see the carry trade laid out (Figure 4.16). The short

TABLE 4.7 Payoff/premium ratio for ATMF calls (6M–3Y tenors)

	6M			12M			2Y			3Y		
	Premium	Payoff	Ratio	Premium	Payoff	Ratio	Premium	Payoff	Ratio	Premium	Payoff	Ratio
AUDUSD	3.19%	4.15%	130.0%	4.45%	6.54%	146.9%	6.19%	12.59%	203.4%	6.85%	16.56%	241.6%
EURAUD	3.06%	2.06%	67.5%	4.39%	2.18%	49.7%	6.06%	1.19%	19.7%	6.59%	0.98%	14.9%
EURCHF	1.47%	1.12%	76.5%	2.07%	1.68%	81.1%	3.17%	1.91%	60.2%	3.00%	0.72%	23.9%
EURCZK	2.02%	0.97%	48.3%	2.82%	1.21%	42.8%						
EURGBP	2.37%	1.97%	82.9%	3.37%	2.89%	85.8%	5.01%	5.58%	111.3%	5.77%	8.15%	141.2%
EURHUF	3.15%	1.69%	53.7%	4.45%	1.64%	36.8%						
EURJPY	3.51%	4.04%	115.1%	4.89%	6.58%	134.4%	7.13%	6.12%	85.8%	8.88%	2.95%	33.2%
EURNOK	2.03%	1.25%	61.9%	2.83%	1.64%	57.9%	4.15%	1.33%	32.0%	4.80%	1.52%	31.7%
EURPLN	3.03%	2.31%	76.4%	4.27%	3.12%	73.0%						
EURUSD	3.09%	3.26%	105.6%	4.38%	4.69%	107.1%	6.05%	3.43%	56.7%	6.70%	2.72%	40.6%
GBPUSD	2.65%	2.52%	94.9%	3.75%	3.36%	89.4%	5.85%	3.13%	53.4%	6.77%	1.55%	22.8%
USDARS	4.73%	0.49%	10.3%	7.98%	0.97%	12.2%						
USDBRL	4.30%	2.58%	60.0%	6.37%	2.86%	44.9%						
USDCAD	2.53%	1.58%	62.3%	3.61%	1.85%	51.2%	5.96%	1.70%	28.5%	7.26%	0.88%	12.1%
USDCHF	3.11%	2.92%	94.0%	4.37%	3.57%	81.7%	5.87%	1.52%	25.9%	6.43%	0.02%	0.4%
USDCLP	3.57%	2.52%	70.7%	5.16%	2.54%	49.2%						
USDCOP	4.27%	2.27%	53.2%	6.54%	1.83%	28.0%						

USDCZK	3.86%	3.22%	83.4%	5.44%	3.51%	64.6%	6.14%	2.69%	43.8%	6.70%	2.84%	42.4%
USDDKK	3.19%	2.65%	83.0%	4.56%	2.95%	64.6%						
USDHKD	0.32%	0.20%	64.2%	0.63%	0.30%	46.8%						
USDIDR	4.14%	2.64%	63.6%	6.47%	3.17%	49.0%						
USDILS	2.35%	1.48%	63.1%	3.29%	1.59%	48.4%						
USDINR	2.59%	2.29%	88.5%	5.18%	3.58%	69.0%						
USDJPY	3.14%	3.65%	116.0%	4.39%	5.20%	118.5%	5.95%	4.24%	71.3%	6.62%	2.89%	43.6%
USDKRW	3.01%	2.20%	73.3%	4.26%	3.24%	76.1%						
USDMXN	3.36%	1.78%	53.0%	4.92%	2.25%	45.8%						
USDNOK	3.47%	2.39%	68.9%	4.89%	2.78%	56.9%	7.15%	2.31%	32.3%	8.01%	1.45%	18.1%
USDPHP	3.50%	1.31%	37.3%	5.16%	1.78%	34.6%						
USDPLN	4.22%	2.55%	60.5%	5.95%	3.17%	53.3%						
USDSEK	3.50%	2.92%	83.5%	4.91%	3.90%	79.3%	7.24%	3.46%	47.8%	8.28%	2.74%	33.0%
USDSGD	1.77%	1.02%	57.4%	2.57%	0.96%	37.5%						
USDTRY	4.19%	2.48%	59.2%	6.35%	2.66%	41.9%						
USDTWD	1.61%	1.73%	108.0%	2.42%	2.45%	101.2%						
USDZAR	4.81%	4.10%	85.2%	6.80%	5.73%	84.4%						

TABLE 4.8 Payoff/premium ratio for ATMF calls, averaged over all currency pairs

Average	Ratio
1W	80.6%
1M	78.4%
3M	75.3%
6M	73.9%
12M	66.0%
2Y	62.3%
3Y	50.0%

TABLE 4.9 Payoff/premium ratio for ATMF puts (1W–3M tenors)

	1W			1M			3M		
	Premium	Payoff	Ratio	Premium	Payoff	Ratio	Premium	Payoff	Ratio
AUDUSD	0.71%	0.62%	86.8%	1.33%	1.26%	94.9%	2.3%	2.1%	91.5%
EURAUD	0.64%	0.62%	96.0%	1.21%	1.34%	111.2%	2.1%	2.7%	126.1%
EURCHF	0.32%	0.27%	83.9%	0.60%	0.55%	92.0%	1.0%	0.9%	90.4%
EURCZK	0.43%	0.36%	82.2%	0.83%	0.76%	91.1%	1.4%	1.4%	101.0%
EURGBP	0.47%	0.41%	87.1%	0.93%	0.82%	89.0%	1.7%	1.4%	84.4%
EURHUF	0.64%	0.56%	87.3%	1.25%	1.14%	91.2%	2.2%	2.3%	105.5%
EURJPY	0.72%	0.63%	87.8%	1.42%	1.24%	87.6%	2.5%	2.2%	87.9%
EURNOK	0.44%	0.38%	85.4%	0.84%	0.81%	96.3%	1.5%	1.5%	101.0%
EURPLN				1.25%	1.09%	87.3%	2.1%	2.2%	100.7%
EURUSD	0.60%	0.54%	89.9%	1.21%	1.15%	95.2%	2.2%	2.0%	94.1%
GBPUSD	0.53%	0.47%	87.8%	1.04%	0.92%	88.1%	1.9%	1.5%	81.0%
USDARS				1.34%	0.92%	68.3%	3.0%	2.7%	90.1%
USDBRL	0.88%	0.87%	98.6%	1.71%	2.16%	126.2%	3.0%	4.9%	164.1%
USDCAD	0.52%	0.50%	96.5%	1.04%	1.03%	99.7%	1.8%	1.9%	105.1%
USDCHF	0.63%	0.60%	95.6%	1.24%	1.27%	102.9%	2.2%	2.2%	100.5%
USDCLP				1.39%	1.34%	96.4%	2.5%	2.8%	113.0%
USDCOP				1.71%	1.74%	102.0%	3.0%	3.6%	120.0%
USDCZK	0.80%	0.76%	94.5%	1.56%	1.70%	108.7%	2.7%	3.1%	112.8%
USDDKK	0.64%	0.53%	83.9%	1.25%	1.20%	95.7%	2.2%	2.0%	91.0%
USDHKD	0.06%	0.02%	36.0%	0.09%	0.03%	32.4%	0.2%	0.0%	26.5%
USDIDR				1.46%	1.17%	80.1%	2.8%	2.4%	87.2%
USDILS				0.99%	1.14%	115.3%	1.7%	2.2%	133.6%
USDINR				0.99%	1.01%	102.6%	1.8%	2.0%	109.1%
USDJPY	0.66%	0.54%	81.8%	1.28%	1.11%	86.3%	2.2%	1.9%	86.6%
USDKRW	0.65%	0.54%	83.3%	1.20%	1.17%	97.6%	2.1%	2.1%	98.8%
USDMXN	0.67%	0.55%	81.1%	1.29%	1.15%	89.4%	2.3%	2.3%	99.7%
USDNOK	0.72%	0.68%	94.5%	1.40%	1.40%	100.3%	2.5%	2.7%	109.9%
USDPHP				1.23%	0.86%	70.2%	2.3%	1.9%	81.7%
USDPLN				1.70%	1.93%	113.5%	3.0%	3.7%	125.3%
USDSEK	0.72%	0.65%	90.9%	1.42%	1.39%	98.0%	2.5%	2.5%	100.7%
USDSGD	0.36%	0.30%	82.3%	0.67%	0.67%	100.6%	1.2%	1.3%	106.1%
USDTRY	0.72%	0.78%	107.5%	1.57%	1.87%	119.1%	2.8%	3.7%	129.4%
USDTWD	0.33%	0.21%	62.8%	0.57%	0.48%	84.0%	1.1%	0.9%	87.0%
USDZAR	1.01%	0.91%	89.4%	1.98%	2.01%	101.3%	3.4%	3.7%	109.7%

TABLE 4.10 Payoff/premium ratio for ATMF puts (6M–3Y tenors)

	6M			12M			2Y			3Y		
	Premium	Payoff	Ratio	Premium	Payoff	Ratio	Premium	Payoff	Ratio	Premium	Payoff	Ratio
AUDUSD	3.19%	3.15%	98.6%	4.44%	4.50%	101.4%	6.21%	2.24%	36.1%	6.88%	0.85%	12.3%
EURAUD	3.06%	4.55%	148.7%	4.37%	7.98%	182.4%	6.09%	15.42%	253.1%	6.63%	22.78%	343.6%
EURCHF	1.47%	1.40%	95.0%	2.07%	2.35%	113.6%	3.23%	7.15%	221.5%	3.11%	10.63%	341.2%
EURCZK	2.01%	2.30%	114.2%	2.82%	3.87%	137.5%						
EURGBP	2.37%	1.87%	79.1%	3.37%	2.46%	73.1%	5.03%	2.12%	42.1%	5.83%	2.42%	41.5%
EURHUF	3.15%	3.51%	111.6%	4.45%	4.58%	102.9%						
EURJPY	3.51%	3.15%	89.8%	4.90%	4.42%	90.2%	7.17%	9.34%	130.3%	8.98%	14.79%	164.7%
EURNOK	2.03%	2.17%	107.0%	2.83%	3.66%	129.5%	4.17%	5.01%	120.2%	4.82%	6.61%	137.2%
EURPLN	3.02%	3.35%	110.9%	4.26%	5.36%	125.9%						
EURUSD	3.08%	2.93%	95.0%	4.37%	3.94%	90.0%	6.09%	3.06%	50.3%	6.75%	3.38%	50.1%
GBPUSD	2.65%	2.24%	84.5%	3.75%	2.96%	79.0%	5.86%	6.94%	118.5%	6.81%	8.83%	129.7%
USDARS	4.82%	4.79%	99.3%	8.00%	8.16%	101.9%						
USDBRL	4.30%	8.97%	208.9%	6.33%	16.37%	258.8%						
USDCAD	2.53%	3.05%	120.9%	3.60%	4.90%	136.3%	5.97%	5.90%	98.9%	7.26%	5.35%	73.7%
USDCHF	3.11%	3.15%	101.4%	4.36%	4.38%	100.5%	5.91%	7.41%	125.3%	6.47%	9.42%	145.7%
USDCLP	3.57%	4.23%	118.4%	5.15%	6.29%	122.3%						
USDCOP	4.24%	5.68%	134.1%	6.45%	7.38%	114.5%						

(continued)

TABLE 4.10 (Continued)

	6M			12M			2Y			3Y		
	Premium	Payoff	Ratio	Premium	Payoff	Ratio	Premium	Payoff	Ratio	Premium	Payoff	Ratio
USDCZK	3.85%	4.62%	120.2%	5.43%	6.25%	115.2%						
USDDKK	3.17%	3.21%	101.1%	4.54%	4.10%	90.1%	6.18%	4.04%	65.4%	6.77%	3.20%	47.2%
USDHKD	0.32%	0.06%	18.7%	0.63%	0.09%	14.7%						
USDIDR	4.16%	4.58%	110.1%	6.39%	7.75%	121.3%						
USDILS	2.35%	3.76%	160.1%	3.29%	6.09%	185.1%						
USDINR	2.61%	2.80%	107.2%	5.15%	3.43%	66.7%						
USDJPY	3.15%	2.68%	85.1%	4.39%	3.46%	78.8%	5.97%	7.68%	128.6%	6.70%	9.74%	145.2%
USDKRW	3.00%	3.36%	111.9%	4.25%	5.18%	122.0%						
USDMXN	3.36%	3.50%	104.1%	4.91%	5.73%	116.7%						
USDNOK	3.47%	4.21%	121.4%	4.88%	6.66%	136.5%	7.18%	6.83%	95.2%	8.08%	6.36%	78.8%
USDPHP	3.48%	3.15%	90.5%	5.12%	5.75%	112.3%						
USDPLN	4.22%	5.85%	138.7%	5.95%	8.94%	150.3%						
USDSEK	3.50%	3.94%	112.6%	4.91%	6.21%	126.6%	7.28%	7.34%	100.8%	8.36%	5.82%	69.6%
USDSGD	1.77%	1.99%	112.5%	2.57%	3.06%	119.2%						
USDTRY	4.18%	6.15%	147.1%	6.29%	10.51%	167.1%						
USDTWD	1.60%	1.27%	79.5%	2.42%	1.51%	62.7%						
USDZAR	4.81%	6.22%	129.4%	6.79%	10.47%	154.2%						

TABLE 4.11 Payoff/premium ratio for
ATMF puts, averaged over all currency pairs

Average	Ratio
1W	80.6%
1M	78.4%
3M	75.3%
6M	73.9%
12M	66.0%
2Y	62.3%
3Y	50.0%

forward (betting against the forward rate) makes money, while the long forward loses it, and can for some cases lose more money than the option premium. These cases would occur when the forward rate is far away from spot (corresponding to a large interest rate differential between the two currencies in the pair) and the premium cost of the option is fairly small (corresponding to fairly low market volatility). In fact, this set of conditions holds more often than might be supposed. Later in the book we will devote a chapter to the phenomena arising in the high yield emerging market currency pairs, where the high carry/low volatility conditions have often persisted for years at a time, making options the best value hedge for some exposures.

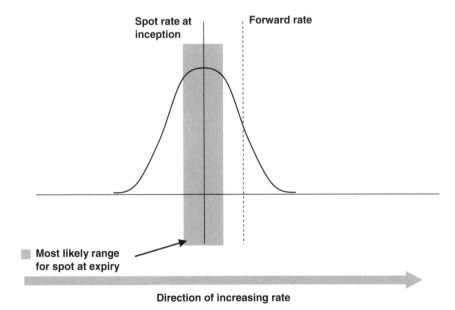

FIGURE 4.13 Spot at inception versus forward, with likely historical range of spot at expiry

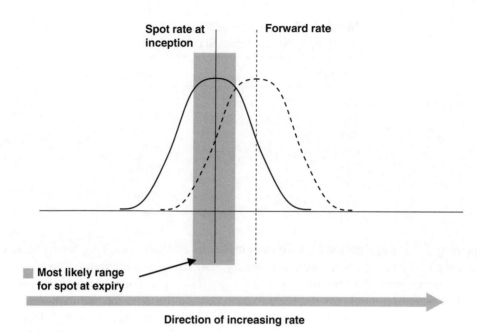

FIGURE 4.14   Implied versus historical rate distributions at expiry

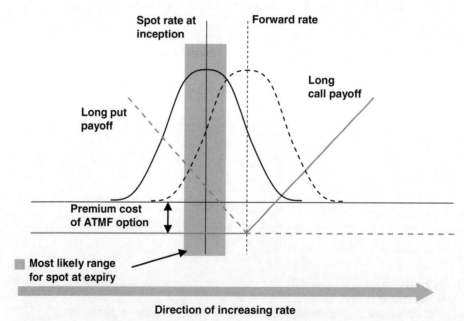

FIGURE 4.15   Option payoffs with implied and historical rate distributions

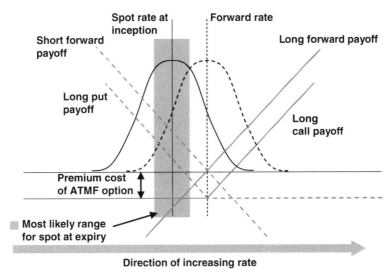

FIGURE 4.16 Option and forward payoffs with implied versus historical distributions

Of course, we would need to reverse these diagrams for the case where the base currency has the higher interest rate, like AUDUSD or USDJPY.

4.4 HAVE WE FOUND A TRADING STRATEGY?

It is always natural, when one sees this degree of inefficiency in a liquid market, to wonder whether there is some kind of money-making strategy waiting to make someone lucky very rich. But it's not clear that this will be the one. The calls and puts do not really diverge for the shorter tenors; the big differences are seen in the 12M tenors and longer. Thus one would not expect to make money in timeframes less than this, and it could be longer. Not many investors would like this pattern of returns. But for those looking to protect their exposures to different currencies, these data are extremely important. They now have information about which option contracts historically do well and which do badly, and additionally which market circumstances are likely to lead to this effect.

The longer dated options do perhaps seem to offer something in the way of returns. For the longest tenors then the volatilities of the interest rates involved become important, but in general trading of interest rates and FX rates are completely separated, with each desk having no mandate or systems to trade in the other's area. Oversight systems are notoriously bad at combining the different types of risk, and traders tend to specialise in their own area, so cross-product knowledge is unusual. Thus, those points on the tenor curve where intelligent combination of the two sets of skills become important could indeed offer opportunity.

4.5 SUMMARY OF RESULTS

We can summarise the results of this chapter for options which are held until maturity as follows:

1. Short dated straddles are on average expensive.
2. Long dated straddles are on average close to fair value.
3. Short dated put and call options are on average expensive.
4. Long dated put options are on average cheap versus payoff where the base currency tends to have lower interest rates, and expensive where the base currency tends to have higher interest rates.
5. Long dated call options are on average expensive versus payoff where the base currency tends to have lower interest rates, and cheap where the base currency tends to have higher interest rates.[4]

REFERENCES

[1] Bilson, J. F. O. (1981) The 'Speculative Efficiency' hypothesis. *Journal of Business* 54(3), 435–451.
[2] Shafer, J. R., Loopesko, B. E., Bryant, R. C. and Dornbusch, R. (1983) Floating exchange rates after ten years. *Brookings Papers on Economic Activity* 1, 1–86.
[3] Fama, E. F. (1984) Forward and spot exchange rates. *Journal of Monetary Economics* 14, 319–338.
[4] James, J., Kasikov, K. and Secmen, A. (2009) Uncovered interest parity and the FX carry trade. *Quantitative Finance* 9(2), 123–127.

---

[4]Recall that cheap and expensive in this context are relative terms that apply to the option in isolation. Our analysis did not take into account any hedges/positions in the underlying.

Out-of-the-Money (OTM) Options: Do Supposedly 'Cheap' OTM Options Offer Good Value?

5.1 INTRODUCTION

In Chapter 4 we discussed the performance of the most liquid foreign exchange options, at-the-money-forward puts and calls. Of course it is possible to trade currency options with less common strike rates, resulting in changes to both premium and payoff characteristics. In this chapter we evaluate the long-term performance of out-of-the-money options and ask how the value offered by these OTM contracts compares with that offered by the ATMF options of the previous chapter.

In order to analyse the performance of out-of-the-money options we will need to take account of the volatility smile; despite the Black-Scholes-Merton model being consistent with implied volatility that is the same for options of different strike rates, this is not true empirically. Plotting quoted implied volatility versus option strike price produces a curved structure, showing that the volatility assumed for the underlying is not constant with strike.

We begin by discussing the shape of the volatility smile – depending on the market considered, its form may better be described as a smirk or even a frown – and reconcile this observed phenomenon with market characteristics; why does the smile look the way it does? Given the observed variation in implied volatility with option strike price, we ask where the best value lies: should a corporate treasurer opt for an at-the-money option when hedging foreign exchange exposure, or would 'cheaper' out-of-the-money options provide a satisfactory hedge at a lower cost?

Readers already familiar with the volatility surface may wish to omit Sections 5.2 to 5.5 and begin reading at Section 5.6.

5.2 PRICE VERSUS VALUE

Out-of-the-money options should cost less than at-the-money options in premium terms. The former, having a strike price some way from the current spot price, are less likely to expire in profit than options with at-the-money strike prices, allowing a clear arbitrage opportunity unless the out-of-the-money option costs less.

We can see how this lower probability of a payoff at expiry is reflected in the prices calculated using the simple option pricing formulae introduced in Chapter 2. Recall that the Black-Scholes-Merton option pricing model is based on a number of assumptions about the underlying asset and financial markets. Geometric Brownian motion is assumed for the underlying and a stochastic partial differential equation formulated. As we have already seen, solving the equation results in analytic expressions for the prices of European put and call options. For a call option, the price is given by:

$$c = S_0 e^{-r_b T} N(d_1) - K e^{-rT} N(d_2)$$

where:

$$d_1 = \frac{\ln(S_0/K) + (r - r_b + \sigma^2/2)T}{\sigma\sqrt{T}}.$$

$$d_2 = \frac{\ln(S_0/K) + (r - r_b - \sigma^2/2)T}{\sigma\sqrt{T}}$$

and:

$$d_2 = d_1 - \sigma\sqrt{T},$$

where T is the tenor, S_0 the spot rate at inception, K the strike rate, r_b and r the risk-free rates for the base and quote currencies respectively and σ the volatility of the underlying asset. $N(.)$ represents the cumulative distribution function of a standard normal distribution.

One can see that for an out-of-the-money call option where the forward rate is such that $K > S$, the higher strike rate will act to reduce the price of the option, $c(S, t)$, while the decrease in the value of $N(d_2)$ will act to increase the call price. However, since $N(d_1)$ also decreases, the net effect of moving the strike rate further out-of-the-money is to reduce the price of the call option.

At the limit when σ is very large, thus maximising the difference between d_1 and d_2, and meaning that $N(d_1) \to 1$ and $N(d_2) \to 0$, the price of an out-of-the-money call option still cannot exceed the price of an at-the-money call option; in both cases the call price now tends towards the spot price. Even at this extreme, the price of an out-of-the-money option can only approach rather than exceed the price of an at-the-money option.

If FX rates really did follow the constant volatility log-normal process assumed under Black-Scholes-Merton, the question of the relative value of out-of-the-money options would be less interesting. Given a well-specified stochastic process, the analytic solutions for prices based on the underlying probability distributions would allow efficient pricing across strike rates as the time value of an option would not be difficult to determine. Fortunately, the world is not nearly so boring!

While we have so far thought in terms of the premium price of options based on a constant volatility process for the underlying, in option markets traders prefer to quote prices in terms of implied volatilities. What is more, it is often said that out-of-the-money options are expensive on this basis. The greater cost of out-of-the-money options in implied volatility terms arises because in reality markets price in different volatilities for an option's underlying depending on the size of the expected move.

As we will show in the coming pages, markets price in higher implied volatilities for larger moves that are likely to be associated with market stress; strikes far out-of-the-money will require very dramatic FX developments if the option is to expire in-the-money. Hence, the idea of a constant volatility process for the underlying must be modified to incorporate experience of previous shocks in markets and the associated behaviour of the option underlying during such episodes. Implied volatility surfaces allow market participants to account for the expectation of future shocks.

The structure of the volatility smile means that, in addition to the variation of option prices suggested by a simple stochastic process for the underlying (with option prices declining as the strike is moved further from the spot rate), there is a conflicting contribution as implied volatilities have a tendency to increase as the strike price is moved further out-of-the-money. Hence, while out-of-the-money options are cheaper in cash terms, it is not clear whether they offer the greatest value in terms of eventual payoff.

We can restate the question of out-of-the-money option value in terms of the pricing of risk associated with large moves in FX rates. If markets tend to overestimate the probability of large moves in FX rates, out-of-the-money options are likely to offer poor value compared to at-the-money options. Conversely, if out-of-the-money implied volatilities are not increased sufficiently to adjust for tail risks, out-of-the-money options should offer better value than at-the-money options. With the shape of the volatility smile varying between currency pairs and with time, it is not obvious whether there are any cases in which out-of-the-money options compare favourably to at-the-money options.

To complicate matters further, in addition to the two conflicting contributions from the probability of exercise and the shape of the volatility smile, we should also be mindful of market liquidity effects. OTM options are less liquid so trading costs may play a role in determining value. It is certainly not easy to find a clear answer about whether out-of-the-money options are 'worth it' in the many books that have been written on options, but we intend to set the record straight!

5.3 THE IMPLIED VOLATILITY SURFACE

In order to derive the Black-Scholes-Merton option pricing model one must make a number of simplifying assumptions relating to both the way in which financial markets function and the way in which market participants behave. Despite the need for these assumptions, the model has proved extremely successful, albeit that we have to account for a number of discrepancies between what the model predicts and what we observe in markets. One could say that, in reality, the Black-Scholes-Merton equations represent a market quoting convention for the more complex models of volatility that now tend to be used.[1]

One key feature of the Black-Scholes-Merton model is the way in which a single volatility is assigned to the underlying. By assuming a constant-volatility log-normal process in the derivation of Black-Scholes-Merton, the model is consistent with a volatility surface like the one shown in Figure 5.1(a). That is, plotting the implied volatility as a function of expiry and strike price produces a flat surface.

Figure 5.1(b) shows a more realistic volatility surface, one that we might actually construct by plotting implied volatilities observed in the market. Implied volatility is clearly not constant, either with the level of the underlying or with the passage of time. This is of course not surprising. The world is too complex to be modelled in the simplistic way that the Black-Scholes-Merton model suggests, though as we will discover in the following section, we are able to rationalise deviations from constant log-normal volatility based on some of the properties of financial markets.

5.4 WHY DO VOLATILITY SURFACES LOOK LIKE THEY DO?

5.4.1 Equity Indices

We begin this section by considering how the volatility surface looks for equity index options. We choose this particular type of option because equity indices have a couple of properties that make the relating of the shape of the volatility surface to market phenomena relatively intuitive. First, when considered as a whole, equity markets are far more likely to move sharply lower than sharply higher (the balance is more even for single stocks). Second, the magnitude of sharp downward moves for equity indices tends to be much larger than the magnitude of sharp moves higher (Figure 5.2).

To see how these market properties may manifest themselves in features of the volatility surface, we begin by considering the slightly simpler case of a reduced dimension volatility structure: the volatility smile. We form such a structure by taking a cross section through the volatility surface for a constant option expiry date, as shown in Figure 5.3. We confine ourselves to the two-dimensional smile here as the effect of option tenor on valuation was considered in detail in Chapter 4.

---

[1]For exotic options the market calculates a theoretical value which is a benchmark, but no standard model exists for pricing. Most traders use a stochastic local volatility model but everyone's calibration is slightly different.

(a) Under the Black-Scholes-Merton model

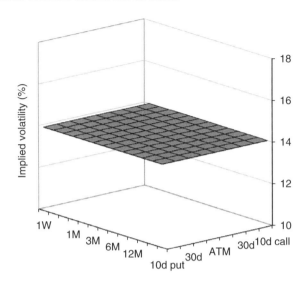

(b) Observed volatility surface for USDSEK as at 28 June 2013

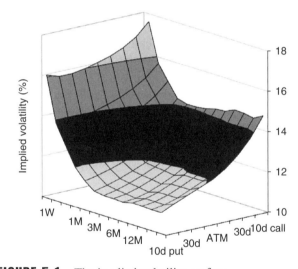

FIGURE 5.1   The implied volatility surface

The first volatility smiles arguably were observed in 1987. Prior to this time option implied volatility as a function of strike price tended to be almost constant, much as predicted by Black-Scholes-Merton. The result was a roughly horizontal line in the volatility versus strike-price plot. The market crash of October 1987, however, meant significant changes for option markets, with traders forced to accept that very large daily losses were possible for equity indices.

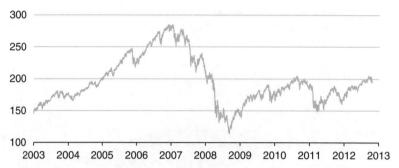

FIGURE 5.2 European equity index – sharp moves lower are more likely than sharp moves higher

We refer to the structure as a smile because, depending on the market, the shape is reminiscent of a mouth with the lips upturned at either end. For equity index options, the shape is often referred to as a skew, or even a smirk, being higher at one end than the other (Figure 5.4). Irrespective of the terminology we choose, we can begin to understand the shape of the equity volatility skew by considering how the structure relates to the key features outlined above.

The astute reader will have noticed that the volatility smile is constructed using implied volatilities for OTM options. This means that for strike prices below the current index level we consider implied volatilities for OTM put options, while for strikes above the current index level, OTM call volatilities are used in the construction of the structure. The fact that the plot of volatility as a function of strike price is skewed tells us that the volatility implied by an OTM put option is higher than the volatility implied by the pricing of comparable OTM call options. Or, put another way, given the relationship between option-implied volatility and price, we can see that equity index put options tend to cost more than equity index call options.

Is this assertion consistent with what we know about equity markets? It would appear so. We have already suggested that very sharp downward moves are more

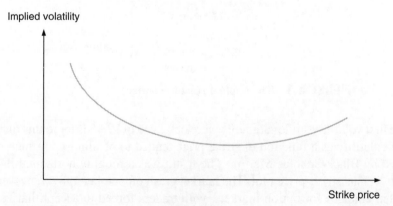

FIGURE 5.3 The implied volatility smile

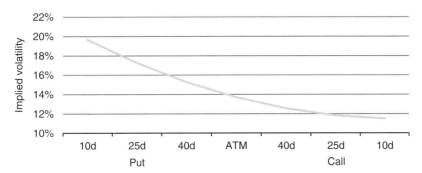

FIGURE 5.4 Schematic implied volatility skew for an equity index

likely than very sharp upward moves in the index. The shape of the volatility skew for equity index options simply confirms that option markets are priced to reflect this; you must pay more for downside protection than for upside participation.[2]

It is perhaps unsurprising that equity investors sometimes turn to the equity option implied volatility skew in order to gauge market sentiment. By comparing how the relative prices of OTM calls and puts develop, taking care to apply an adjustment for the prevailing level of market volatility, one can get an indication of the strength of demand for protection and thus the degree to which the market anticipates a sell-off.

5.4.2 Foreign Exchange Markets

For currency markets, our primary interest here, the situation is less clear. We have already noted that implied volatilities tend to be greater when related to moves that are strongly risk-averse. However, for vanilla currency options where the underlying is an exchange rate it may be the case that the outcome of a spike in volatility for the underlying is uncertain, or may be seen to change over time. Put another way, while rising risk aversion invariably means a sell-off in equity markets, the direction in which a spot rate moves as risk assets decline in value is not always obvious.

For a currency pair that includes a 'hard' currency such as the US dollar and a 'soft' currency (e.g. an emerging market currency) safe-haven flows are most likely to mean the selling of the latter and increased demand for the former. Thus, in cases where a currency pair contains a clear safe-haven currency we may expect the shape of the volatility smile to be skewed so that it resembles an equity index implied volatility 'smirk', with volatility higher for strike prices that involve a strong depreciation of the more risky currency. Depending on how we quote the exchange rate, the smirk may

---

[2]The reason for the skew is supply and demand. Most investors tend to be long shares. With new information in a falling market everyone wants to liquidate at the same time, which causes increased volatility in the price action. To protect against these adverse movements net demand is to buy put options. Conversely, to gain an additional yield, owners of shares may sell out-of-the-money call options.

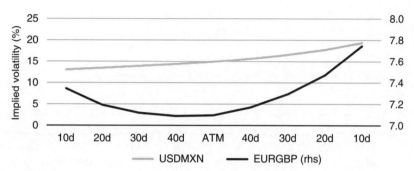

FIGURE 5.5 Volatility smiles for USDMXN and EURGBP as at 28 June 2013

slope in the opposite direction; we should expect the exchange rate to rise in times of crisis if the US dollar is specified as the base currency.

For cross rates where two 'hard' currencies appear, the volatility structure may be more symmetrical: closer to a smile than a smirk. Figure 5.5 shows two volatility smiles that support this argument. For USDMXN the skew structure has a definite smirk shape, with OTM calls on the rate implying a higher volatility than OTM puts. For EURGBP, however, a case where it is less clear whether a rise or fall in the exchange rate should be considered a risk-off event, the skew structure is almost symmetric.

Finally, to complete our ride on the emotional roller coaster of volatility structures, in addition to the existence of smiles and smirks, we must also consider the possibility of a volatility frown. A volatility frown may arise in the case of a binary event that may cause a sharp step either higher or lower in an asset price. For example, a company subject to the outcome of litigation may see its stock price step higher or lower by 10% depending on the announcement of the result [1].

In currency markets, a volatility frown is relatively rare. The phenomenon is normally restricted to very short dated options (under one-week maturity) around the time of significant events. Such an example would be EURUSD options over the release of non-farm payroll (NFP) data in the US. This is typically a market-moving event so volatility is expected, but once the event risk has passed volatilities tend to decline. Traders look to exploit this characteristic by trading ATMF options against the wings of the volatility smile. Given the findings presented in this book volatility frowns in the FX market ought perhaps to be more common.

5.5 PARAMETERISING THE VOLATILITY SMILE

Now that we have introduced the volatility smile, those of a more mathematical background will no doubt feel a strong urge to quantify the degree of skew present. Hopefully most readers will be at least slightly curious about how one may easily identify the various shapes of implied volatility skews in order to gauge what markets are pricing in regarding tail risks.

To introduce a degree of confusion, as is often the case in finance, the exact terminology used to this end is dependent on the market in question. Once we know the market conventions, however, we will be able to see that the different methods used to describe the shape of the smile are broadly similar. As before, we begin by considering the case for equity markets.

Out-of-the-money equity index options have historically tended to have their strike prices quoted in percent of the spot rate. The measure of asymmetry of the smile commonly used in this market is the 90–110% equity implied volatility skew. As one might imagine, this quantity represents the difference in implied volatility for options with strike prices of 90% and 110% of the spot rate.

Figure 5.6(a) illustrates the construction of the measure. The lower the value (for a given prevailing level of volatility), the lower the relative cost of put options to call options. One may interpret a particularly low level of equity implied volatility skew as an indicator of complacency among investors.

In foreign exchange markets, OTM options tend to be quoted in terms of delta rather than as a percentage of spot. Considering the difference in implied volatility for 25-delta OTM put and call options gives a similar indication of the amount of skew in the FX option volatility smile. For foreign exchange options a particular terminology is adopted for this spread, with market participants often referring to the '25-delta risk reversal' (Figure 5.6(b)). By analogy to the equity implied volatility skew for equity index options, FX risk reversals contain information about the directional outlook of market participants.[3]

Beyond the simple measure of symmetry provided by risk reversals, we can gauge the curvature of the implied volatility smile by considering the butterfly spread. If markets are liquid and we can expect the same volatility for all values of the underlying, we should anticipate a flat Black-Scholes-Merton volatility surface. However, in reality unlikely events can occur and markets can react wildly to shocks. In such cases we should expect much higher volatility away from the current spot price and the smile curve will be shaped more like a letter 'U' than a horizontal line.

To provide an example, the market in EURUSD is a well-established one. There is great liquidity and even if the spot rate moves strongly we can expect an orderly market. These facts are reflected in a shallow smile – imagine the cross section of a saucer for a teacup. In contrast, some emerging markets have much wilder gyrations in exchange rates and as a result a much more convex volatility smile – imagine the cross section of the teacup rather than its saucer. This is a relatively easy concept to imagine and is captured by an FX option butterfly. A long butterfly strategy consists of buying an ATM straddle and selling put and call options of equal delta.

---

[3]In addition to being a convenient label for the difference in implied volatility of put and call options of the same delta, the term risk reversal also refers to an option strategy that involves buying an OTM call option and selling an OTM put option.

(a) Schematic illustration of the equity index 90%–110% implied volatility skew

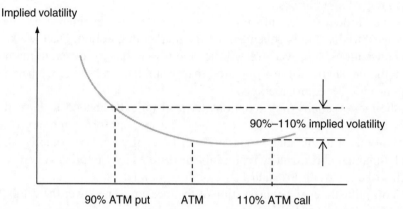

(b) Schematic representation of a 25-delta risk reversal

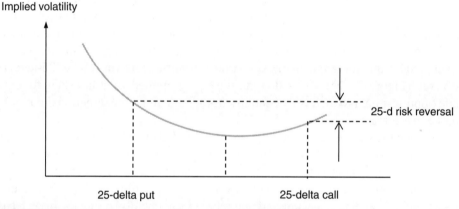

FIGURE 5.6   Measures of skewness for the volatility smile

Trading a butterfly spread in the market is relatively easy even if understanding exactly how the spread is constructed is a little more complicated. The market calculates the butterfly volatility as:

$$\sigma_{butterfly/25\text{-}delta} = [(\sigma_{call/25\text{-}delta} + \sigma_{put/25\text{-}delta})/2] - \sigma_{ATM}.$$

Using this derived volatility the strikes for the butterfly are then calculated. Hence the 25-delta put strike for a butterfly is not the same as the 25-delta put strike for a risk reversal (Figure 5.7).

In simple terms, the butterfly spread allows us to observe the probability of larger moves in the exchange rate that are priced into the options market.

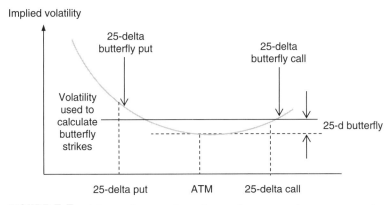

FIGURE 5.7 A butterfly spread can be used to gauge the steepness of the volatility smile

THE VOLATILITY SMILE AND OPTION TRADING

In Chapter 2 we discussed some basic risk management techniques for option trading. However, our simplified explanations ignored the fact that option implied volatility is not constant for different strikes and tenors and in fact forms a contoured surface. Trading an option using only delta ignores the fact that as spot moves the volatility surface may shift too. Given that the value of the option actually changes with spot *and* with the expected change in volatility as the underlying moves, the exact delta of the option may not be the most useful figure for hedging. In fact this simplified approach will lead to over-hedging or under-hedging as the spot rate changes.

A lot of work has gone into understanding how volatility surfaces change and what the 'correct' delta for an option is. Arguably, more work goes into understanding risk and the trading of risk than goes into establishing whether the assumptions used to calculate a price are really accurate. The findings presented in this book certainly appear to support this argument.

To highlight the problem faced by traders, let us consider an example.

An ATMF option has a volatility of 10% and the 25-delta call has a volatility of 16%. A 25-delta call option is purchased and the Black-Scholes-Merton spot market delta hedge is sold for 25% of the notional. Now imagine a scenario where spot jumps but everything else remains the same (time to maturity, interest rates etc.) and the option is now ATMF. Let us also assume the volatility surface remains the same. Instead of being priced with a volatility of 16%, the option is now priced for an implied volatility of 10%.

The owner of the option has gained in absolute premium terms, but given the lower volatility not quite as much as they might have expected. This difference could be made up by assuming a slightly modified delta at inception, namely selling less than 25% of the notional amount. This modified delta can be calculated from the expected shortfall due to the move in the smile and is known as the smile delta.

This was a very basic example. In fact the difference between delta and the smile delta depends on how the volatility surface is expected to move. Most traders will develop an in-built sense of this concept and will often think in terms of whether the volatility smile will be an accurate predictor or not. Thoroughly understanding this effect and other subtleties becomes extremely important for those managing large option portfolios.

5.6 MEASURING RELATIVE VALUE IN ATMF AND OTM FOREIGN EXCHANGE OPTIONS

In the preceding sections we described the nature of the volatility smile for different markets and related the shape of the structure to observable phenomena. We then described how the shape of the smile can be quantified by using simple volatility spread measures.

Having got the formalities out of the way, we are now in a position to turn our attention to the question posed in the chapter title: do supposedly 'cheap' out-of-the-money options offer good value? Given that we know that option prices can vary strongly with strike price (which may be expressed in terms of delta), where on the volatility smile does the best value lie?

We have already explained how, despite the reduction in option prices in premium terms as one moves away from the ATMF strike (due solely to arguments based on the likelihood of the option expiring in-the-money), we must look a little deeper if we are to determine the real value of options. We have also explained that in terms of implied volatilities out-of-the-money options are often more 'expensive'. Now we get to the nub of the matter regarding option relative value: how do the increased implied volatilities for changes in spot price that would correspond to significant market stress relate to the actual likelihood of such events occurring? That is, do markets over- or underestimate the probability of such events happening, corresponding to poor or attractive value bought out-of-the-money options respectively on average?

Before we can arrive at an answer regarding option relative value, we will need to be more specific; the definition of value will clearly depend on the application. We may begin by asking how much out-of-the-money and at-the-money options pay out on average in relation to their premiums. A simple question maybe, but a difficult one to answer all the same. We may then wish to know how this relative valuation can be applied to a specific case: the hedging of foreign exchange exposure by corporations, for example.

While the former question relates purely to the percentage loss or gain that has on average been realised, the latter question relating to value in the context of hedging may include a broader set of considerations. For example, how does the relative cost compare to an alternative hedging product, and how do the respective cash flow structures compare?

5.6.1 The Analysis

A good place to begin in our attempt to ascertain the relative value of ATMF and OTM options is to ask how much the options cost. We have already described how we can identify which option is more expensive in volatility terms from the volatility smile, but how does that translate into premium terms with respect to option notional value – recall that the out-of-the-money option has a lower probability of expiring in-the-money and so should have a lower price than an ATMF option for the same implied volatility.

Before we get to the results we will briefly discuss our dataset and methodology. In Chapter 4 we considered straddles/strangles in order to reduce the sensitivity of the strategy to overall directionality of the exchange rate.[4] For each of the currency pairs we calculated premiums and payoffs for a range of tenors (1W, 1M, 3M, 6M, 12M, 2Y and 3Y) between 2004 and 2013 where possible. All calculations were performed for at-the-money options, 25-delta options and 10-delta options.[5] We chose a period of 10 years because that was the period for which we were able to source good quality data for 10-delta options. In general we would try to use all available data but when our objective is a direct comparison of ATMF and OTM options then it is necessary to be more selective.

Irrespective of the tenor involved we calculated the performance of one option per week over the back-test period. As discussed in Chapter 3, costs were imposed based on market spreads for the periods in question, and in all cases we calculated premiums in percentages of underlying notional value in the base currency. We considered static option positions only – we did not account for any delta-hedging of risk.

Because payoff information for the longer dated options was not available near the end of the evaluation window, we also calculated premiums and payoffs for the period only to 2012. We found that the results were not significantly different and we therefore present the findings for the full 10-year period.

---

[4]A long straddle involves purchasing both a call and a put option. The combination has a payoff that is not particularly sensitive to the direction of spot moves – the purchaser can benefit if the spot rate moves strongly in either direction. A strangle is similar, but involves options with different strike prices.

[5]As discussed earlier in the chapter, out-of-the-money FX option strike prices are usually expressed in terms of delta. A delta of 0.25 (sometimes written as 25) tells us that we should expect the option price to change by one-quarter of a unit for a one-unit change in underlying price.

5.6.2 Option Premium

In simple terms, Figure 5.8 shows that, on average, halving the delta of an option reduces the cost of that option by approximately 50%. For our dataset, a 3M ATMF option typically costs 3–5% of the notional amount while a 3M 25-delta OTM option costs nearer 1–2% of the notional. A similar percentage reduction in price occurs when we move from 25-delta out to 10-delta. Again the change is broadly in line with our rule of thumb from Chapter 2: halving option delta corresponds to roughly halving the probability that the vanilla option will expire in-the-money. In short, in terms of premium the probability of expiring in-the-money clearly outweighs the impact of the volatility smile on option prices.

5.6.3 Option Payoff

Considering the payoff side of option performance (Figure 5.9), we found a similar relationship: as expected, the reduced premiums of OTM options result in smaller payoffs too.[6] Once again, halving the delta roughly speaking halved the size of the payment.

So far this is all as expected and not especially exciting; however, things will start to become more interesting when we go a step further and combine the information presented in Figure 5.8 and Figure 5.9 in order to compare the historical payoff-to-premium performance of ATMF and OTM options.

Currency-by-currency average premiums and payoffs for all of the tenors are tabulated in the Appendix.

5.6.4 Payoff-to-Premium Ratios

By comparing historical premium and payoff data, we were able to generate payoff/premium ratios for all of the currency-pair/tenor combinations. In a cost-free world a ratio of 100% would suggest that on average an option has been priced efficiently over the period covered by the analysis. Since we have included transaction costs in our analysis, efficient pricing should be expected to result in ratios of slightly less than 100%.

Figure 5.10 gives us our first look at the relative historical performance of OTM and ATMF options. For 1M contracts, the results are fairly conclusive: in almost all cases OTM options paid out less than ATMF options as a percentage of the premium paid.

However, as we move to longer tenors the picture becomes slightly less clear. At the 3M tenor for the majority of currency pairs considered, ATMF options paid out a greater percentage of the premium invested on average, with 25-delta options

---

[6]Payoffs are discounted to account for the period of time that passes between an upfront premium being paid and any payout being received.

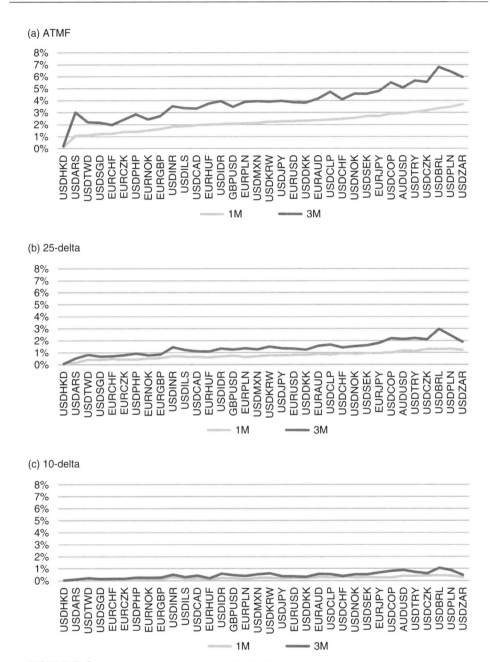

FIGURE 5.8   Average premiums for ATMF, 25-delta and 10-delta straddles/strangles in percent of notional amount for 2004–2013 inclusive

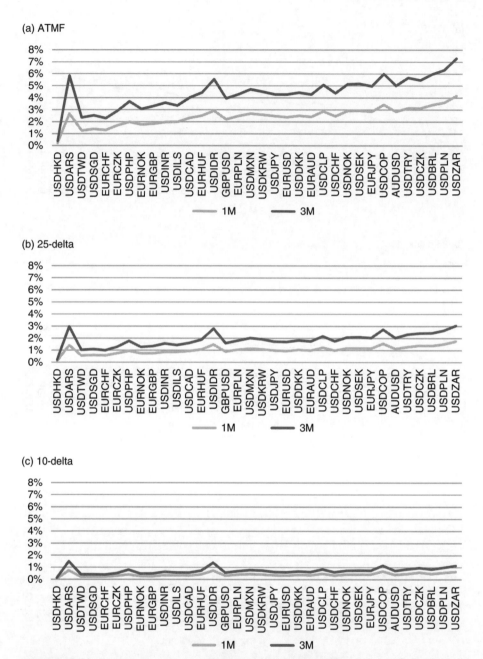

FIGURE 5.9 Average payoffs for ATMF, 25-delta and 10-delta straddles/strangles in percent of notional amount for 2004–2013 inclusive

(a) 1M tenor

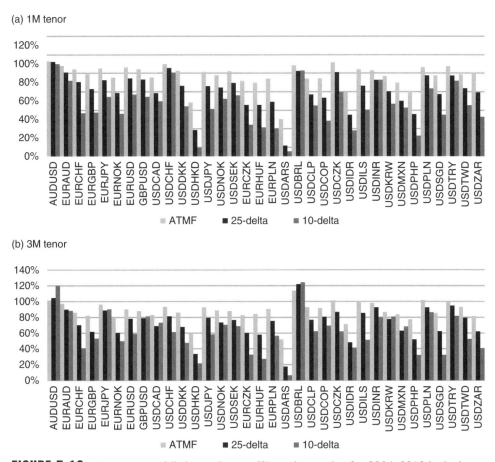

(b) 3M tenor

FIGURE 5.10   Average straddle/strangle payoff/premium ratios for 2004–2013 inclusive

coming out second best ahead of 10-delta options. However, this was not true for all pairs, with the ranking by payoff-to-premium ratio being reversed for AUDUSD and USDBRL.

Having combined payoffs and premiums in order to provide a measure of historical performance for individual currency pairs, we went a step further. We aggregated the results for the currency pairs, grouping them into G10 and EM baskets. Note that we did not take into account the fact that different cross rates had different amounts of data; the averages are simple averages over the currency pairs.

Based on this aggregation, Figure 5.11 shows how OTM options performed as a whole over the period of our back-test. The variation in payoff-to-premium ratios hinted at in Figure 5.10 is evident for both G10 and EM currency pairs. For the shorter tenors OTM options offer much worse value than ATMF options – paying out roughly half as much on average at the one-week tenor. As we move to longer tenors there

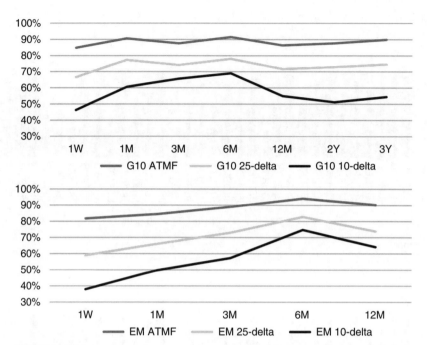

FIGURE 5.11   Average straddle/strangle payoff/premium ratios by tenor for 2004–2013 inclusive

is some evidence that OTM options offer slightly better value, but the overall picture is clear: payoff-to-premium ratios are significantly higher for ATMF options than for OTM options right across the board.

We might ask ourselves whether the differences between ATMF and OTM options highlighted by Figure 5.11 are simply a reflection of the greater liquidity of ATMF options. Recall that out-of-the-money options are less liquid than at-the-money options and hence incur greater transaction costs in the form of a bid-ask spread.

Figure 5.12 sheds some light on this issue. The payoff ratios in this instance are calculated using mid-market data (the average of bid and ask quotes) in order to omit the effect of the bid-ask spread. Whilst there is naturally a change in the form of the charts versus those shown in Figure 5.11, we note that the at-the-money options still offer better value. While trading costs may contribute to the differences between ATMF and OTM options, they cannot account for the large differences we observe.

We finally compared the average payoff ratios by tenor for the G10 and emerging market currency baskets. As shown in Figure 5.13, while the effect is not a large one, the structures for the EM basket are steeper for both ATMF and OTM options. That is, the variation of value with tenor appears to be greater for currency pairs that include an emerging-market currency than for the G10 exchange rates.

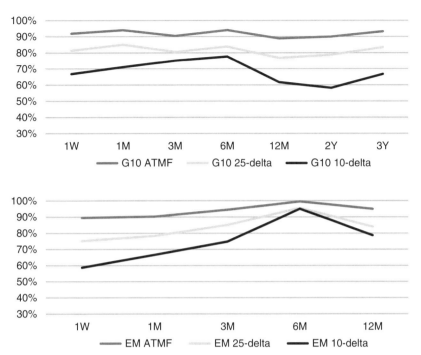

FIGURE 5.12 Average straddle/strangle payoff/premium ratios by tenor for 2004–2013 inclusive. In this instance calculations are performed at mid-market rates in order to exclude the bid-ask spread

5.6.5 Discussion

We have shown that despite their apparent 'cheapness' – as a rule of thumb the premium cost of a 25-delta option is around half that of an ATMF option – out-of-the-money options on the whole offer poor value. The tendency for implied volatilities to be higher for OTM strikes helps to increase the cost of out-of-the-money options

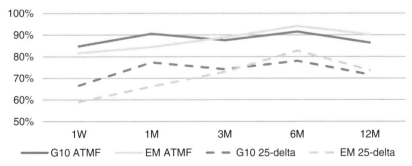

FIGURE 5.13 Average payoff-to-premium ratios by tenor for 2004–2013 inclusive

beyond a level consistent with their probability of expiring in-the-money. We note that results for G10 and EM exchange rates are broadly comparable though not identical – we will discuss differences between G10 and EM options in detail in Chapter 6.

The difference in payoff-to-premium ratios for ATMF and OTM options is most exaggerated for the shorter tenors and deeply out-of-the-money strikes; for G10 currency pairs the payoff-to-premium ratio for one-week 10-delta options is around 45%, versus around 85% for at-the-money options. A similar picture is evident, on average, for exchange rates including an EM currency.

The difference, however, appears to be somewhat smaller for longer tenors. For G10 crosses, 6M 25-delta options have a payoff-to-premium ratio of 70% compared to a c. 90% ratio for 6M ATMF options.

In addition to a lessening of the 1W OTM versus ATMF performance deficit at longer tenors, our analysis also reveals some interesting results regarding outright OTM value with tenor. The results show that, as is the case for at-the-money options, longer dated bought OTM options tend to offer better value than very short dated OTM options. We discuss possible reasons for the relative outperformance of longer tenor options in Chapters 4 and 6.

We note with reference to Figure 5.13 that the market's apparently inaccurate perception of long-term risk seems to have been slightly different for G10 exchange rates and EM exchange rates. There is some evidence that overall long-term risks have historically been underestimated slightly for EM versus G10 currencies. Meanwhile, short-term risks appear to have been overestimated to a greater degree for EM currencies than for G10 currencies.

Finally, it is worth bearing in mind that for the period examined the variation of straddle value with tenor is smaller than with the larger period considered in Chapter 4, particularly for G10 – indeed, if we had originally done the study using this smaller dataset we might not have been as surprised by it and might not have gone on to look at the puts and calls individually.

A more detailed discussion of the performance of individual ATMF and OTM put and call options can be found in Chapter 6.

5.6.6   Alternative Measures of OTM Option Worth

Before we summarise the main points of this chapter it is worth putting the findings in context. Because the analysis may be applied to, say, the problem of hedging a company's FX exposure, we should acknowledge that factors other than outright value may be important. Despite the apparent lack of payoff-to-premium value in out-of-the-money options, we cannot agree that these instruments are not valuable in other respects.[7]

---

[7]In addition to the issues discussed in this section, OTM options have more subtle benefits such as the provision of convexity for dynamic traders and the hedging of exotic options. While these features may not be of general interest, we mention them here for completeness.

For example, companies with a mandatory hedging policy may find out-of-the-money options an ideal vehicle for occasions when they are of the view that 'insurance' is very unlikely to be called upon. In a scenario in which a hedged currency steadily appreciates during a hedging period, an OTM option could provide compulsory hedge at less than half the cost of an ATMF option. The comparison to an FX forward hedge is even more favourable; not only would a corporate benefit from the appreciation, but the small 'insurance' cash flow of an OTM option replaces the potentially large negative cash flow that would fall due under the forward hedge.

Finally we note that in times of high volatility, when options that expire out-of-the-money may appear to offer especially poor value due to elevated premiums, alternative benefits may be greatest. The opportunity to remain exposed to moves in the underlying, for example, may be especially beneficial.

5.7 SUMMARY

In this chapter we revisited the fundamentals behind option pricing formulae and identified the reasons for out-of-the-money options being cheaper in premium terms given a flat volatility smile. We also introduced the volatility skew for equity and FX markets and considered the shape of the skew for different currency pairs. We discussed whether risk was likely to be over- or underestimated for OTM options and how such a systematic bias might affect option relative value.

The findings of our analysis strongly suggest that OTM options are overpriced in nearly all cases. Whether emerging or G10 currency, long tenor or short, the payoff-to-premium ratio is higher for ATMF options than for the OTM equivalent. The greater liquidity of ATMF options cannot fully explain the differences.

We found that the relative pricing of long and short-term risk in G10 and EM markets may have been subject to a systematic bias. While short-term risk in EM markets appears to be overestimated relative to the risk for G10 currencies, at the longer tenors EM risk appears to be underestimated versus risk for the G10 universe.

The warning for market participants appears clear: OTM options are nearly universally expensive versus ATMF equivalents. In the light of this clear evidence, one must carefully consider whether the benefits of entering OTM option positions offer sufficient compensation for the bias present in the market pricing of the instruments.

REFERENCE

[1] Hull, J. (2012) *Options, Futures and Other Derivatives*, 8th edition (London: Pearson).

CHAPTER 6

G10 vs EM Currency Pairs

6.1 WHY CONSIDER EM AND G10 OPTIONS SEPARATELY?

At first glance it's not clear why we would look at these cases separately. Indeed, the phrase 'emerging markets' is itself a little odd. What do we mean? It cannot mean 'small' when, at the time of writing, the Chinese currency is usually placed in this category, and China has the second-largest economy in the world. But it makes a little more sense when one looks at the history of the data series. Emerging markets tend to be those which are more illiquid or have the possibility of becoming illiquid. This may be due to a number of factors such as the size of the market, the degree of governmental control or that the markets have been liquidly traded for a relatively short period. In most cases, they tend to have higher interest rates than the more mature G10 markets.

This is the first of the reasons for taking a separate look at the two cases – many of the effects which we have seen are at least partly due to interest rate differentials, so it makes sense to split them up and see if the data are dominated by a few EM pairs. If this were the case then the 'averages' we are seeing would be less useful and interesting. Additionally, the EM pairs have less data in general, so we will be able to see if recent data are skewing the results.

We can repeat some of the analysis seen in Chapter 4, where we discovered that longer dated ATMF options on average tend to be better value, and this effect is mostly driven by the interest rate differentials (the effect is largest in general in the put options). Additionally, where there is sufficient data, we can take a look at OTM contracts as well.

6.2 HOW WOULD EM FX OPTIONS BE USED?

While one might think that options in EM pairs would be quite a complex and possibly expensive way to hedge an FX risk, in fact there are cases where they have historically

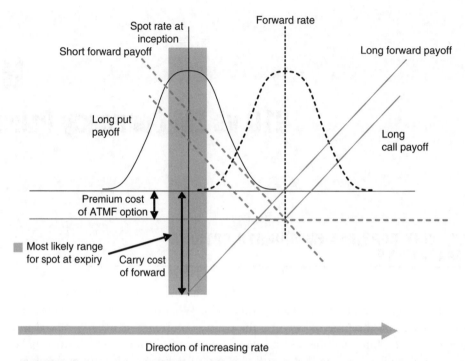

Direction of increasing rate

FIGURE 6.1   Forward and option payoffs for high interest rate differentials

been much cheaper than the apparently simpler forward hedge. Consider Figure 6.1, which is an exaggerated version of the final figure in Chapter 4.

We have exaggerated the difference between the spot rate and the forward rate at inception (i.e. assumed a large interest rate differential). It can be seen that if a hedge contract is taken out to protect against rate increases, the 'carry cost' can be much larger than the 'premium cost' if the rate at expiry is most likely to be close to the spot at inception. Even in emerging markets, history tells us that this is indeed the case.

6.3   STRADDLE RESULTS

In Figures 6.2, 6.3, 6.4 and 6.5 and Tables 6.1 and 6.2 we show the average results for G10 and EM pairs. Looking initially at the graphs, we see that on the whole both show the same pattern. Long dated straddles are better value on average than short dated straddles, with the longest tenors tending to come close to breaking even. Thus the effect is not dominated by one sector or type of currency pair. The longest tenors have of course the poorest and shortest data series and should be regarded sceptically.

Next, let us look at the currency pair breakdown in Figures 6.4 and 6.5. These are essentially the same data for the straddles as were displayed in Chapter 4, but

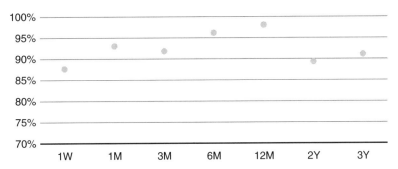

FIGURE 6.2   Payoff/premium ratio for ATMF G10 straddles – average over 14 pairs

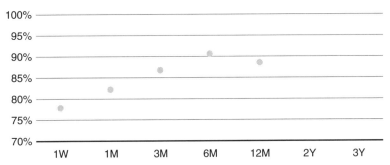

FIGURE 6.3   Payoff/premium ratio for ATMF EM straddles – average over 20 pairs

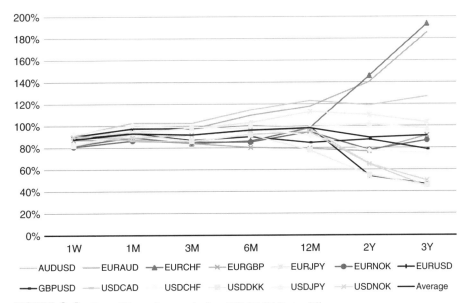

FIGURE 6.4   Payoff/premium ratio for ATMF G10 straddles

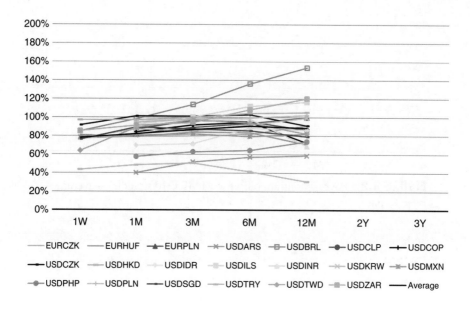

FIGURE 6.5 Payoff/premium ratio for ATMF EM straddles

TABLE 6.1 Average payoff/premium ratio for ATMF G10 straddles

Tenor	Ratio
1W	87.6%
1M	93.0%
3M	91.9%
6M	96.2%
12M	98.0%
2Y	89.3%
3Y	91.1%

TABLE 6.2 Average payoff/premium ratio for ATMF EM straddles

Tenor	Ratio
1W	77.9%
1M	82.2%
3M	86.8%
6M	90.6%
12M	88.5%

differently broken out. We can say that the EM pairs seem to hold to the pattern a little more consistently than the G10; perhaps unsurprising as the effect is at least partly due to the carry trade. A comparison using different time periods is not useful here as any differences will almost inevitably be due to the fact that the EM data series are much shorter than the G10.

To avoid long series of tables in this discussion, from now on the detailed currency-by-currency results will be tabulated in the Appendix.

6.3.1 Comparison of ATMF Put and Call Options

Overall, for straddles, EM and G10 pairs show similar results. Let us now look at puts and calls, which may show larger differences due to the interest rate differentials. Figures 6.6 and 6.7, and Tables 6.3 and 6.4, summarise the put and the call results. The puts are similar in both G10 and EM cases, though the EM puts show a steeper gradient; short dated contracts are relatively more expensive than in the G10 case, and long dated contracts are relatively better value. But the calls show a very distinct difference. They are universally much worse value for EM pairs than for G10 pairs. On average, long dated calls for EM pairs pay back only about 50% of their initial cost.

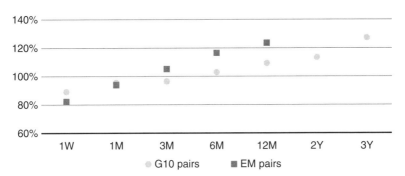

FIGURE 6.6 Payoff/premium ratio for ATMF puts

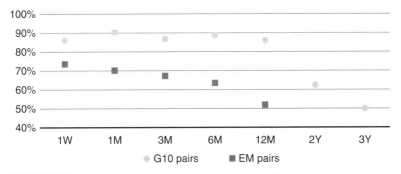

FIGURE 6.7 Payoff/premium ratio for ATMF calls

TABLE 6.3   Average payoff/premium ratio for ATMF puts

Tenor	G10 Ratio	EM Ratio
1W	89.1%	82.3%
1M	95.5%	93.9%
3M	96.4%	105.1%
6M	102.9%	116.4%
12M	109.1%	123.6%
2Y	113.3%	
3Y	127.2%	

TABLE 6.4   Average payoff/premium ratio for ATMF calls

Tenor	G10 Ratio	EM Ratio
1W	86.1%	73.5%
1M	90.3%	70.1%
3M	86.8%	67.3%
6M	88.7%	63.5%
12M	86.1%	52.0%
2Y	62.3%	
3Y	50.0%	

Can we explain this, using our understanding of the effect of large interest rate differentials on the value of options? We can certainly make some progress. Let's look once more at the payoff diagram when interest rate differentials are large (Figure 6.8).

Once it's clearly laid out, we can see what is happening. EM pairs have a larger interest rate differential on average, so their forward rates lie further from the spot rate at inception (they also have slightly more expensive options, represented by larger premium costs). As the forward rate lies to the 'depreciation' side of the spot, call options only pay out for large depreciation moves. We know these are unlikely, though they do sometimes happen. Because on average they happen only occasionally, buying calls will over time lose money, so both the G10 and EM calls tend to lose money. But, when these large moves do happen, both the higher premium and the larger interest rate differential for EM pairs mean that they will pay out less. Thus EM calls are on average worse value than G10 calls.

How about puts? In Figure 6.9 we now focus on the put payoffs and we see that the cheaper premium for G10 vs EM now acts in opposition to the effect from the smaller interest rate differential. The puts from both G10 and EM will pay off for normal small moves, so we would expect them on average to be much better value than the calls for both G10 and EM – which is indeed the case, as shown in Figure 6.6. But the difference in payoff is now much smaller and there is room for other effects to

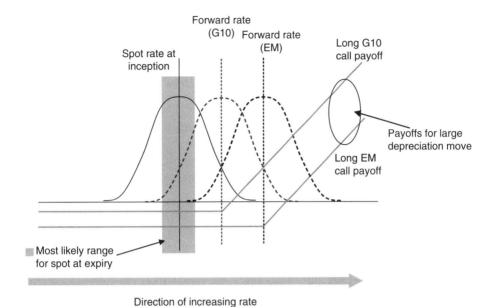

FIGURE 6.8 Payoff diagram for large and small interest rate differentials for calls

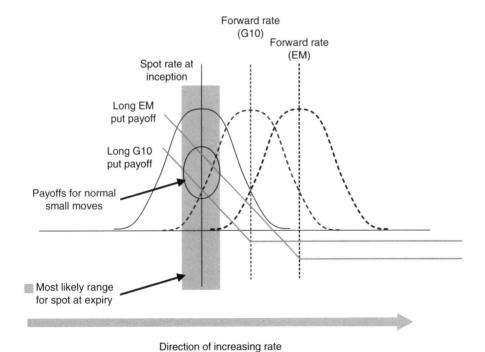

FIGURE 6.9 Payoff diagram for large and small interest rate differentials for puts

come into play, like the width of the implied volatility distributions. Thus puts show a much smaller difference which is more dependent upon tenor.

6.3.2 Comparison of OTM Put and Call Options

It is now worth turning our attention to the case for OTM options. The 25-delta and the 10-delta cases all have enough data to study, though it is worth remembering that the 10-delta series often start later than the rest. Tables 6.5 and 6.6 show the payoff ratios for the put options, grouping them by delta and by G10 and EM pairs. The data for the ATMF options are shown in Tables 6.3 and 6.4; the 25-delta and 10-delta put results are in Tables 6.5 and 6.6; and the OTM call results are presented in Tables 6.7 and 6.8. The data for ATMF and OTM puts and calls are graphed in Figures 6.10 and 6.11. Currency-by-currency results are as before in the Appendix.

Both G10 and EM pairs have a clear tendency for short dated puts to be expensive, and long dated puts to be cheap, echoing results found in Chapter 5, though we are now splitting up the results into puts and calls rather than considering straddles. The further out-of-the-money the puts are, the worse value they become. The main difference between the G10 and EM cases is that the short dated tenors for the EM pairs show a more extreme mispricing; they are relatively even more expensive than

TABLE 6.5 Payoff/premium ratio for 25-delta puts

Tenor	G10 Ratio	EM Ratio
1W	75.1%	64.4%
1M	85.9%	79.4%
3M	87.2%	90.9%
6M	91.6%	108.3%
12M	100.0%	118.6%
2Y	96.2%	
3Y	117.4%	

TABLE 6.6 Payoff/premium ratio for 10-delta puts

Tenor	G10 Ratio	EM Ratio
1W	58.9%	43.3%
1M	72.0%	64.0%
3M	77.3%	71.6%
6M	75.8%	97.4%
12M	87.7%	110.5%
2Y	60.3%	
3Y	90.0%	

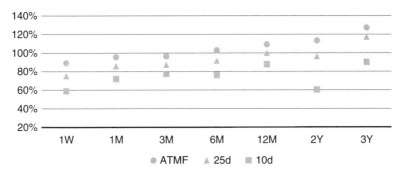

FIGURE 6.10   Payoff/premium ratio for G10 puts

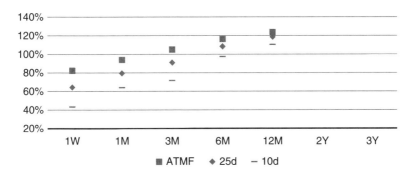

FIGURE 6.11   Payoff/premium ratio for EM puts

their G10 counterparts. By the time the 1Y tenor is reached, however, the EM OTM puts have come close to the EM ATMF puts in value. In the G10 case, the differential is not really reduced and the longer tenors remain poor value for OTM puts relative to ATMF puts. In Figures 6.12 and 6.13 we have broken out the data to compare the 25-delta and 10-delta cases for the EM and G10 pairs directly.

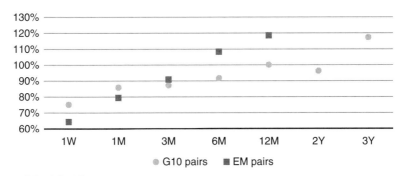

FIGURE 6.12   Payoff/premium ratio for 25-delta puts

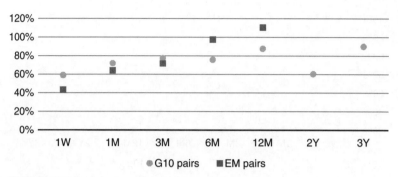

FIGURE 6.13 Payoff/premium ratio for 10-delta puts

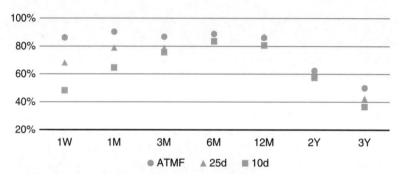

FIGURE 6.14 Payoff/premium ratio for G10 calls

As can be seen, the G10 and EM pairs show similar characteristics for the OTM put options, the major difference being that the EM pairs have a steeper difference in value between shorter and longer tenors.

We now examine the data for the call options. As can be seen in Figures 6.14 and 6.15, the OTM calls are much worse value relative to ATMF than the puts, particularly for short tenors. The longer tenors show less difference between OTM and ATMF.

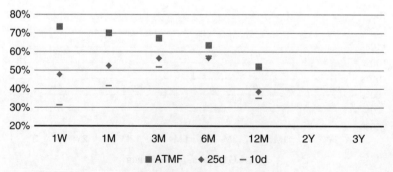

FIGURE 6.15 Payoff/premium ratio for EM calls

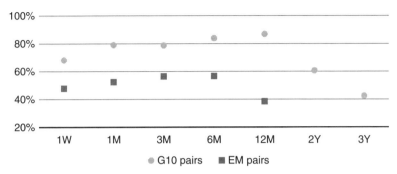

FIGURE 6.16 Payoff/premium ratio for 25-delta calls

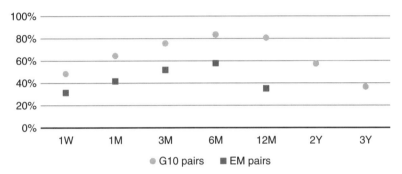

FIGURE 6.17 Payoff/premium ratio for 10-delta calls

This is a feature for both G10 and EM pairs; for the puts it was only evident for the EM pairs. There is also something of a 'humped' shape for the OTM calls which is absent for the puts, where the shortest and longest tenors have worse value for these strikes.

We also break the data out for G10 vs EM, graphed in Figures 6.16 and 6.17, tabulated in Tables 6.7 and 6.8. The OTM calls are very much worse value for EM than for G10, showing the effect laid out in Figure 6.8 very clearly.

TABLE 6.7 Payoff/premium ratio for 25-delta calls

Tenor	G10 Ratio	EM Ratio
1W	68.2%	47.7%
1M	79.0%	52.4%
3M	78.7%	56.4%
6M	83.9%	56.6%
12M	86.9%	38.4%
2Y	60.5%	
3Y	42.4%	

TABLE 6.8   Payoff/premium ratio for 10-delta calls

Tenor	G10 Ratio	EM Ratio
1W	48.3%	31.4%
1M	64.6%	41.6%
3M	75.7%	51.7%
6M	83.5%	57.7%
12M	80.6%	35.0%
2Y	57.3%	
3Y	36.6%	

We have a couple of effects still to explain. Why are OTM calls much worse value than ATMF calls, but the AMTF and OTM options more similar for puts? And why does this difference narrow for longer tenors?

First, let's look at the case simply for ATMF vs OTM calls. The OTM calls are worse value, particularly for short tenors. In Figure 6.18 we show a diagram of what happens. The calls, being the wrong side of the forward rate, pay off only for large depreciation moves. The OTM calls will suffer twice: once for paying off less for the same move, but once more for only paying off for the very largest moves. Every move which pays off for the OTM option pays off more for the ATMF option; but many moves for which the ATMF option makes money do not produce a payoff under the OTM contract. Thus we can explain simply why OTM call options are much worse value than ATMF call options.

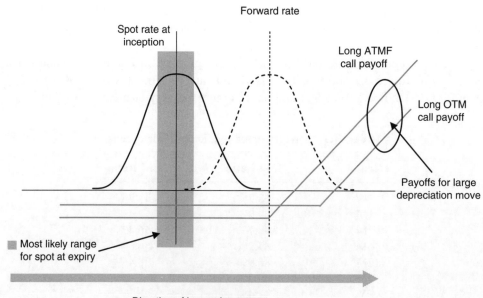

FIGURE 6.18   Payoff diagram for ATMF vs OTM calls

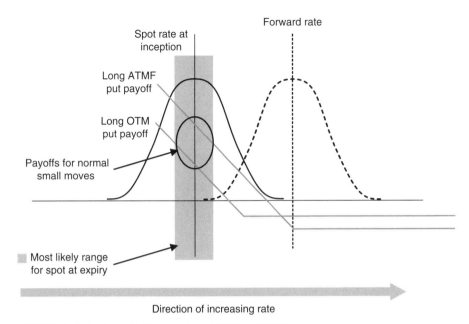

FIGURE 6.19   Payoff diagram for ATMF vs OTM puts

For the puts, Figure 6.19 shows the payoffs for ATMF vs OTM options. We can see that although the OTM payoff is lower both payoffs lie in the most probable region – in effect, they are highly likely to occur. So the OTM options only have one disadvantage, not two as in the case of the calls. Thus the difference between ATMF and OTM is less for puts. We can also, to a certain extent, account for the 'humped' shape of the call graphs which is not seen in the puts. For both puts and calls, the short dated OTM options show the greatest overpricing due to implied volatility being higher than realised. This effect diminishes with tenor. But for the calls, the carry then comes in to again reduce the payoff/premium ratio in the long tenors; they have a 'sweet spot' in the middle where both of the effects are smaller. For the puts, both the carry and the tendency for longer dated OTM volatility to be relatively less overvalued act to increase the payoff/premium ratio for longer tenors and reduce it for shorter tenors, so the 'hump' is not seen.

6.3.3   The Effect of Tenor

For both G10 and EM calls, short dated OTM options show much worse value at short tenors relative to ATMF calls. The difference narrows to almost zero for longer tenors. This pattern is not reproduced for puts so how can we explain this call option behaviour?

First, let us consider the earlier diagram in Figure 6.18. This would correspond well to a long dated option where the forward rate and the spot rate at inception

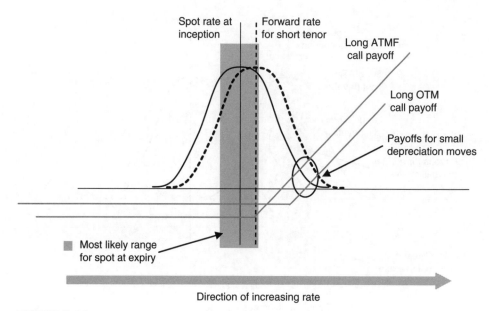

FIGURE 6.20   Payoff diagram for the case of small interest rate differentials

are widely separated. In this situation, both the ATMF and the OTM calls are very unlikely to pay off. They are both very far out-of-the-money.

Now let us look at Figure 6.20, where the case for a short dated option is presented. In this situation the forward rate will be much closer to the spot, and so the ATMF option is significantly more likely to actually have a payoff than the OTM. So there is a bigger difference between ATMF calls for short tenors than for long tenors. We don't need to draw another set of diagrams to show that this is much less the case for puts.

Another effect coming in here for puts is that there are two phenomena: carry is dominant, but also we know from Chapter 5 that there is a tendency for the market to overestimate volatility to a larger degree for OTM options. This will be more evident at shorter tenors where carry is smaller. Thus for puts the tendencies tend to offset each other at shorter tenors, while for calls they add up, meaning that calls show a greater change of relative value with tenor. It is fascinating to see the interplay of effects; for the short tenors in Figures 6.14 and 6.15, the poor value offered by the OTM options dominates. This is probably largely due to overestimation of the probability of large moves in the tails, as found in Chapter 5. As this effect gets smaller with tenor, the carry comes into play, so the curve has a humped shape, with both ends offering poor value due to different effects, which are smaller in the central tenors.

So, most of the features of the apparently anomalous patterns of payoff in options are in fact natural consequences of the carry trade, sometimes complicated by the fact that there is a tendency for implied volatility to be somewhat expensive, especially for OTM options. While this is interesting, and should be useful information for those looking to invest in foreign assets or hedge FX exposures, there is one case where the consequences of the various anomalies lead to a truly surprising result for those looking to hedge high yield exposures.

6.4 HEDGING WITH FORWARDS VS HEDGING WITH OPTIONS

Various entities that have exposure to EM currencies face an unpleasant problem. Consider the situation where there is an expected cash flow of 100 million BRL in three months' time. The person who expects the cash flow is based in EUR. Thus, if the BRL depreciates suddenly against the EUR, the cash flow will be worth much less. The BRL certainly has a history of such depreciations, so the risk is very real.

So how to protect against this risk? Initially one might think that a full forward hedge would be safest. But, the problem is that such a hedge will lock in the negative carry – costing the investor on average perhaps several percent of the notional amount. This is because the rate that corresponds to a depreciation of BRL is unlikely to be realised; the various BRL depreciations happen sufficiently rarely that on average the forward rate is quite incorrect.

Recall in Figure 6.1 we showed that, under certain circumstances, options were likely to be a less costly hedge than forwards. In Figure 6.21 we show the situation

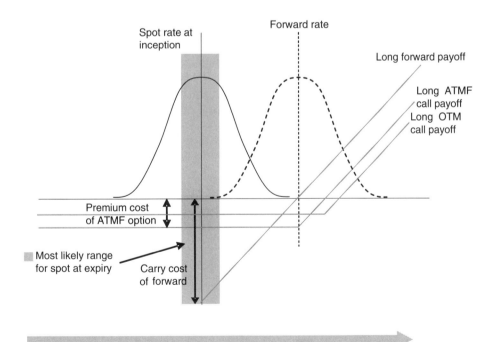

FIGURE 6.21 Payoffs for forwards, ATMF calls and OTM calls for the case of high interest rate differentials

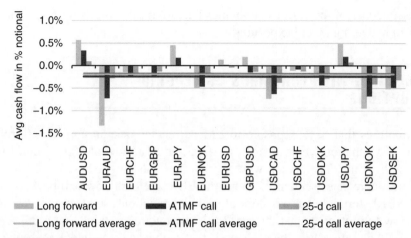

FIGURE 6.22   Average cash flow for 3M G10 hedges (positive exposure)

for the ATMF and OTM calls and the long forwards, which would be the appropriate hedges when the risk to the investor is from EM currency depreciation, i.e. he or she has a positive exposure.

As can be seen, in the likely range for the spot rate to end up, both option contracts have a limited loss of their premium, while the forward rate can have a much larger loss. Because the distance between the forward rate and the spot will increase with tenor, this potential loss on the forward contracts will be larger for longer tenors. Also, we expect that this effect will dominate in EM pairs; in G10 pairs, the carry is not as large and sometimes switches sign, so we expect the effect to be smaller.

Figures 6.22 and 6.23 show the results for 3M hedges, where the exposure is positive, i.e. the risk being hedged is depreciation of the quote currency. Each bar

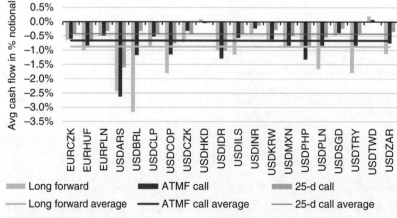

FIGURE 6.23   Average cash flow for 3M EM hedges (positive exposure)

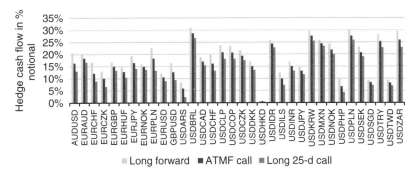

FIGURE 6.24 Hedge cash flow in percent of notional for period of worst depreciation

is the average hedge cash flow, including premium, payoff and costs, for hedging quarterly with the various contracts. Please see the Appendix for tabulated results.

We see that the result is much as might have been anticipated. For the G10 currencies, there is little consistency. Those where the quote currency tends overall to have higher interest rates have cost money to hedge, while those where the quote currency has had generally lower interest rates (USDJPY, AUDUSD etc.) have paid back the hedger. Overall hedging has cost money, but option hedges and forward hedges have on average cost similar amounts. It is worth pointing out that the ordering of value of the different contracts in any individual currency pair does show the effect of cheaper option hedges where the base currency tends to have higher interest rates – for example in AUDUSD.

What a different case it is for EM currency pairs! In this case, though all hedges lose money, the forwards lose the most, followed by the ATMF option, then the OTM option. We might wonder why the OTM option seems to offer better value to the hedger than the ATMF option but the answer is not hard to find – because neither option is likely to pay out, the fact that the OTM costs less is more important than the fact that the ATMF will pay out more in the rare event of a big depreciation move.

Let us now look at exactly those big depreciation moves in Figure 6.24 and Table 6.9, because, for a hedger, it is no use buying the cheapest hedge if it is not very effective when it is needed most.

There is little need to separate G10 and EM cases here; we see that, on average, all three hedge contracts have extremely similar returns. So where options offer cheaper hedges, on the whole they still offer similar protection.

We can now consider the case for puts vs short forwards, i.e. hedges for appreci-ation risk. In this case one might be hedging a future liability in a different currency, and the risk would be that the currency would appreciate, leaving more to pay under the contract. We give a picture of the payoffs in Figure 6.25. As we might expect, the forward hedge produces the highest payoff, followed by the ATMF option, followed by the OTM option. We have placed the forward rate slightly closer to the spot to

TABLE 6.9   Worst depreciation quarter hedge cash flow

	ATMF call	Long forward	Long 25-delta call
AUDUSD	16.4%	20.6%	13.0%
EURAUD	18.3%	20.2%	16.7%
EURCHF	12.1%	16.7%	8.9%
EURCZK	10.1%	13.0%	6.6%
EURGBP	14.9%	16.8%	13.3%
EURHUF	12.8%	14.9%	10.5%
EURJPY	16.4%	19.5%	14.1%
EURNOK	14.8%	16.1%	13.6%
EURPLN	18.2%	22.8%	13.3%
EURUSD	10.5%	12.2%	9.0%
GBPUSD	12.6%	16.3%	9.4%
USDARS	5.9%	8.3%	2.4%
USDBRL	28.7%	30.9%	26.8%
USDCAD	17.0%	18.8%	15.5%
USDCHF	16.1%	20.0%	13.3%
USDCLP	20.9%	23.7%	18.1%
USDCOP	20.7%	23.4%	18.1%
USDCZK	19.3%	21.7%	17.5%
USDDKK	15.1%	17.0%	13.4%
USDHKD	0.6%	0.7%	0.5%
USDIDR	24.4%	25.9%	22.8%
USDILS	9.9%	12.4%	7.3%
USDINR	15.0%	16.9%	13.1%
USDJPY	13.1%	14.6%	11.7%
USDKRW	27.6%	29.7%	25.6%
USDMXN	24.4%	25.8%	23.4%
USDNOK	21.9%	24.4%	20.0%
USDPHP	6.7%	10.2%	4.3%
USDPLN	27.6%	29.9%	25.9%
USDSEK	20.7%	23.0%	19.0%
USDSGD	8.4%	9.4%	7.3%
USDTRY	25.3%	28.1%	22.8%
USDTWD	8.2%	9.3%	7.1%
USDZAR	25.9%	29.5%	22.9%

approximate more of a G10 case; in this situation we would expect the forward to make money but the options, depending on strike and volatility, may or may not have a positive return. For the EM case in Figure 6.26, we would expect at least the ATMF option to have a chance of making money.

In Figures 6.27 and 6.28 that is exactly what we see. For G10 currency pairs, the carry trade shows up as an overall positive return to the short forward contract,

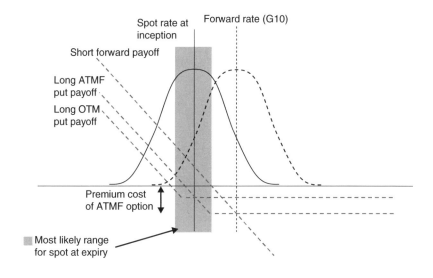

FIGURE 6.25 Payoffs for forwards, ATMF puts and OTM puts for the case of moderate interest rate differentials

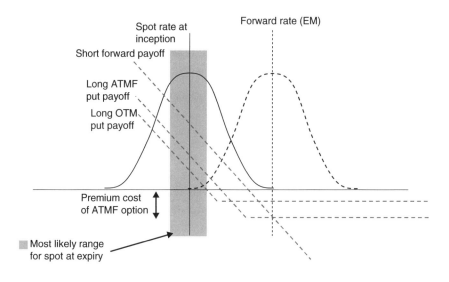

FIGURE 6.26 Payoffs for forwards, ATMF puts and OTM puts for the case of high interest rate differentials

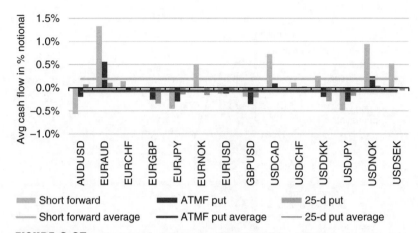

FIGURE 6.27   Average cash flow for 3M G10 hedges (negative exposure)

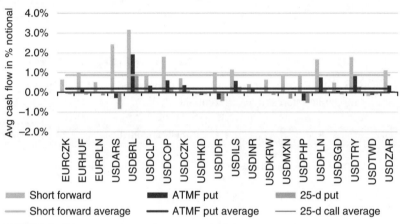

FIGURE 6.28   Average cash flow for 3M EM hedges (negative exposure)

but the options don't on average make money. For the EM pairs, the carry trade has much higher returns and the ATMF options just about make money, though the OTM on average do not. It is difficult to tell the ATMF and 25-delta average lines apart on Figure 6.27 but the data are tabulated in Table 6.10; both are slightly negative on average. Detailed currency-by-currency results can be found in the Appendix.

TABLE 6.10   Average cash flow in percent of notional for 3M hedges

	Long forward	ATMF call	25-delta call	Short forward	ATMF put	25-delta put
G10 Average	−0.17%	−0.22%	−0.16%	0.17%	−0.07%	−0.09%
EM Average	−0.92%	−0.59%	−0.33%	0.92%	0.30%	0.03%

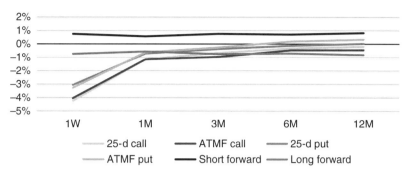

FIGURE 6.29 Average cash flow in percent of notional for different hedge tenors, averaged over G10 currency pairs

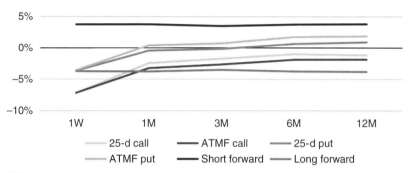

FIGURE 6.30 Average cash flow in percent of notional for different hedge tenors, averaged over EM currency pairs

Finally, let us turn our attention to the effect of tenor. We repeated the entire analysis above, initially done on 3M options, on 1W, 1M, 6M and 12M options. The results are aggregated in Figures 6.29 and 6.30, and Tables 6.11 and 6.12. In all cases, we multiplied the average cash flows by their annual frequency (factor of 4 for 3M cash flows, 12 for 1M cash flows, etc.) to be able to compare the annual hedging cost.

TABLE 6.11 Average annual cost of hedging in percent of notional for different G10 currency pairs

Tenor	25-delta call	ATMF call	25-delta put	ATMF put	Short forward	Long forward
1W	−4.24%	−4.04%	−3.06%	−3.26%	0.75%	−0.75%
1M	−1.14%	−1.14%	−0.72%	−0.62%	0.56%	−0.56%
3M	−0.67%	−0.97%	−0.37%	−0.26%	0.76%	−0.76%
6M	−0.33%	−0.47%	−0.13%	0.20%	0.71%	−0.71%
12M	−0.20%	−0.45%	0.02%	0.34%	0.82%	−0.82%

TABLE 6.12   Average annual cost of hedging in percent of notional for different EM currency pairs

Tenor	25-delta call	ATMF call	25-delta put	ATMF put	Short forward	Long forward
1W	−7.21%	−7.17%	−3.64%	−3.56%	3.74%	−3.74%
1M	−2.43%	−3.24%	−0.46%	0.41%	3.76%	−3.76%
3M	−1.72%	−2.64%	−0.16%	0.74%	3.49%	−3.49%
6M	−1.00%	−1.89%	0.65%	1.75%	3.75%	−3.75%
12M	−1.16%	−1.84%	0.91%	1.89%	3.82%	−3.82%

We see now a clear pattern emerging for the average results from many years of data. The effect is tenor dependent, with all tenors of 3M and upwards seeing an advantage to hedging with options for positive exposure. In this case the OTM options offer the best value hedge. For negative exposure, there is a clear advantage for short forward hedges. The shorter tenors do not show this effect and are far worse value; this is certainly due to the carry being smaller, and may also be due to an overestimation of volatility in the option market.

The differences between EM and G10 currency pairs are mainly the scale of the cash flows, with EM gains and losses being considerably larger, and the tenor at which options come to offer good value over forward hedges. For EM pairs, even 1M tenors have an advantage, while for G10 pairs it is not till the 6M tenor that all options including ATMF become better value than forwards. As this effect is driven by the difference between spot and forward, it is exactly as we would expect.

6.5 SUMMARY OF RESULTS

We can summarise the results of this chapter as follows:

1. Short dated straddle options are on average expensive for both G10 and EM currency pairs.
2. Long dated straddle options are on average close to fair value for both G10 and EM currency pairs.
3. Short dated put and call options are on average expensive for both G10 and EM currency pairs.
4. Long dated put options are on average cheap where the base currency tends to have lower interest rates, and expensive where the base currency tends to have higher interest rates. The results are similar for G10 and EM.
5. Long dated call options are on average expensive where the base currency tends to have lower interest rates, and cheap where the base currency tends to have higher

interest rates. The results for EM are more extreme than for G10; in general the call options are much worse value.

6. Short dated and long dated OTM put options are worse value than ATMF put options for G10 currency pairs. For EM pairs this effect diminishes with tenor.

7. Short dated OTM call options are worse value than ATMF call options for G10 currency pairs. For EM and G10 pairs this effect diminishes with tenor.

8. All EM OTM call options are worse value than OTM G10 call options.

9. EM OTM put options and G10 OTM put options offer similar value.

10. For both G10 and EM hedging of depreciation risk, options offer better value in longer tenors. For EM pairs this tenor is anything above 1M; for G10 the point is 6M.

11. For both G10 and EM hedging of appreciation risk, forwards offer better value in all cases, averaged over time.

Trading Strategies

7.1 INTRODUCTION

What is the intention of this chapter? We hope that the readers have not been hanging on waiting for the magical trading strategy, for it will not be found in the next few pages! If there were a simple, powerful way of making money in the FX markets, in a low risk way, then clearly it would have been found long before this book was written. And if the authors had found such a thing, probably they would not be writing about it in this book! But what we can show is that persistent anomalies have existed, which have not led to risk-free returns but which do convey a plentiful quantity of information to those who need to make decisions about the underlying value of options in FX. This could be hedgers, or investors, or pure speculators.

We do not propose to investigate option strategies further than showing the reader whether simple consistent strategies have worked; that would be the subject of an entire new book! But it will be a useful starting point for those involved to understand what the underlying strategies deliver, when they have worked, and when they have not.

Initially, we will focus on the simple carry trade, which has dominated so much of the data we have seen so far, before moving on to option trading strategies in general.

7.2 HISTORY OF THE CARRY TRADE

What is the carry trade? We have talked about it before but it is worth discussing it in detail, as it is so critical to the option mispricings we discover. To understand it properly we need to go back in time, before the FX option market began, to when FX spot rates began to trade in a freely floating fashion.

In 1944 the Bretton-Woods system of monetary management was established which included fixed exchange rates between the world's developed economies, which could be adjusted at intervals [1]. Each country was obliged to maintain its exchange rate with the US dollar, which itself was pegged to the value of gold. This was intended to guarantee post-war stability and prevent competitive devaluation of currencies, which had been a major source of conflict in the earlier part of the century. However, the gold peg proved difficult to maintain and led to increasing pressure on the US dollar to depreciate. In 1971 the peg to gold was removed, which was the beginning of the end for the fixed exchange rate regime.

After that date, exchange rates gradually became free floating until by the 1980s most were trading freely. The behaviour of these new market rates was expected to follow a few simple rules; in particular, they were supposed to have their underlying value determined by interest rates and inflation in their own country. A country with high inflation will have high interest rates. Each year the government can 'print' more money to keep up with inflation (and use it to pay debts or invest) in a process called seigniorage. Thus if 5% more money is printed, the currency will theoretically devalue by 5%, and high interest rates will be closely linked to weaker currencies.

This led to the idea (in fact first discussed in Keynes' theories from the 1920s [2]) of Uncovered Interest Parity (UIP) – that FX rates will evolve to on average track the forward rates determined by the relative interest rates between two currency areas. However, it became clear early on in the free-floating FX regime that in fact FX rates utterly decline to obey these rules; as early as 1981, 1983 and 1984 papers were published by Bilson, Shafer and Fama [3], [4], [5] concluding that forward exchange rates have little power as forecasts of future spot rates. Published papers up to the present day continue to agree [6]. The main focus of the discussion has moved to trying to explain the UIP breakdown and finding special conditions under which the theory might hold in practice.

7.3 THEORY

The theory underlying the carry trade, and the profits which can be made if UIP does not hold, are simply derived. Uncovered Interest Parity claims that, in the environment of risk-free arbitrage and risk-neutral investors, the forward exchange rate F at time t for time $t + k$ (expressed in units of quote currency per one unit of base currency) equals the spot exchange S rate at time t multiplied by the ratio of interest rates I with maturity $t + k$ (where b denotes the base currency):

$$F_{t,t+k} = S_t \times \frac{(1 + I_{t,t+k})}{\left(1 + I^b_{t,t+k}\right)}$$

Taking logs (indicated by lower case letters) and re-arranging gives:

$$f_{t,t+k} - S_t = i_{t,t+k} - i^b_{t,t+k}$$

In order for there to be no arbitrage between foreign exchange and interest rate markets, the expected spot exchange rate for time $t + k$ must equal the forward rate.

If there is a systematic bias for $f_{t,t+k} - S_t$ to differ from $i_{t,t+k} - i^b_{t,t+k}$, then UIP does not hold and profit opportunities can arise. In particular, if on average the spot rate at the start of the period is the best predictor of the spot rate at the end, then the average

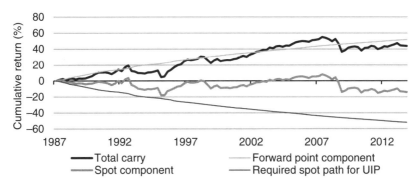

FIGURE 7.1 G10 carry trade returns with spot and interest rate components

profit is simply given by the interest rate differential; if one interest rate is 5% and the other is 3%, the carry trade would on average deliver 2% to the investor.

7.4 G10 CARRY TRADE RESULTS

Figure 7.1, which is essentially an update of [6], shows that this has indeed happened.

It shows the result, including costs, of the profits which would have accumulated to an investor in the carry trade, in each of the 45 possible G10 currency crosses, once per quarter since 1987.[1] Not bad for a job which only requires you to come into the office four times per year! But breaking it down into components reveals some interesting features.

1. The actual profits (Total carry) closely track the forward point component. This is the theoretical 'perfect carry trade' which would have resulted if the spot rates and the end of each deal were the same as those at the start. On average, the carry trade delivers almost exactly the interest rate differential.
2. UIP does not hold – if it did, the spot rate would have followed the required spot path for UIP.
3. The spot component (contribution delivered by the spot rate movements) has at different times enhanced or reduced the carry returns. Thus from 1995 to 2006, the spot movements roughly doubled the return from the carry component, leading to a flood of investment money. This was abruptly reversed in 2008, since when the returns have been closer to the mean.

We want, of course, to check that this result is not due to one or two anomalous currency pairs. Thus, in the following charts (Figures 7.2 to 7.11 and Table 7.1), we

---

[1]That is, we pursue a quarterly carry trade strategy separately in each of the 45 crosses, and average the result.

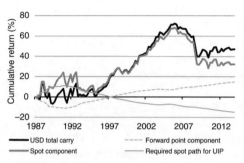

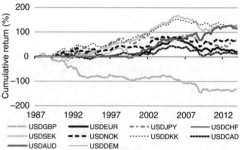

FIGURE 7.2 USD crosses

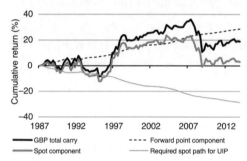

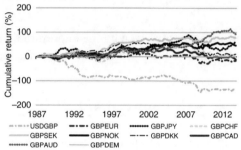

FIGURE 7.3 GBP crosses

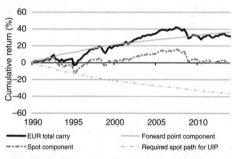

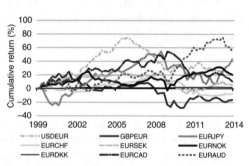

FIGURE 7.4 EUR (DEM prior to 1999) crosses

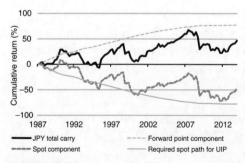

FIGURE 7.5 JPY crosses

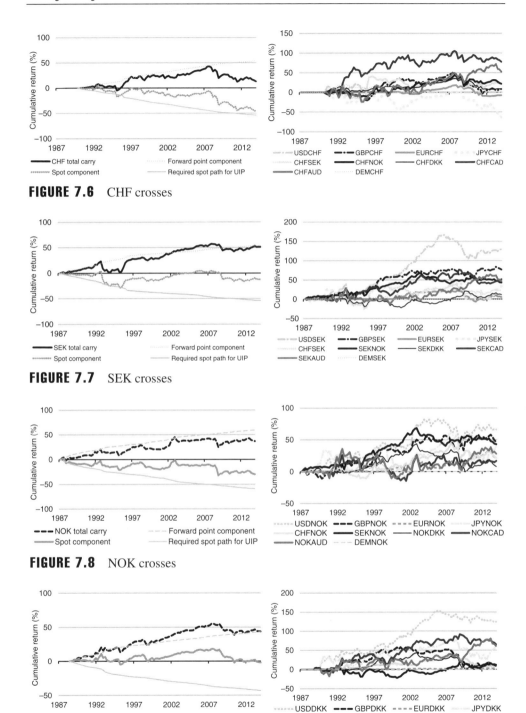

FIGURE 7.6 CHF crosses

FIGURE 7.7 SEK crosses

FIGURE 7.8 NOK crosses

FIGURE 7.9 DKK crosses

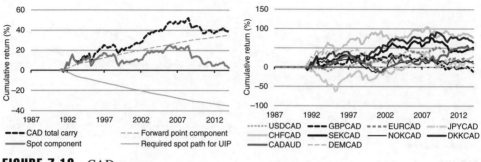

FIGURE 7.10   CAD crosses

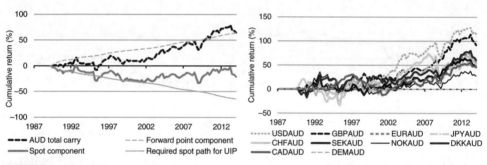

FIGURE 7.11   AUD crosses

TABLE 7.1   Detailed G10 carry trade quarterly results. Average quarterly contributions and annualised quarterly volatilities (%)

	Fwd pt component	Required spot path	Spot component	Vol of spot component	Total carry	Vol of total carry
USDGBP	−1.3%	1.3%	−0.2%	10.5%	−1.2%	10.7%
USDDEM	0.6%	−0.6%	0.2%	12.3%	1.0%	12.3%
USDEUR	−0.1%	0.1%	0.4%	10.3%	0.4%	10.6%
USDJPY	0.7%	−0.7%	0.4%	12.0%	0.7%	12.3%
USDCHF	0.5%	−0.5%	−0.6%	11.6%	−0.3%	12.0%
USDSEK	0.6%	−0.6%	0.5%	12.7%	1.3%	11.7%
USDNOK	0.6%	−0.6%	−0.1%	11.5%	0.7%	11.4%
USDDKK	0.4%	−0.4%	0.8%	10.8%	1.3%	10.7%
USDCAD	0.3%	−0.3%	−0.2%	7.3%	0.1%	7.4%
USDAUD	0.3%	−0.3%	1.2%	13.3%	1.9%	12.9%
GBPDEM	0.7%	−0.7%	0.4%	8.8%	0.8%	9.4%
GBPEUR	0.2%	−0.2%	−0.3%	8.1%	−0.3%	8.4%
GBPJPY	0.9%	−0.9%	0.1%	12.8%	0.6%	13.7%
GBPCHF	0.7%	−0.7%	−0.3%	9.7%	0.1%	10.4%
GBPSEK	0.3%	−0.3%	0.5%	8.4%	0.7%	8.3%

TABLE 7.1 (*Continued*)

	Fwd pt component	Required spot path	Spot component	Vol of spot component	Total carry	Vol of total carry
GBPNOK	0.4%	−0.4%	0.1%	8.0%	0.4%	8.0%
GBPDKK	0.3%	−0.3%	−0.1%	8.1%	0.1%	8.5%
GBPCAD	0.3%	−0.3%	−0.3%	9.4%	−0.1%	9.3%
GBPAUD	0.4%	−0.4%	0.5%	11.5%	0.9%	11.4%
DEMJPY	0.7%	−0.7%	−0.3%	12.4%	−0.3%	12.7%
DEMCHF	0.3%	−0.3%	0.2%	4.6%	0.4%	4.6%
DEMSEK	0.7%	−0.7%	−0.8%	9.8%	0.0%	9.4%
DEMNOK	0.4%	−0.4%	−0.1%	5.2%	0.2%	5.1%
DEMDKK	0.4%	−0.4%	0.0%	2.5%	0.3%	2.8%
DEMCAD	0.4%	−0.4%	1.2%	14.1%	1.2%	13.4%
DEMAUD	0.7%	−0.7%	−0.7%	16.5%	0.3%	16.1%
EURJPY	0.6%	−0.6%	0.5%	12.3%	0.7%	12.6%
EURCHF	0.3%	−0.3%	−0.4%	4.7%	−0.1%	4.9%
EURSEK	0.2%	−0.2%	0.0%	5.9%	0.1%	5.6%
EURNOK	0.4%	−0.4%	−0.1%	7.3%	0.3%	6.8%
EURDKK	0.0%	0.0%	0.0%	0.2%	0.0%	0.3%
EURCAD	0.2%	−0.2%	0.2%	10.5%	0.2%	10.1%
EURAUD	0.7%	−0.7%	0.1%	11.3%	0.9%	10.9%
JPYCHF	0.1%	−0.1%	−0.8%	12.3%	−0.7%	11.8%
JPYSEK	0.7%	−0.7%	−0.9%	15.9%	0.3%	14.4%
JPYNOK	0.8%	−0.8%	−0.9%	15.9%	0.4%	14.1%
JPYDKK	0.6%	−0.6%	−0.4%	13.3%	0.6%	12.8%
JPYCAD	0.7%	−0.7%	−0.8%	15.8%	0.3%	14.4%
JPYAUD	0.9%	−0.9%	−0.8%	17.3%	0.7%	16.3%
CHFSEK	0.8%	−0.8%	−0.8%	10.2%	0.2%	11.4%
CHFNOK	0.7%	−0.7%	−0.7%	8.6%	0.2%	8.1%
CHFDKK	0.5%	−0.5%	−0.5%	5.1%	0.1%	5.1%
CHFCAD	0.5%	−0.5%	0.2%	13.6%	0.9%	12.7%
CHFAUD	0.9%	−0.9%	−0.8%	15.0%	0.6%	14.5%
SEKNOK	0.4%	−0.4%	0.0%	6.1%	0.4%	6.2%
SEKDKK	0.3%	−0.3%	−0.1%	6.6%	0.1%	7.1%
SEKCAD	0.3%	−0.3%	0.3%	10.6%	0.6%	10.7%
SEKAUD	0.6%	−0.6%	−0.2%	11.0%	0.5%	11.1%
NOKDKK	0.3%	−0.3%	−0.2%	5.9%	0.1%	6.1%
NOKCAD	0.4%	−0.4%	−0.1%	10.7%	0.2%	10.5%
NOKAUD	0.6%	−0.6%	−0.3%	11.8%	0.3%	11.6%
DKKCAD	0.3%	−0.3%	0.6%	11.4%	0.7%	11.0%
DKKAUD	0.7%	−0.7%	−0.3%	13.0%	0.6%	12.6%
CADAUD	0.5%	−0.5%	−0.1%	8.4%	0.5%	8.4%

give the results for each set of crosses – all the USD crosses first, then GBP, etc. There is of course some overlap – USDGBP results are the same as GBPUSD results – but the reader can get some idea of the universality of the trade.

What can we say about these more detailed results? The first thing is that the carry trade is universal, and applies to all the G10 currencies. While there are some individual exceptions, like GBPUSD, overall the evidence is overwhelming. Additionally, in most graphs there is evidence of some distinct regimes. The run-up to 2007 shows almost universal positive returns in all the graphs, largely driven by spot rates, and similarly the 2008 drawdown is present in all cases. After that, there is more divergence, with a spread of results in the post-crisis period – though, on average, the delivered profit is the carry, just as before.

7.5 EM CARRY TRADE RESULTS

We now look at perhaps the better known case of carry for EM currencies. We present results only for exchange rates to the EUR and USD; intra-market crosses are often very illiquid with poor data, and in any case would be actually traded via the EUR or USD.

We see in Figure 7.12 that the results are very similar indeed to the G10. The EM pairs on average deliver higher returns, but this is to be expected; they have higher interest differentials. And just like the G10, the average rate of return is very similar to the forward point component (albeit a little less). So once more, the carry trade delivers approximately the carry over the long term.

As with the G10, let us convince ourselves that this is not due to one or two outliers. Below in Figures 7.13 and 7.14 and Table 7.2 are the currency-by-currency results.

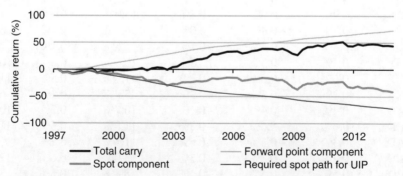

FIGURE 7.12 EM carry trade returns with spot and interest rate components

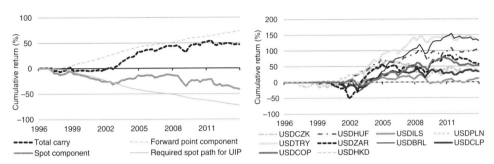

FIGURE 7.13 USD crosses

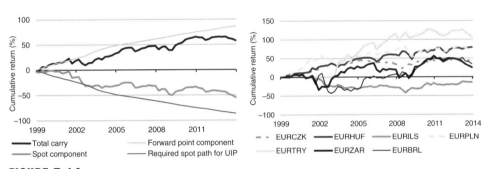

FIGURE 7.14 EUR crosses

Once more, the carry trade is almost universal regardless of base or quote currency. Moreover, interestingly, it does not appear to show signs of disappearing.

7.6 WHAT IS GOING ON?

As always, let us take a look at the diagram of what the market predicts versus what really happens. This is probably the simplest of all cases. If the spot rate is likely to remain near its starting value, then we are likely to make money by going short of the forwards.[2] This is the carry trade, as shown in Figures 7.15 and 7.16. As might be expected, it is more extreme for EM cases. It is easy to see that if, as is indeed the case, spot rates tend to stay close to the initial spot rate, then the carry trade will make money, and the EM carry trade, with a larger average interest rate differential, will make more money.

---

[2]As long as the forward rate is higher than the spot rate; this condition is fulfilled when the quote currency has a higher interest rate than the base currency. As discussed there are the anomalous carry pairs where this is often not the case.

TABLE 7.2 Detailed EM carry trade quarterly results. Average quarterly contributions and annualised quarterly volatilities (%)

	Fwd pt component	Required spot path	Spot component	Vol of spot component	Total carry	Vol of total carry
USDCZK	0.3%	−0.3%	−0.1%	14.0%	0.5%	14.2%
USDHUF	1.5%	−1.5%	−0.3%	15.5%	1.8%	15.5%
USDILS	0.5%	−0.5%	−0.4%	8.8%	0.2%	8.8%
USDPLN	1.2%	−1.2%	−0.9%	15.5%	0.8%	15.3%
USDTRY	3.5%	−3.5%	−0.8%	14.9%	3.0%	17.6%
USDZAR	1.6%	−1.6%	−1.3%	17.5%	1.0%	17.8%
USDBRL	2.5%	−2.5%	−0.9%	19.3%	2.5%	18.8%
USDCLP	0.5%	−0.5%	−0.2%	13.2%	0.6%	13.1%
USDCOP	1.1%	−1.1%	−0.5%	13.0%	1.0%	13.3%
USDHKD	0.1%	−0.1%	0.0%	0.4%	0.1%	0.5%
USDIDR	1.8%	−1.8%	−0.3%	10.6%	0.7%	7.3%
USDINR	1.3%	−1.3%	−0.7%	7.6%	0.6%	7.3%
USDKRW	1.3%	−1.3%	−0.7%	7.6%	0.6%	7.3%
USDPHP	1.3%	−1.3%	−0.6%	6.6%	0.7%	6.6%
USDSGD	0.3%	−0.3%	−0.5%	5.4%	−0.2%	5.4%
USDTWD	0.1%	−0.1%	−0.1%	5.4%	0.1%	5.4%
EURCZK	0.2%	−0.2%	0.3%	6.7%	0.6%	6.4%
EURHUF	1.5%	−1.5%	−0.3%	9.7%	1.3%	10.2%
EURILS	0.5%	−0.5%	−0.8%	8.9%	−0.3%	8.4%
EURPLN	1.2%	−1.2%	−0.2%	11.9%	1.4%	11.5%
EURTRY	3.7%	−3.7%	−1.7%	16.0%	2.4%	17.3%
EURZAR	1.7%	−1.7%	−1.8%	17.6%	0.4%	16.4%
EURBRL	1.5%	−1.5%	−2.0%	21.2%	0.7%	18.6%

7.7 OPTION TRADING STRATEGIES – BUYING PUTS

The carry trade, as is now very clear, is overall profitable. Indeed, depending on exactly how it is implemented, it usually comes out with a better risk-return ratio than holding an equity index. But it certainly is not without risk; the drawdown in 2008 wiped out about five years of accumulated profit. Not an event that anyone wants to explain to their manager! But, investments are inevitably associated with risk, and this is no exception.

So far so simple. But can we be a bit clever? What if, instead of doing the more volatile forward trade, we simply bought put options, whose risk is limited to the premium paid? Looking at Figure 7.17, it has the potential to work well.

We see that the option will never pay out as much as the forward when there is a positive payoff; it is always lower by the amount of its premium. But which is worth more on average will just depend on how often we end up in the different

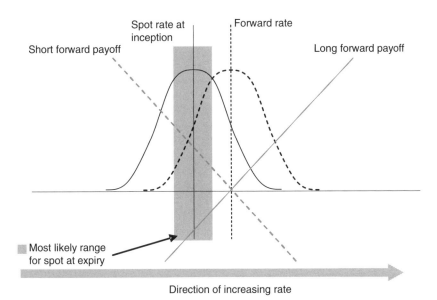

FIGURE 7.15 G10 carry trade

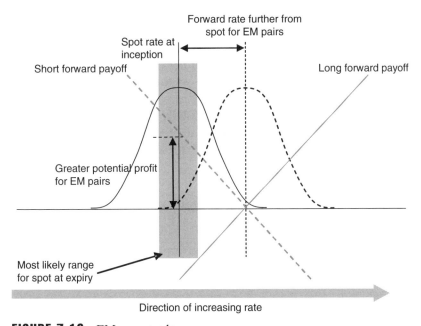

FIGURE 7.16 EM carry trade

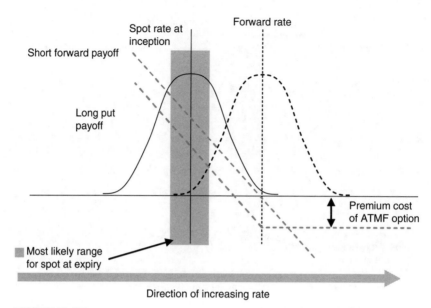

FIGURE 7.17   Potential profitable payoff when buying put options

regions – if the exchange rate clings close to spot at the start, then the option will on average pay out less than the forward. If on the other hand it tends to devalue violently (this will be in the direction of the increasing rate) then there will be many instances where the forward loses money and the option has the advantage. So it is possible that systematically buying options could perform better than just doing forward trades. Even if performance is lower, the profile of returns could be more attractive, with fewer and less violent drawdowns.

The next question is what put option to buy. In theory we should choose the longest tenor; in practice the two- and three-year tenors have very few data. Below in Figure 7.18 and Table 7.3 we show the returns for systematically buying and holding put options of different tenors.

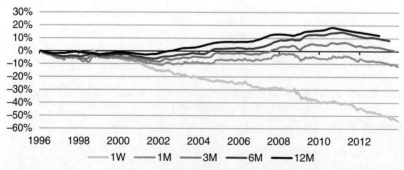

FIGURE 7.18   Average cumulative returns for buying ATMF puts

TABLE 7.3   Detailed results for average annualised (payoff – premium) for ATMF put buying

	1W	1M	3M	6M	12M
AUDUSD	−4.9%	−0.8%	−0.9%	−0.1%	0.0%
EURAUD	−1.3%	1.8%	2.4%	3.2%	3.8%
EURCHF	−2.7%	−0.6%	−0.4%	−0.1%	0.3%
EURCZK	−4.0%	−0.9%	0.1%	0.6%	1.1%
EURGBP	−3.2%	−1.3%	−1.1%	−1.1%	−0.9%
EURHUF	−4.2%	−1.3%	0.6%	0.8%	0.2%
EURJPY	−4.5%	−2.1%	−1.1%	−0.6%	−0.4%
EURNOK	−3.4%	−0.4%	0.1%	0.3%	0.9%
EURPLN		−1.9%	0.1%	0.6%	1.1%
EURUSD	−3.2%	−0.7%	−0.5%	−0.3%	−0.4%
GBPUSD	−3.3%	−1.4%	−1.4%	−0.8%	−0.8%
USDARS		−4.9%	−0.8%	0.4%	0.4%
USDBRL	−0.6%	5.5%	8.0%	9.6%	10.3%
USDCAD	−0.9%	0.0%	0.4%	1.1%	1.4%
USDCHF	−1.4%	0.5%	0.1%	0.1%	0.0%
USDCLP		−0.6%	1.4%	1.4%	1.2%
USDCOP		0.5%	2.6%	3.1%	1.1%
USDCZK	−2.4%	1.7%	1.6%	1.7%	0.9%
USDDKK	−5.4%	−0.6%	−0.7%	0.1%	−0.4%
USDHKD	−1.9%	−0.8%	−0.5%	−0.5%	−0.5%
USDIDR		−3.3%	−1.2%	1.1%	1.5%
USDILS		1.8%	2.3%	2.8%	2.8%
USDINR		0.4%	0.7%	0.4%	−1.6%
USDJPY	−6.2%	−2.1%	−1.1%	−0.9%	−0.9%
USDKRW	−5.7%	−0.3%	−0.1%	0.6%	1.0%
USDMXN	−6.6%	−1.6%	0.1%	0.4%	0.9%
USDNOK	−2.1%	0.1%	1.1%	1.6%	1.9%
USDPHP		−4.4%	−1.6%	−0.6%	0.7%
USDPLN		2.8%	3.1%	3.2%	3.1%
USDSEK	−3.5%	−0.3%	0.1%	0.9%	1.4%
USDSGD	−3.4%	0.1%	0.4%	0.5%	0.5%
USDTRY	2.9%	3.7%	3.5%	4.1%	4.4%
USDTWD	−6.4%	−1.1%	−0.5%	−0.6%	−0.9%
USDZAR	−5.4%	0.4%	1.5%	3.0%	3.8%

There is a noticeable difference between the 1W and the other tenors but this is explained by competing effects along the tenor curve. The carry is in general favourable to puts, but for short tenors the carry has less effect and the tendency for short dated options to be expensive becomes dominant. Recall from Chapters 4 and 6 that, for 1W puts, premium is typically more than payoff, for 1M puts they are very similar on average, but for all longer tenors premium is on average less than the payoff, and buying puts makes money.

As can be seen, this is much as we would expect. The short dated options lose money, while the longer dated options on average make money. Before the reader becomes too excited, however, and starts thinking that this is a marvellous risk-free way to run the carry trade, there are a few things to note:

- The returns are variable and in a market regime where volatilities are declining the strategy is likely to lose money.
- The early years have only a few data series before 2000.
- The returns seem low but that is in fact not true. They are given as a percentage of notional amount but in fact the amount of money 'invested' would be more like the premium cost, or perhaps an amount calculated on the likely risk and drawdowns of the strategy. As premiums are only a few percent of notional amount one can see that the return on invested capital could be very high.
- The average numbers given in Figure 7.18 will not precisely match averages calculated using Table 7.3, due to the different amounts of data in different series.
- The profile of the returns is quite desirable, as it tends to perform better than traditional investments in times of rising risk.

Notwithstanding the caveats above, it is remarkable that a simple effort at a trivial option buying strategy has returned very reasonable returns.

Let us now look currency by currency at the path taken to get to the apparent profitability above. We can take the 1M and 12M results to assess the effect of different tenors.

As we see in Figures 7.19 and 7.20, by the time we get to the 12M tenors, the strategies are solidly profitable overall. Additionally, they have some absolutely desirable properties – they actually make money when risk is rising, and the returns are positively skewed, in that they have sharp upward moves, but smoother smaller downward moves. These are both very much sought after by investors, as they help protect and diversify portfolios in risky times, and reduce the probability of large losses in a short period. However, we have to set against that the fact that the strategy can lose money slowly for several years in a row. That would take a great deal of patience to tolerate, and by the time the money started to arrive, the investor might well have lost faith.

7.8   OPTION TRADING STRATEGIES – SELLING CALLS

From Chapter 6, we know that OTM options will not be better value than their ATMF counterparts, so there is little point investigating whether the trade could be done more profitably with OTM options. However, there is one final idea to investigate. Rather than buy put options, which are effectively 'cheap', we could sell call options, which

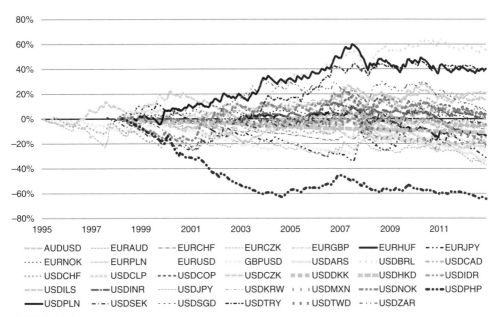

FIGURE 7.19 Cumulative returns of put buying for 1M options

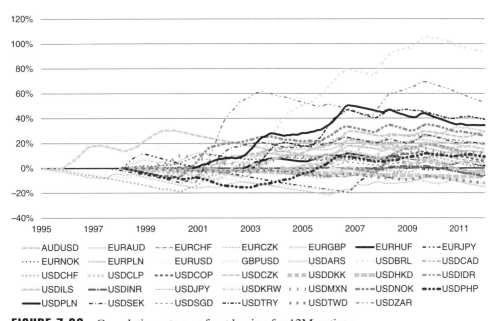

FIGURE 7.20 Cumulative returns of put buying for 12M options

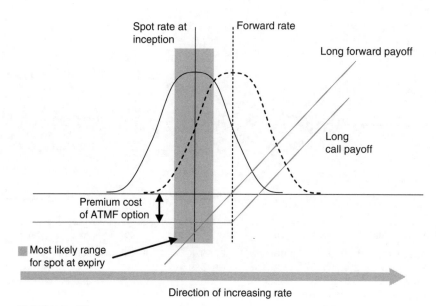

FIGURE 7.21   Potential profitable payoff when selling call options

we would expect to be particularly expensive. However, we would now think that the best returns would lie in the short dated options; looking at Figure 7.21, we would expect that the options would expire worthless most of the time so selling them to collect the premium would be a good idea.

We show the results in Figure 7.22 and Table 7.4 and, indeed, once more, it is what we expect.

All the calls are profitable to sell, though the short dated ones do best. We might expect that the longer dated ones would do better, though they do not. Here for once something else than the carry trade is coming into play; the likely explanation is that implied volatilities in the short dated end of the curve tend to be somewhat higher than realised, which makes an additional difference. This is also due to the shorter

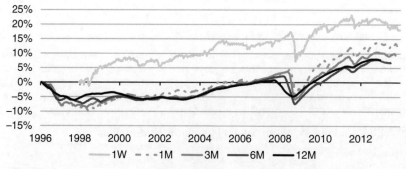

FIGURE 7.22   Average cumulative returns for selling ATMF calls

TABLE 7.4 Detailed results for average annualised [payoff – premium] for ATMF call selling

	1W	1M	3M	6M	12M
AUDUSD	−1.8%	−2.2%	−1.7%	−2.1%	−2.3%
EURAUD	0.8%	1.4%	2.4%	1.6%	2.0%
EURCHF	−0.3%	0.3%	0.6%	0.5%	0.2%
EURCZK	1.5%	2.1%	1.8%	1.6%	1.3%
EURGBP	0.0%	1.0%	0.7%	0.6%	0.4%
EURHUF	2.8%	3.5%	2.6%	2.4%	2.5%
EURJPY	−1.6%	−1.0%	−1.1%	−1.4%	−1.9%
EURNOK	1.5%	1.6%	1.4%	1.2%	1.0%
EURPLN		2.0%	1.2%	0.9%	0.8%
EURUSD	0.3%	−0.4%	−0.3%	−0.5%	−0.4%
GBPUSD	0.0%	−0.3%	0.3%	0.1%	0.3%
USDARS		9.0%	7.1%	6.3%	5.5%
USDBRL	6.0%	4.7%	3.9%	2.9%	3.2%
USDCAD	1.0%	2.8%	2.2%	1.7%	1.6%
USDCHF	0.3%	−0.3%	0.0%	0.2%	0.6%
USDCLP		1.7%	0.9%	1.2%	2.0%
USDCOP		3.3%	2.7%	2.8%	3.9%
USDCZK	−5.3%	−1.6%	−0.1%	0.4%	1.3%
USDDKK	0.9%	0.5%	1.2%	0.8%	1.4%
USDHKD	0.2%	−0.1%	0.0%	0.1%	0.2%
USDIDR		2.8%	2.3%	1.0%	1.9%
USDILS		1.8%	1.7%	1.4%	1.5%
USDINR		0.7%	0.1%	0.0%	1.1%
USDJPY	2.6%	−0.8%	−1.2%	−1.2%	−0.9%
USDKRW	3.2%	1.9%	1.6%	1.1%	0.7%
USDMXN	2.9%	3.1%	2.7%	2.7%	2.3%
USDNOK	0.4%	2.8%	2.2%	1.8%	1.9%
USDPHP		2.6%	2.1%	2.1%	1.8%
USDPLN		3.2%	2.5%	2.7%	2.3%
USDSEK	0.9%	1.5%	1.4%	0.8%	0.8%
USDSGD	1.5%	1.0%	1.1%	1.2%	1.4%
USDTRY	1.9%	3.4%	2.8%	2.9%	3.3%
USDTWD	2.0%	−0.4%	−0.8%	−0.6%	−0.3%
USDZAR	1.6%	2.3%	1.9%	0.7%	0.6%

dataset for the 1W options, which is responsible for much of the difference between that tenor and the rest.

However, it's clear to see that once more we have not discovered a magical trading strategy. All option selling strategies are inherently risky and this is no exception – the violent drawdown in 2008 would have wiped out multiple years of profit. But again, a very trivial implementation of an idea has shown itself to be potentially profitable.

WARNING ON SELLING OPTIONS

It might well seem to the reader that selling options is a profitable strategy. This is certainly true under the right circumstances. But we cannot say strongly enough that there are inbuilt risks to option selling and that it can incur sudden catastrophic losses. Returns to option selling are highly negatively skewed, with small frequent gains offset by rare and large losses. When the loss events occur, markets are likely to be highly illiquid and difficult to trade, so losses may become very difficult to stem.

Traders enter a position on a risk/reward basis, with a take-profit and stop-loss in mind. There is no point in being right on a position, but not being able to lock the profit in. Or worse still being wrong on a position and not being able to exit, particularly with options where the P/L profile is so asymmetric. For this reason selling options only against a known cash flow to enhance the rate may be the maximum amount of leverage a company may want to take.

Once again we look, currency by currency, at the path taken to get to the apparent profitability of selling call options, focusing on the 1M and 12M tenors.

As can be seen in Figures 7.23 and 7.24 there are only a few currencies which are exceptions to the profitability rule, and these are in general the anomalous carry currencies like USDJPY and AUDUSD. However, the severe drawdown experienced in 2008, visible in both long and short-term options gives a warning to those hoping to make money from this kind of strategy. The 12M option strategy looks very smooth but this is simply due to the fact that we assume that an option is sold each week, so the series is highly overlapping. The returns are scaled to take account of the overlap, of course.

7.9 OPTION TRADING STRATEGIES – TRADING CARRY WITH OPTIONS

Now that we have investigated buying puts and selling calls, it seems natural to take the final step and actively trade the carry with options. The obvious way to do this would be to either buy puts or calls depending upon the direction of the interest rate differential. This means that anomalous currency pairs like AUDUSD and USDJPY will no longer distort the results, and also that some G10 pairs where the carry has historically changed direction could be used to deliver returns more effectively.

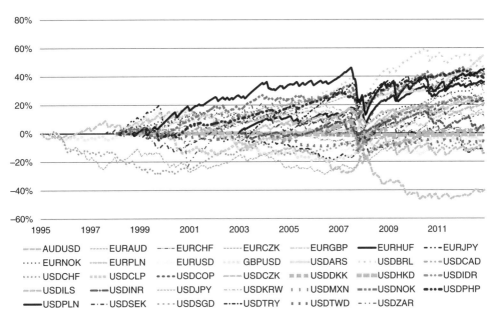

FIGURE 7.23 Cumulative returns of call selling for 1M options

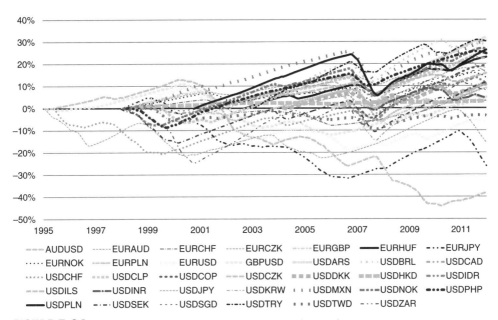

FIGURE 7.24 Cumulative returns of call selling for 12M options

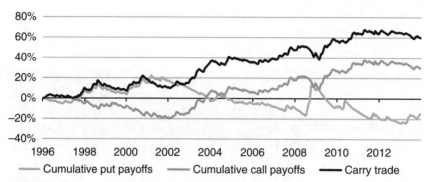

FIGURE 7.25   AUDUSD carry trade for 1M options

To trade the carry with options, we define some very simple rules. The sign of the interest rate differential at the start defines the direction of the trade, so we will buy puts when the quote currency has a higher yield, and buy calls when the base currency yield is higher. For longer tenors, it might be that the interest rate curves change between inception and payoff so that the carry 'flips', but in this case we will not change any trades which are already live, though new trades will obey the new signal.

Figures 7.25 and 7.26 show the results for the carry trade, in AUDUSD, for 1M and 12M options. We have chosen this currency pair as it's a perfect example of the trade working well. The combination trade is far better than either of the constituent buying of puts or calls.

We next show the returns to the 1M and 12M carry trade for G10 and EM currencies. The results are shown in Figures 7.27 to 7.32. As can be clearly seen, particularly for the G10 pairs, taking the carry as a signal is a great improvement over either buying only puts or only calls. We would absolutely expect this effect to be much more significant for G10 than EM – in the latter there are hardly any occasions when one would do other than buy puts and the data reflect this.

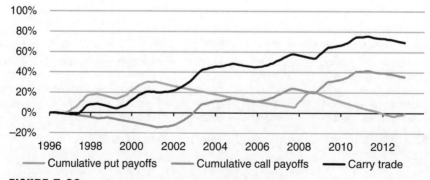

FIGURE 7.26   AUDUSD carry trade for 12M options

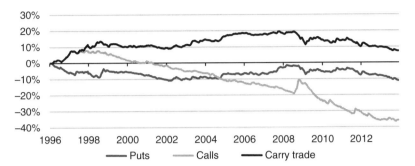

FIGURE 7.27   Carry trade for 1M options – All

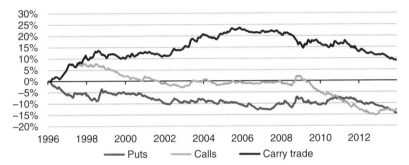

FIGURE 7.28   Carry trade for 1M options – G10

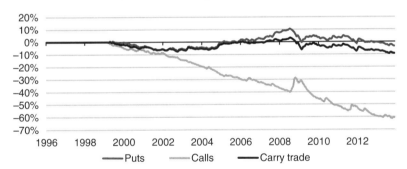

FIGURE 7.29   Carry trade for 1M options – EM

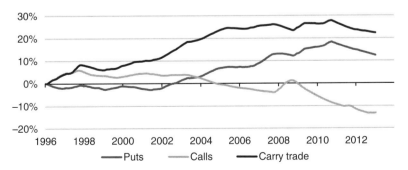

FIGURE 7.30   Carry trade for 12M options – All

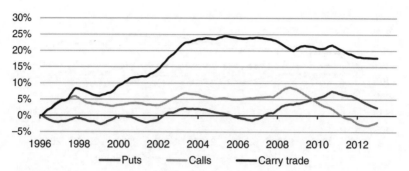

FIGURE 7.31   Carry trade for 12M options – G10

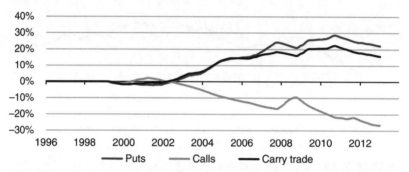

FIGURE 7.32   Carry trade for 12M options – EM

The results in Table 7.5 show the overall improvement in returns to the carry trade as the tenor gets longer. However, these are the average returns per trade, which can be as long as a year or as short as a week. The final line of the table annualises the returns by multiplying by the number of periods of the contract per year. We also plot these overall results in Figures 7.33 and 7.34. Now we can get an idea of how the trade would perform as an investment strategy – clearly the longer tenors are more interesting, though the difference between G10 and EM pairs is less than one might expect.

Is it a good strategy? It's interesting but perhaps not a panacea. The last few years of generally declining volatility have seen purchased options at a disadvantage. Though the returns look quite low we recall that they are quoted as returns on the notional amount, so it would be reasonable to apply a leverage of perhaps three to equalise volatility of returns with that of an equity index. But they point the way to the fact that options are an interesting source of return where some very simple rules already generate positive and fairly smooth payoffs.

7.9.1   Premium and Payoff vs MTM Calculations

When we consider trading strategies, we have an important caveat to add to the results in the previous graphs. This is that the results include only premium and payoff, not

TABLE 7.5 Average quarterly carry trade returns

	1W	1M	3M	6M	12M
AUDUSD	−0.01%	0.28%	0.88%	2.02%	4.09%
EURAUD	−0.02%	0.15%	0.61%	1.58%	3.77%
EURCHF	−0.06%	−0.08%	−0.24%	−0.34%	−0.39%
EURGBP	−0.06%	−0.10%	−0.32%	−0.91%	−1.56%
EURJPY	−0.08%	−0.13%	0.15%	0.53%	1.69%
EURNOK	−0.08%	−0.08%	−0.09%	0.07%	0.63%
EURUSD	−0.03%	0.08%	0.30%	0.50%	1.37%
GBPUSD	−0.06%	−0.06%	−0.22%	−0.28%	−0.45%
USDCAD	−0.02%	−0.10%	−0.26%	−0.25%	0.40%
USDCHF	−0.08%	−0.03%	−0.19%	−0.30%	−0.95%
USDDKK	−0.14%	−0.23%	−0.75%	−1.15%	−2.92%
USDJPY	−0.10%	0.00%	0.18%	0.58%	0.81%
USDNOK	−0.05%	0.00%	0.21%	0.68%	1.32%
USDSEK	−0.03%	0.15%	0.37%	0.95%	2.21%
EURCZK	−0.08%	−0.15%	−0.04%	0.27%	0.73%
EURHUF	−0.08%	−0.11%	0.15%	0.42%	0.20%
EURPLN		−0.16%	0.02%	0.32%	1.14%
USDARS		−0.41%	−0.19%	0.18%	0.41%
USDBRL	−0.01%	0.46%	1.99%	4.82%	10.31%
USDCLP		−0.10%	0.36%	0.49%	0.26%
USDCOP		−0.07%	0.46%	1.36%	1.00%
USDCZK	−0.05%	−0.05%	−0.45%	−1.17%	−3.03%
USDHKD	−0.03%	−0.03%	−0.04%	−0.09%	−0.26%
USDIDR		−0.17%	−0.02%	0.67%	1.53%
USDILS		0.08%	0.22%	0.47%	1.34%
USDINR		0.05%	0.22%	0.23%	−1.68%
USDKRW	−0.13%	−0.17%	−0.32%	−0.39%	−0.36%
USDMXN	−0.13%	−0.13%	0.02%	0.18%	0.89%
USDPHP		−0.38%	−0.51%	−0.36%	0.37%
USDPLN		0.10%	0.29%	0.55%	0.45%
USDSGD	−0.08%	−0.07%	−0.27%	−0.45%	−1.56%
USDTRY	0.06%	0.31%	0.88%	2.07%	4.36%
USDTWD	−0.13%	−0.04%	0.08%	0.01%	−0.14%
USDZAR	−0.10%	0.03%	0.37%	1.51%	3.81%
Average	−0.06%	−0.03%	0.11%	0.43%	0.88%
Ann. Average	−3.31%	−0.41%	0.45%	0.87%	0.88%

the interim value of the options on all the days in between. This marked-to-market (MTM) value can vary very significantly and thus would inevitably introduce more volatility, and worsen drawdowns. So investors thinking to implement strategies based on premium and payoff values would do well also to investigate how MTM changes will affect their back-tested results.

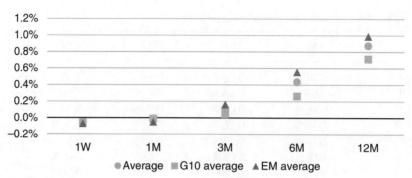

FIGURE 7.33   Average quarterly option carry trade returns (payoff – premium)

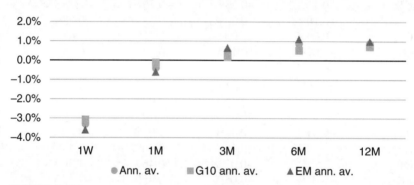

FIGURE 7.34   Average annualised carry trade returns

7.10   SUMMARY OF RESULTS

We can summarise the results of this chapter as follows:

1. The carry trade has worked since the start of the floating FX rate market in the 1980s.
2. It is possible to trade the carry trade by buying put options, the longer tenor the better.
3. One can make money selling call options as they tend to expire worthless – though once more we emphasise that this is an average and they have the capacity to lose large amounts of money in a short time.
4. The carry trade may also be executed by buying put or call options as indicated by the interest rate differential.
5. None of the strategies is without risk, however, and they serve as a starting point for trading strategy development.

REFERENCES

[1] Proceedings and Documents of the United Nations Monetary and Financial Conference, Bretton Woods, New Hampshire, 1–22 July 1944.

[2] Isard, P. (2006) Uncovered interest parity. IMF Working Paper No.WP/06/96, April.

[3] Bilson, J. F. O. (1981) The 'Speculative Efficiency' hypothesis. *Journal of Business* 54(3), 435–451.

[4] Shafer, J. R., Loopesko, B. E., Bryant, R. C. and Dornbusch, R. (1983) Floating exchange rates after ten years. *Brookings Papers on Economic Activity* 1, 1–86.

[5] Fama, E. F. (1984) Forward and spot exchange rates. *Journal of Monetary Economics* 14, 319–338.

[6] James, J., Kasikov, K. and Secmen, A. (2009) Uncovered interest parity and the FX carry trade. *Quantitative Finance* 9(2), 123–127.

REFERENCES

Summary

8.1 A CALL TO ARMS

We started this book by saying that we wanted to show what had really been happening in the FX option market, from its early beginnings up to the present day. We hope that the reader now appreciates that there were good reasons for this! The fact that the market has so persistently misvalued such a widely traded set of instruments will surely come as a surprise to many. Though there are reasons that this has not been generally known up to this point, as discussed in Chapter 1, it is surely now time that these market behaviours should be made clear to those who need to know about them.

But more generally, there would never have been a need to write this book if from the start the markets had taken a different attitude. If the post-trade performance of different contract types had been considered to be important from the start, then there would have been regular evaluation of the situation, and the fact that the carry trade effectively 'breaks' the option market would always have been clear. Instead, the overwhelming focus of market participants has been on the price at the point of sale and whether it conforms to the various pricing assumptions and no-arbitrage conditions which are set out at inception. Even when the carry trade itself started to be noticed, it was dismissed by large segments of the market and the academic community, who tended to argue that it could or should not exist rather than examining the evidence.

It doesn't have to be like this. Options are not the only products where we should be collecting regular data to evaluate performance. They only happen to be the ones where the data series fortunately exist and are long enough to enable us to come to some firm conclusions. Indeed, though we have used the Bloomberg dataset, there are others which exist within different banks which are longer and more detailed – but which nobody wants to share. One of the authors has worked with proprietary data on FX options which went back to 1988, critically including the 1992 European ERM crisis. Though that longer dataset came to exactly the same conclusions as the

Bloomberg set, we cannot use it here as it is not available to those outside the company. This is a ridiculous situation. Pooled datasets would hugely improve the transparency and help the reputation of the financial industry.

Consider products like barriers, path dependent options, knock-outs. The data needed to price them are more extensive than those for vanilla options, and are not commonly stored anywhere. Thus, popular products, with billions of flow dollars spent on them each year, are utterly unknown entities when it comes to calculating their average payback. This is not clever.

Now is the perfect time for the financial world to review this situation. Increased scrutiny and regulation mean that banks have an urgent need to increase transparency, and to be seen to be doing so. Additionally, commoditisation of vanilla products means that banks tend to design more complex contracts – not necessarily a bad thing, but surely as soon as a product becomes widely traded, its performance should be tracked?

Banks are not the only culprits. Academia, usually so focused on data, has neglected the fact that historical data are of poor quality and patchy. Study after study on financial markets is done on tiny datasets with poor quality control, and nobody appears to complain. It would be appropriate for regulatory bodies to require that high quality databases of prices and performance of widely used instruments are maintained and made generally available to those seeking to enter into contracts. Academics should be encouraged to publish studies on this wide dataset. This would add hugely to the information available to companies seeking to hedge exposures. There would be no need for detailed or proprietary information to be made available; we are talking about products which are widely traded and whose prices do not differ significantly among different institutions.

8.2   SUMMARY OF RESULTS FROM THIS BOOK

So, we are now in a position to summarise what we have learned from our data analysis exercise. From our previous chapters we have the following historical facts:

1. Short dated straddle options are on average expensive.
2. Long dated straddle options are on average close to fair value.
3. Short dated put and call ATMF options are on average expensive.
4. Long dated put options are on average cheap where the base currency tends to have lower interest rates, and expensive where the base currency tends to have higher interest rates. The results are similar for G10 and EM.
5. Long dated call options are on average expensive where the base currency tends to have lower interest rates, and cheap where the base currency tends to have higher interest rates. The results for EM are more extreme than for G10; in general the call options are much worse value.

6. In general, OTM options are overvalued relative to ATMF options.
7. Short dated and long dated OTM put options are worse value than ATMF put options for G10 currency pairs. For EM pairs this effect diminishes with tenor.
8. Short dated OTM call options are worse value than ATMF call options for G10 currency pairs. For EM and G10 pairs this effect diminishes with tenor.
9. All EM OTM call options are worse value than OTM G10 call options.
10. EM OTM put options and G10 OTM put options offer similar value.
11. For both G10 and EM hedging of depreciation risk, options offer better value in longer tenors. For EM pairs this tenor is anything above 1M; for G10 the point is 6M.
12. For both G10 and EM hedging of appreciation risk, forwards offer better value in all cases.
13. The carry trade has worked since the start of the floating FX rate market in the 1980s.
14. It is possible to trade the carry trade by buying put options, the longer the tenor the better.
15. One can make money selling call options as they tend to expire worthless where the base currency has lower interest rates. For exchange rates where the base currency tends to have higher interest rates one can make money selling put options.

All of these effects are explained by a few simple underlying facts about the way the market moves. These are:

1. The carry trade exists; spot rates at the start of a deal are a better estimate of rates at the end than are the forward rates.
2. Implied volatility is an overestimate of realised volatility, most acutely in short tenors.
3. Implied volatility for OTM options is a more extreme overestimate of the realised volatility.

Nothing of this requires genius. It doesn't even require calculus. Just a thoughtful look at the data and an understanding of the products and their payoffs.

8.3 BUILDING UP A PICTURE

To put everything together, it is useful to look at the situation in graphics. In the figures following (Figures 8.1 to 8.7), we build up to the different situations from the very beginning. Note that these diagrams hold for the case where the base currency has lower interest rates; for anomalous carry currencies then the situations need to

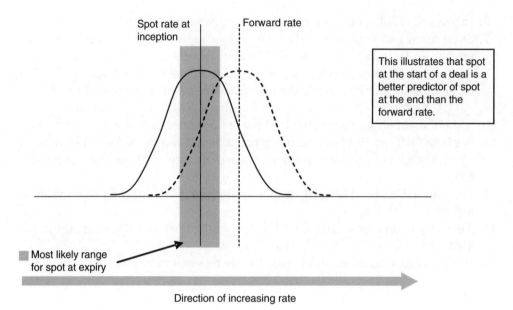

FIGURE 8.1   Forward and spot rates with distributions

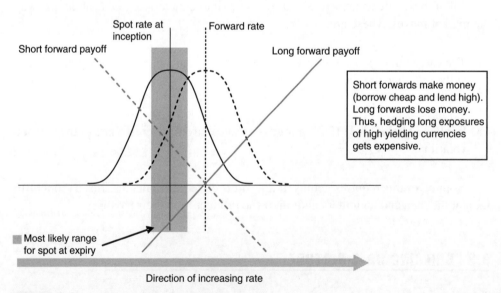

FIGURE 8.2   Why the carry trade works

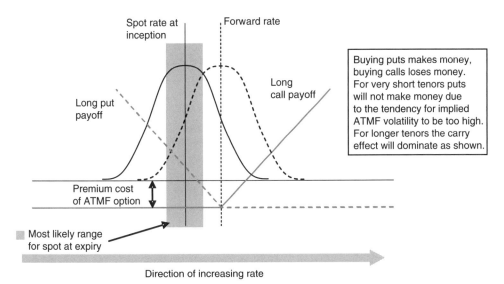

FIGURE 8.3 ATMF put and call options

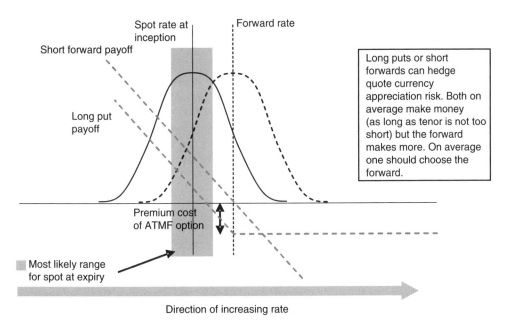

FIGURE 8.4 Hedging quote currency appreciation risk

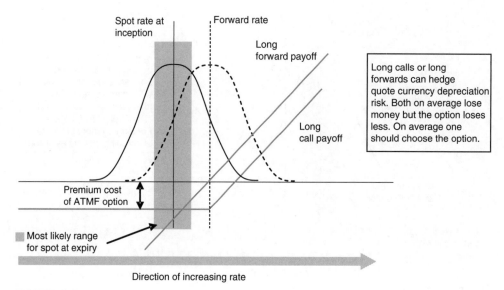

FIGURE 8.5   Hedging quote currency depreciation risk

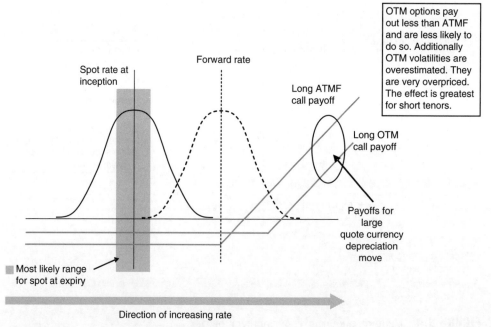

FIGURE 8.6   ATMF vs OTM call option

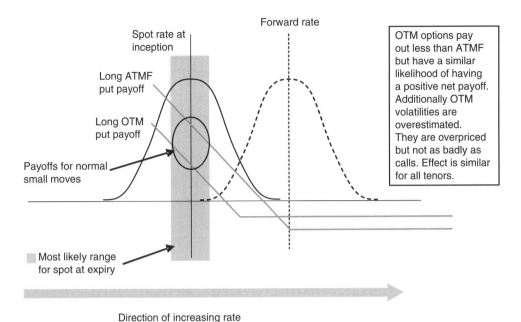

FIGURE 8.7 ATMF vs OTM put option

be changed around. As a reminder, the contracts discussed here are options on the exchange rate so that:

- A long EURUSD forward contract is long of the EUR.
- A call option on EURUSD pays out if the EUR rises vs the USD, i.e. if the FX rate rises.
- A put option on EURUSD pays out if the USD rises vs the EUR, i.e. if the FX rate falls.

8.3.1 What Does This Mean in Practice?

There are two broad classes of people who will be interested in these results: hedgers and investors. For the hedgers, they would like to understand what the most cost effective protection strategies have been. For the investors, we can show where there are likely opportunities to find profitable trading strategies. Below, then, is the final set of suggestions derived from our historical analysis. Recall that for anomalous carry currencies the effects will be reversed. Also recall that selling options to make money is a high risk strategy! Investors are well advised to ensure they have some kind of large risk insurance policy, like a bought option further out-of-the-money.

1. Hedging quote currency appreciation risk

    Choose a short forward contract on the exchange rate. No particular tenor is strongly favoured. Effect is strongest for EM markets.

2. Hedging quote currency depreciation risk

   Choose a call option on the exchange rate, OTM if available. The fact that the payoff is unlikely to occur outweighs the fact that OTM volatilities are poor value. The tenor effect is variable; review Chapter 6 for details.

3. Trading forward contracts to make money

   Do a short forward to access the carry trade.

4. Buying options to make money

   Buy long dated puts.

5. Selling options to make money

   Sell short dated calls.

8.4 FINAL WORD

We wrote this book after we realised that the series of papers we had been working on revealed a set of anomalies which were largely unknown but very important. We hope that we have added to the knowledge on the subject and helped to kick-start a change in attitude with respect to historical market data and valuation. We also hope that folk who have to make important hedging and investment decisions will find material to help them become more informed about the FX market they trade. This market has become more interesting the more we have looked into it, and its imperfections have become part of its fascination.

Appendix

CHAPTER 1

What 'Should' an Option Cost?

This is an interesting question and has had different answers as markets have evolved. Let's take an imaginary trip through history as we trace the development of option-like products.

1. **Pooled insurance.** In this peer-to-peer arrangement, each of a group of merchants would agree to pay a small amount into an emergency fund every year. The moneys in the fund were available to cover a catastrophic loss for any one of them, like the loss of a ship. Each of them had a claim on the fund, and they were thus covered by a primitive kind of insurance. In this case, on average, a merchant would expect to receive what he put in, over a lifetime or similar. Apart from any banking costs, the fund moneys were there purely to cover the payoffs and smooth the risk of the group of merchants.

   Case 1: Average Premium = Average Payoff

2. **Insurance company.** Seeing a desire for smoothed risk, insurance companies arise to fulfil the need. They take in premiums, keep them safe in a pool and pay out for legitimate claims from the pool. They also expect to make a profit sufficient to pay salaries and dividends. They are taking one-way risk: they only pay out on claims which are probably large, and they only take in premiums which are small. So they would also desire to build up something of a protective reserve amount to buffer large claims. Thus we would expect premiums on average to be slightly more than payoffs.[1]

   Case 2: Average Premium > Average Payoff

3. **Old-fashioned trading desk.** The original mechanism for making money on a trading desk was to take in both bids and offers with a spread between them. For

---

[1] A modern insurance company actually expects to make a lot of its money from returns on investing the premiums – which poses a problem when global interest rates are low.

an option trading desk, the first few years tended to look more like an insurance company as corporations wanted to buy options but there were few natural sellers. As the market became more liquid a desk could take a middleman position and buy and sell, taking a mostly riskless spread in between. Not every trade had to be matched as long and short positions could be aggregated. As the risks to this type of trading were lower, the desk required less reserve than an equivalent insurance company. Therefore the difference between payoff and premium would be the bid-offer cost, which could be small.

Case 3: Average Premium slightly > Average payoff

4. **Modern trading desk.** The desk makes money partly from bid-offer spread and partly by intelligent handling of positions. Bid-offer spread is small. Thus the premium and the payoff will be similar.

Case 4: Average Premium very slightly > Average payoff

So it can now be seen that for a modern buyer or seller of options there is not much reason for this liquid and commoditised contract to have a premium which differs very much for its payoff from simple value considerations.

ISO codes

Code	Currency	Locations using this currency
ARS	Argentine peso	Argentina
AUD	Australian dollar	Australia, Australian Antarctic Territory, Christmas Island, Cocos (Keeling) Islands, Heard and McDonald Islands, Kiribati, Nauru, Norfolk Island, Tuvalu
BRL	Brazilian real	Brazil
CAD	Canadian dollar	Canada
CHF	Swiss franc	Switzerland, Liechtenstein
CLP	Chilean peso	Chile
CNY	Chinese yuan	China
COP	Colombian peso	Colombia
CZK	Czech koruna	Czech Republic
DEM	German mark	Germany (pre-euro)
DKK	Danish krone	Denmark, Faroe Islands, Greenland
EUR	Euro	Andorra, Austria, Belgium, Cyprus, Estonia, Finland, France, Germany, Greece, Guadeloupe, Ireland, Italy, Kosovo, Latvia, Luxembourg, Malta, Martinique, Mayotte, Monaco, Montenegro, the Netherlands, Portugal, Reunion, Saint Barthélemy, San Marino, Saint Pierre and Miquelon, Slovakia, Slovenia, Spain, Vatican City

Code	Currency	Locations using this currency
GBP	Pound sterling	United Kingdom, Isle of Man, Jersey, Guernsey, South Georgia and South Sandwich Islands, British Indian Ocean Territory, Tristan da Cunha, British Antarctic Territory
HKD	Hong Kong dollar	Hong Kong, Macao
HUF	Hungarian forint	Hungary
IDR	Indonesian rupiah	Indonesia
ILS	Israeli new shekel	Israel, State of Palestine
INR	Indian rupee	India
JPY	Japanese yen	Japan
KRW	South Korean won	South Korea
MXN	Mexican peso	Mexico
MYR	Malaysian ringgit	Malaysia
NOK	Norwegian krone	Norway, Svalbard and Jan Mayen, Bouvet Island, Queen Maud Land, Peter I Island
PHP	Philippine peso	Philippines
PLN	Polish złoty	Poland
RUB	Russian ruble	Russia, Abkhazia, South Ossetia, Crimea
SEK	Swedish krona	Sweden
SGD	Singapore dollar	Singapore, auxiliary in Brunei
THB	Thai baht	Thailand
TRY	Turkish lira	Turkey, Northern Cyprus
TWD	New Taiwan dollar	Taiwan
USD	United States dollar	United States, American Samoa, Barbados, Bermuda, British Indian Ocean Territory, British Virgin Islands, Caribbean Netherlands, Ecuador, El Salvador, Federated States of Micronesia, Guam, Haiti, Marshall Islands, Northern Mariana Islands, Palau, Panama, Puerto Rico, Timor-Leste, Turks and Caicos Islands, US Virgin Islands, Zimbabwe
ZAR	South African rand	South Africa

FX Market Conventions

Like many other fields of specialisation, each area of finance has its own arcane vocabulary or jargon. Even in expressing daily performance, colleagues sitting very near to each other on a trading floor may use completely different language. For a credit trader, it may be perfectly natural to talk of spreads tightening, widening or even blowing out, while a sovereign debt specialist will usually talk in terms of yields. Equity traders may talk in terms of percentage changes, while FX dealers are more likely to be concerned with pips and big figures. And that is before we even consider derivative instruments. For option traders, volatilities, correlations and surfaces are very important.

The area of foreign exchange, being long established, has an especially interesting vocabulary. The exchange rate between pounds sterling and US dollars, for example, GBPUSD, is commonly referred to as cable. In this case at least there is some logic to the description, which refers to the time when the exchange rate was transmitted under the Atlantic by means of a steel cable – since replaced by fibre optic links.

Foreign exchange quotation conventions and notation can frequently lead to confusion among those outside the FX community. First, the order in which currencies appear in quotations is itself subject to a series of conventions that can take some getting used to and which must be noted when reading rates printed in the financial pages. For example, it is traditional for the exchange rate between the US dollar and Japanese yen to be written as USDJPY, the price of one dollar in yen. A rising rate thus means that the dollar is strengthening. The exchange rate between the US dollar and the euro, however, is written as EURUSD, the price of one euro in dollars. In this case a rising rate means a weakening dollar.

What is perhaps more confusing is the way in which the currencies in an FX quotation are identified; it is difficult to find a consensus on this issue even among FX professionals. Among non-FX people, merely asking the question has been known to cause eyes to glaze over. However, it is difficult for us not to broach this subject. First, readers may come across differing conventions in other publications or during the course of their studies. We should at least be clear about how our definitions compare to those of others. Second, as we will see, clearly defining the currency in which an option trade's notional amount is stated is very important. When describing which is the notional currency for a collection of exchange rates it would be nice to avoid saying things like: 'the left hand (or first) currency in the exchange rate'. We discuss some alternative naming conventions below before explaining the approach adopted during the remainder of this book.

Describing the first and second currencies in a quotation as the asset and base currencies respectively is perhaps the easiest approach to explain as there is a direct analogy with other financial markets. For example, when considering an equity share it is clear that it (the asset) can have its price described in terms of the number of units of some base currency – one share may cost $1.50.

By analogy, in the exchange rate EURUSD it is the EUR that is the asset currency and USD the base; a rate of 1.5000 means that one euro (the asset) costs $1.50 or 1.5 units of the base currency. There is a simple mnemonic to remember which currency is which: A comes before B in the alphabet, so the first part of the quote is the asset and the second the base.

So far, so good. However, it turns out that other conventions exist, and that these alternatives are at odds with the Asset/Base labels. Those studying the CFA Institute's Learning Outcome Statements will be familiar with the labels Base and Quote and some corporate treasurers with Base and Risk currencies. Note that in both cases the base currency is now the one on the left of the exchange rate. Other alternatives include Base/Term, Foreign/Domestic and Fixed/Variable.

We may all have to agree to disagree on the right description for the currencies in an exchange rate, or else perhaps acknowledge that different terminology is required depending on the circumstances. In this book we shall adopt the names base and quote to describe the first and second currencies in an exchange rate respectively. To be explicit, in quoting EURUSD we will refer to EUR as the base currency and USD as the quote currency.

CHAPTER 2

European- and American-style Options

Vanilla European-style options are only exercisable at maturity. Comparable American-style options are exercisable at any point during the life of the option with spot delivery. So an American option premium will always be more than the corresponding European option. Volatility for an American option is usually very close to the corresponding vanilla option. However, exceptions can exist, such as on a highly skewed currency pair where high volatility is foreseen. In this instance if spot moves, just when you may want to exercise the American feature, the volatility will be rising and the option may be worth more. This was a feature of the USDJPY market in the 1990s.

CHAPTER 4

Payoff/Premium Ratios for Straddles, by Time Period

TABLE A.1 Payoff/premium for ATMF straddles, 31/12/1995–12/12/2001 (1W–3M tenors)

	1W			1M			3M		
	Premium	Payoff	Ratio	Premium	Payoff	Ratio	Premium	Payoff	Ratio
AUDUSD	1.52%	1.30%	85.5%	2.50%	2.47%	98.8%	4.15%	3.76%	90.4%
EURAUD									
EURCHF	0.50%	0.38%	76.9%	1.00%	0.71%	71.7%	1.60%	1.17%	73.1%
EURCZK	0.69%	0.55%	80.4%	1.39%	1.04%	75.1%	2.58%	1.92%	74.5%
EURGBP	1.11%	1.04%	94.4%	2.12%	1.76%	82.8%	3.72%	3.09%	83.0%
EURHUF									
EURJPY	1.66%	1.70%	102.2%	3.29%	3.09%	93.9%	5.66%	5.63%	99.6%
EURNOK	0.76%	0.59%	77.6%	1.44%	1.16%	80.2%	2.50%	2.02%	80.8%

(*continued*)

TABLE A.1 (*Continued*)

	1W			1M			3M		
	Premium	Payoff	Ratio	Premium	Payoff	Ratio	Premium	Payoff	Ratio
EURPLN									
EURUSD	1.35%	1.28%	95.0%	2.67%	2.47%	92.5%	4.67%	4.71%	100.8%
GBPUSD	1.02%	0.80%	77.8%	1.96%	1.65%	84.2%	3.48%	2.44%	70.0%
USDARS									
USDBRL									
USDCAD	0.74%	0.56%	75.5%	1.47%	1.19%	80.9%	2.51%	1.71%	68.2%
USDCHF	1.33%	1.25%	93.4%	2.51%	2.50%	99.7%	4.45%	4.58%	102.9%
USDCLP				2.27%	2.33%	102.7%	4.28%	4.36%	101.8%
USDCOP									
USDCZK									
USDDKK									
USDHKD				0.17%	0.03%	19.5%	0.35%	0.07%	20.4%
USDIDR									
USDILS									
USDINR									
USDJPY	1.53%	1.25%	82.1%	2.86%	2.82%	98.6%	5.01%	5.31%	105.9%
USDKRW				2.04%	1.73%	84.7%	3.80%	2.70%	70.9%
USDMXN	0.72%	0.55%	76.4%	2.24%	1.93%	85.9%	4.57%	3.67%	80.2%
USDNOK	1.34%	1.10%	82.0%	2.63%	1.80%	68.5%	4.59%	3.14%	68.4%
USDPHP				3.78%	1.80%	47.5%	6.79%	3.74%	55.0%
USDPLN				3.20%	2.75%	86.1%	5.42%	3.88%	71.6%
USDSEK	1.41%	1.26%	89.8%	2.75%	2.24%	81.5%	4.72%	3.62%	76.8%
USDSGD				1.24%	1.46%	117.5%	2.28%	2.74%	119.9%
USDTRY									
USDTWD				0.93%	0.89%	96.2%	1.74%	2.04%	116.9%
USDZAR	1.34%	1.16%	86.8%	2.71%	2.52%	93.2%	4.63%	5.18%	112.0%

TABLE A.2 Payoff/premium for ATMF straddles, 31/12/1995–12/12/2001 (6M–3Y tenors)

	6M			12M			2Y			3Y		
	Premium	Payoff	Ratio	Premium	Payoff	Ratio	Premium	Payoff	Ratio	Premium	Payoff	Ratio
AUDUSD	5.56%	5.73%	103.2%	7.65%	10.02%	131.0%	11.18%	15.38%	137.6%	12.43%	17.60%	141.6%
EURAUD												
EURCHF	2.26%	1.61%	71.2%	3.14%	2.04%	65.1%						
EURCZK	3.89%	3.76%	96.6%	5.67%	7.22%	127.2%						
EURGBP	5.20%	3.45%	66.4%	7.18%	4.82%	67.1%						
EURHUF												
EURJPY	8.03%	8.46%	105.4%	10.98%	13.48%	122.8%						
EURNOK	3.50%	3.01%	86.0%	4.82%	5.90%	122.2%						
EURPLN												
EURUSD	6.52%	5.89%	90.4%	9.00%	10.75%	119.5%						
GBPUSD	4.91%	2.94%	59.8%	6.80%	4.29%	63.1%						
USDARS												
USDBRL												
USDCAD	3.48%	2.07%	59.5%	4.74%	2.91%	61.3%						
USDCHF	6.26%	6.12%	97.9%	8.66%	8.69%	100.4%						
USDCLP	6.41%	6.61%	103.2%	9.30%	7.51%	80.7%						

(continued)

TABLE A.2 (*Continued*)

| | 6M | | | 12M | | | 2Y | | | 3Y | | |
	Premium	Payoff	Ratio	Premium	Payoff	Ratio	Premium	Payoff	Ratio	Premium	Payoff	Ratio
USDCOP												
USDCZK												
USDDKK												
USDHKD	0.75%	0.13%	16.8%	1.59%	0.27%	16.7%						
USDIDR												
USDILS												
USDINR												
USDJPY	7.06%	7.87%	111.5%	9.76%	10.34%	106.0%						
USDKRW	5.55%	4.50%	81.1%	7.94%	8.18%	103.0%						
USDMXN	6.97%	5.76%	82.6%	10.84%	9.43%	87.1%						
USDNOK	6.36%	4.79%	75.2%	8.72%	10.90%	125.1%						
USDPHP	10.01%	5.23%	52.3%	14.06%	9.25%	65.7%						
USDPLN	7.74%	6.21%	80.2%	10.23%	11.58%	113.2%						
USDSEK	6.51%	5.54%	85.1%	8.90%	10.51%	118.1%						
USDSGD	3.40%	2.49%	73.2%	4.96%	3.09%	62.3%						
USDTRY												
USDTWD	2.76%	3.08%	111.8%	4.50%	5.04%	112.0%						
USDZAR	6.53%	8.94%	136.9%	9.17%	14.03%	153.1%						

TABLE A.3 Payoff/premium for ATMF straddles, 31/12/1995–12/12/2001 averaged over all currency pairs

Tenor	Ratio
1W	85.1%
1M	83.7%
3M	83.8%
6M	83.9%
12M	96.5%
2Y	137.6%
3Y	141.6%

TABLE A.4 Payoff/premium for ATMF straddles, 31/12/2001–12/12/2007 (1W–3M tenors)

	1W			1M			3M		
	Premium	Payoff	Ratio	Premium	Payoff	Ratio	Premium	Payoff	Ratio
AUDUSD	1.17%	1.12%	96.0%	2.28%	2.43%	106.6%	3.99%	4.08%	102.3%
EURAUD	1.02%	0.91%	89.4%	1.79%	1.68%	93.9%	3.16%	2.31%	72.9%
EURCHF	0.46%	0.38%	82.1%	0.85%	0.79%	93.0%	1.49%	1.35%	90.3%
EURCZK	0.77%	0.57%	74.1%	1.46%	1.17%	80.3%	2.46%	2.05%	83.0%
EURGBP	0.71%	0.64%	90.3%	1.37%	1.29%	94.2%	2.45%	2.23%	90.7%
EURHUF	1.01%	0.77%	76.5%	1.96%	1.61%	82.1%	3.52%	2.98%	84.6%
EURJPY	1.05%	0.94%	90.1%	2.05%	1.91%	93.3%	3.58%	3.11%	87.0%
EURNOK	0.78%	0.64%	81.5%	1.48%	1.43%	96.9%	2.54%	2.56%	100.5%
EURPLN				2.24%	1.87%	83.4%	3.86%	3.42%	88.6%
EURUSD	1.02%	0.91%	89.4%	2.03%	2.03%	99.8%	3.63%	3.70%	102.1%
GBPUSD	0.92%	0.84%	91.4%	1.82%	1.93%	106.2%	3.22%	3.09%	96.0%
USDARS				1.13%	0.66%	58.3%	2.23%	1.48%	66.5%
USDBRL	1.60%	1.36%	85.0%	3.07%	3.27%	106.4%	5.44%	6.61%	121.5%
USDCAD	0.95%	0.88%	93.3%	1.89%	1.85%	97.6%	3.18%	3.50%	110.3%
USDCHF	1.11%	0.98%	88.0%	2.20%	2.17%	98.4%	3.90%	3.73%	95.6%
USDCLP				2.49%	2.18%	87.3%	4.49%	4.32%	96.3%
USDCOP				3.47%	3.30%	95.1%	5.55%	6.64%	119.6%
USDCZK	1.18%	0.98%	83.3%	2.17%	2.25%	103.6%	3.82%	3.90%	101.9%
USDDKK	0.93%	0.76%	81.4%	1.77%	1.69%	95.4%	3.13%	2.65%	84.7%
USDHKD	0.14%	0.06%	42.4%	0.21%	0.12%	57.7%	0.40%	0.27%	67.8%
USDIDR				1.87%	1.80%	96.4%	3.19%	1.87%	58.8%
USDILS				1.63%	1.65%	100.8%	2.74%	3.13%	114.5%
USDINR				1.19%	1.17%	98.5%	2.15%	2.62%	122.1%
USDJPY	1.08%	0.92%	85.2%	2.09%	2.04%	97.4%	3.58%	3.43%	95.6%
USDKRW	0.83%	0.65%	77.8%	1.61%	1.57%	97.1%	2.95%	2.97%	100.6%
USDMXN	1.01%	0.79%	77.9%	2.02%	1.55%	76.5%	3.68%	2.67%	72.5%
USDNOK	1.25%	1.17%	93.9%	2.37%	2.53%	106.9%	4.16%	4.54%	109.2%
USDPHP				2.24%	1.21%	53.9%	4.36%	2.81%	64.4%
USDPLN				2.64%	2.76%	104.2%	4.59%	4.70%	102.4%
USDSEK	1.20%	1.08%	89.6%	2.36%	2.45%	103.8%	4.17%	4.34%	104.2%
USDSGD	0.60%	0.45%	74.6%	1.07%	0.96%	89.6%	1.91%	1.66%	86.9%
USDTRY	1.35%	1.35%	99.9%	3.17%	3.24%	102.2%	5.83%	6.77%	116.2%
USDTWD	0.41%	0.23%	55.9%	0.98%	0.96%	98.4%	1.79%	1.93%	108.1%
USDZAR	2.22%	1.80%	80.9%	4.27%	4.20%	98.4%	7.15%	7.28%	101.8%

TABLE A.5 Payoff/premium for ATMF straddles, 31/12/2001–12/12/2007 (6M–3Y tenors)

	6M			12M			2Y			3Y		
	Premium	Payoff	Ratio	Premium	Payoff	Ratio	Premium	Payoff	Ratio	Premium	Payoff	Ratio
AUDUSD	5.57%	6.48%	116.4%	7.67%	10.99%	143.4%	10.23%	14.18%	138.6%	11.88%	15.98%	134.5%
EURAUD	4.46%	3.36%	75.3%	6.24%	4.31%	69.0%	8.54%	5.86%	68.6%	9.75%	11.54%	118.3%
EURCHF	2.12%	2.08%	98.0%	2.98%	3.50%	117.5%	3.44%	5.61%	163.2%	4.16%	6.09%	146.5%
EURCZK	3.43%	3.13%	91.4%	4.73%	5.00%	105.7%						
EURGBP	3.51%	3.40%	96.8%	4.96%	5.38%	108.5%	5.81%	12.34%	212.5%	7.19%	15.08%	209.6%
EURHUF	5.04%	4.58%	90.9%	7.12%	6.89%	96.8%						
EURJPY	5.04%	4.46%	88.5%	7.04%	8.25%	117.3%	8.64%	15.37%	177.9%	9.88%	17.92%	181.4%
EURNOK	3.54%	3.08%	87.0%	4.91%	4.09%	83.2%	5.99%	3.37%	56.4%	7.22%	4.51%	62.4%
EURPLN	5.38%	5.25%	97.6%	7.47%	8.70%	116.4%						
EURUSD	5.18%	6.02%	116.3%	7.31%	8.96%	122.6%	8.74%	7.40%	84.7%	10.33%	6.53%	63.2%
GBPUSD	4.57%	4.78%	104.6%	6.38%	8.01%	125.5%	8.06%	14.80%	183.5%	9.59%	15.96%	166.4%
USDARS	3.60%	2.43%	67.5%	6.38%	3.97%	62.3%						
USDBRL	7.91%	12.77%	161.5%	11.60%	26.32%	226.8%						
USDCAD	4.40%	5.37%	121.9%	6.25%	8.80%	140.8%	8.17%	8.59%	105.2%	9.44%	4.48%	47.4%
USDCHF	5.53%	5.55%	100.4%	7.75%	7.55%	97.5%	9.10%	6.63%	72.8%	10.68%	6.40%	59.9%

USDCLP	6.42%	6.10%	95.1%	9.15%	9.20%	100.5%						
USDCOP	7.47%	11.26%	150.7%	7.58%	12.16%	160.3%						
USDCZK	5.41%	7.05%	130.2%	6.27%	7.54%	120.3%						
USDDKK	4.45%	4.79%	107.7%				8.56%	8.33%	97.3%	10.03%	7.09%	70.6%
USDHKD	0.67%	0.40%	59.9%	1.38%	0.57%	41.6%						
USDIDR	4.25%	1.95%	45.8%	6.28%	7.72%	122.9%						
USDILS	3.84%	5.18%	134.9%	5.39%	8.41%	156.1%						
USDINR	3.07%	4.14%	135.1%									
USDJPY	4.98%	4.87%	97.9%	6.87%	6.70%	97.6%	8.32%	10.16%	122.1%	9.70%	11.62%	119.7%
USDKRW	4.10%	4.43%	108.0%	5.84%	8.33%	142.7%						
USDMXN	5.35%	3.45%	64.4%	7.80%	5.64%	72.3%						
USDNOK	5.87%	6.71%	114.3%	8.21%	9.99%	121.6%	10.26%	9.59%	93.5%	12.02%	7.82%	65.0%
USDPHP	6.64%	4.58%	68.9%	9.71%	7.99%	82.3%						
USDPLN	6.43%	7.32%	113.8%	8.96%	13.09%	146.1%						
USDSEK	5.89%	7.03%	119.3%	8.27%	11.04%	133.5%	10.23%	11.23%	109.7%	11.55%	6.63%	57.4%
USDSGD	2.77%	2.42%	87.2%	3.96%	3.32%	83.7%						
USDTRY	8.69%	11.16%	128.3%	12.92%	19.08%	147.7%						
USDTWD	2.64%	2.81%	106.1%	3.91%	3.33%	85.3%						
USDZAR	9.90%	11.72%	118.3%	13.81%	19.29%	139.6%						

TABLE A.6 Payoff/premium for ATMF straddles, 31/12/2001–12/12/2007 averaged over all currency pairs

Tenor	Ratio
1W	82.8%
1M	92.7%
3M	94.7%
6M	102.9%
12M	115.2%
2Y	120.4%
3Y	107.3%

TABLE A.7 Payoff/premium for ATMF straddles, 31/12/2007–12/12/2013 (1W–3M tenors)

	1W			1M			3M		
	Premium	Payoff	Ratio	Premium	Payoff	Ratio	Premium	Payoff	Ratio
AUDUSD	1.62%	1.49%	91.9%	3.21%	3.28%	102.3%	5.67%	6.34%	111.9%
EURAUD	1.36%	1.21%	89.3%	2.69%	2.64%	98.1%	4.80%	5.08%	105.9%
EURCHF	0.88%	0.73%	83.4%	1.64%	1.53%	93.2%	2.88%	2.40%	83.3%
EURCZK	1.03%	0.81%	78.7%	2.00%	1.58%	79.2%	3.40%	2.78%	81.9%
EURGBP	1.11%	0.92%	82.7%	2.19%	1.87%	85.3%	3.95%	3.19%	80.7%
EURHUF	1.47%	1.22%	83.0%	2.89%	2.24%	77.5%	5.06%	4.23%	83.6%
EURJPY	1.72%	1.52%	88.3%	3.41%	3.24%	95.0%	5.98%	6.19%	103.6%
EURNOK	1.04%	0.85%	81.7%	2.00%	1.60%	80.1%	3.47%	2.60%	74.9%
EURPLN				2.74%	2.20%	80.2%	4.73%	4.19%	88.6%
EURUSD	1.33%	1.19%	89.6%	2.68%	2.61%	97.5%	4.82%	4.43%	91.8%
GBPUSD	1.22%	1.12%	91.3%	2.45%	2.20%	89.7%	4.41%	4.09%	92.6%
USDARS				2.92%	1.16%	39.8%	6.45%	3.43%	53.2%
USDBRL	1.88%	1.60%	85.1%	3.65%	3.38%	92.7%	6.34%	6.85%	108.1%
USDCAD	1.25%	1.17%	93.5%	2.54%	2.04%	80.5%	4.46%	3.31%	74.1%
USDCHF	1.35%	1.30%	96.1%	2.71%	2.79%	102.9%	4.81%	4.64%	96.5%
USDCLP				3.18%	2.70%	85.0%	5.59%	5.41%	96.8%
USDCOP				3.41%	2.78%	81.7%	6.02%	5.23%	86.9%
USDCZK	1.80%	1.70%	94.3%	3.56%	3.57%	100.3%	6.17%	6.29%	101.9%
USDDKK	1.43%	1.19%	82.8%	2.84%	2.58%	91.1%	5.00%	4.30%	85.9%
USDHKD	0.10%	0.05%	44.0%	0.17%	0.09%	51.4%	0.33%	0.15%	44.6%
USDIDR				3.01%	2.03%	67.3%	5.75%	4.15%	72.2%
USDILS				2.31%	2.12%	91.6%	3.95%	3.56%	90.3%
USDINR				2.53%	2.26%	89.6%	4.64%	4.12%	88.7%
USDJPY	1.40%	1.15%	82.1%	2.76%	2.36%	85.5%	4.82%	4.47%	92.7%
USDKRW	1.70%	1.32%	77.6%	3.33%	2.76%	82.9%	5.77%	4.66%	80.9%
USDMXN	1.69%	1.33%	78.7%	3.25%	2.64%	81.4%	5.66%	4.95%	87.5%
USDNOK	1.65%	1.49%	89.9%	3.29%	2.75%	83.4%	5.81%	5.08%	87.5%
USDPHP				2.08%	1.46%	70.3%	3.87%	2.65%	68.5%
USDPLN				4.22%	3.82%	90.4%	7.43%	7.20%	97.0%
USDSEK	1.69%	1.46%	86.3%	3.36%	2.93%	87.2%	5.91%	5.13%	86.8%
USDSGD	0.84%	0.64%	76.9%	1.62%	1.39%	85.8%	2.97%	2.50%	84.0%
USDTRY	1.52%	1.45%	95.5%	3.11%	2.97%	95.5%	5.53%	4.98%	90.0%
USDTWD	0.70%	0.45%	64.5%	1.41%	1.14%	81.0%	2.65%	2.29%	86.1%
USDZAR	2.16%	1.94%	89.5%	4.26%	3.55%	83.4%	7.54%	6.22%	82.6%

TABLE A.8 Payoff/premium for ATMF straddles, 31/12/2007–12/12/2013 (6M–3Y tenors)

	6M			12M			2Y			3Y		
	Premium	Payoff	Ratio	Premium	Payoff	Ratio	Premium	Payoff	Ratio	Premium	Payoff	Ratio
AUDUSD	8.12%	9.69%	119.4%	11.69%	12.08%	103.3%	16.27%	14.98%	92.1%	18.26%	19.16%	105.0%
EURAUD	6.94%	8.26%	119.1%	10.11%	13.77%	136.2%	14.55%	24.06%	165.3%	16.23%	34.33%	211.4%
EURCHF	4.16%	3.42%	82.2%	6.05%	5.73%	94.6%	8.41%	11.33%	134.7%	7.99%	15.88%	198.7%
EURCZK	4.73%	3.37%	71.4%	6.64%	4.21%	63.4%						
EURGBP	5.79%	4.46%	77.0%	8.53%	5.59%	65.5%	12.66%	4.64%	36.7%	15.25%	6.48%	42.5%
EURHUF	7.23%	5.67%	78.4%	10.34%	5.63%	54.5%						
EURJPY	8.60%	9.50%	110.4%	12.32%	13.07%	106.1%	18.05%	16.30%	90.3%	21.52%	18.85%	87.6%
EURNOK	4.88%	4.12%	84.4%	6.97%	6.72%	96.4%	9.87%	8.45%	85.6%	11.69%	11.26%	96.3%
EURPLN	6.72%	6.03%	89.7%	9.70%	8.11%	83.7%						
EURUSD	7.01%	6.54%	93.3%	10.26%	6.95%	67.7%	14.41%	5.88%	40.8%	16.10%	5.69%	35.3%
GBPUSD	6.46%	6.65%	102.9%	9.55%	6.70%	70.2%	14.09%	7.13%	50.6%	17.05%	5.84%	34.2%
USDARS	10.59%	5.89%	55.6%	17.68%	10.33%	58.4%						
USDBRL	9.07%	10.65%	117.4%	13.45%	14.03%	104.3%						
USDCAD	6.52%	5.23%	80.1%	9.63%	6.71%	69.7%	14.39%	7.16%	49.8%	17.68%	7.63%	43.1%
USDCHF	6.89%	6.52%	94.8%	9.89%	7.52%	76.1%	13.60%	10.37%	76.3%	14.84%	12.07%	81.3%

(continued)

TABLE A.8 (Continued)

	6M			12M			2Y			3Y		
	Premium	Payoff	Ratio	Premium	Payoff	Ratio	Premium	Payoff	Ratio	Premium	Payoff	Ratio
USDCLP	8.07%	7.51%	93.1%	11.86%	9.02%	76.0%						
USDCOP	8.70%	7.27%	83.6%	12.89%	9.42%	73.1%						
USDCZK	8.78%	8.25%	94.0%	12.57%	8.53%	67.9%						
USDDKK	7.26%	6.30%	86.7%	10.57%	6.67%	63.1%	14.81%	5.55%	37.5%	16.51%	4.99%	30.2%
USDHKD	0.53%	0.18%	34.4%	0.95%	0.24%	25.4%						
USDIDR	8.66%	7.82%	90.3%	13.39%	11.65%	87.0%						
USDILS	5.54%	5.30%	95.6%	7.85%	6.81%	86.7%						
USDINR	6.81%	5.72%	84.0%	10.29%	7.16%	69.6%						
USDJPY	6.89%	6.28%	91.2%	9.85%	9.25%	93.9%	14.28%	13.83%	96.9%	16.56%	14.59%	88.1%
USDKRW	8.23%	7.25%	88.0%	11.85%	8.64%	72.9%						
USDMXN	8.08%	7.06%	87.3%	11.74%	10.09%	86.0%						
USDNOK	8.34%	7.45%	89.4%	12.12%	8.30%	68.5%	17.10%	8.82%	51.6%	19.77%	7.76%	39.2%
USDPHP	5.83%	4.01%	68.8%	8.85%	6.39%	72.2%						
USDPLN	10.62%	9.73%	91.6%	15.33%	10.88%	71.0%						
USDSEK	8.44%	7.41%	87.8%	12.19%	8.74%	71.8%	17.44%	10.35%	59.4%	19.92%	9.57%	48.0%
USDSGD	4.38%	3.71%	84.7%	6.52%	5.08%	78.0%						
USDTRY	8.13%	7.03%	86.4%	12.33%	9.15%	74.3%						
USDTWD	4.00%	3.18%	79.6%	6.06%	4.20%	69.2%						
USDZAR	10.86%	9.61%	88.5%	15.74%	14.26%	90.6%						

TABLE A.9 Payoff/premium for ATMF straddles, 31/12/2007–12/12/2013 averaged over all currency pairs

Tenor	Ratio
1W	83.9%
1M	84.7%
3M	86.5%
6M	87.7%
12M	77.9%
2Y	76.2%
3Y	81.5%

Payoff/Premium Ratios for ATMF Puts, by Time Period

TABLE A.10 Payoff/premium for ATMF puts, 31/12/1995–31/12/2013 (full period) (1W–3M tenors)

	1W			1M			3M		
	Premium	Payoff	Ratio	Premium	Payoff	Ratio	Premium	Payoff	Ratio
AUDUSD	0.71%	0.62%	86.8%	1.33%	1.26%	94.9%	2.30%	2.11%	91.5%
EURAUD	0.64%	0.62%	96.0%	1.21%	1.34%	111.2%	2.13%	2.69%	126.1%
EURCHF	0.32%	0.27%	83.9%	0.60%	0.55%	92.0%	1.03%	0.94%	90.4%
EURCZK	0.43%	0.36%	82.2%	0.83%	0.76%	91.1%	1.43%	1.45%	101.0%
EURGBP	0.47%	0.41%	87.1%	0.93%	0.82%	89.0%	1.65%	1.39%	84.4%
EURHUF	0.64%	0.56%	87.3%	1.25%	1.14%	91.2%	2.21%	2.33%	105.5%
EURJPY	0.72%	0.63%	87.8%	1.42%	1.24%	87.6%	2.47%	2.17%	87.9%
EURNOK	0.44%	0.38%	85.4%	0.84%	0.81%	96.3%	1.45%	1.47%	101.0%
EURPLN				1.25%	1.09%	87.3%	2.15%	2.16%	100.7%
EURUSD	0.60%	0.54%	89.9%	1.21%	1.15%	95.2%	2.16%	2.03%	94.1%
GBPUSD	0.53%	0.47%	87.8%	1.04%	0.92%	88.1%	1.85%	1.50%	81.0%
USDARS				1.34%	0.92%	68.3%	2.95%	2.66%	90.1%
USDBRL	0.88%	0.87%	98.6%	1.71%	2.16%	126.2%	2.99%	4.91%	164.1%
USDCAD	0.52%	0.50%	96.5%	1.04%	1.03%	99.7%	1.78%	1.87%	105.1%
USDCHF	0.63%	0.60%	95.6%	1.24%	1.27%	102.9%	2.19%	2.20%	100.5%
USDCLP				1.39%	1.34%	96.4%	2.48%	2.80%	113.0%
USDCOP				1.71%	1.74%	102.0%	2.97%	3.56%	120.0%
USDCZK	0.80%	0.76%	94.5%	1.56%	1.70%	108.7%	2.72%	3.07%	112.8%
USDDKK	0.64%	0.53%	83.9%	1.25%	1.20%	95.7%	2.21%	2.01%	91.0%
USDHKD	0.06%	0.02%	36.0%	0.09%	0.03%	32.4%	0.18%	0.05%	26.5%
USDIDR				1.46%	1.17%	80.1%	2.78%	2.42%	87.2%
USDILS				0.99%	1.14%	115.3%	1.68%	2.24%	133.6%

(continued)

TABLE A.10 (*Continued*)

	1W			1M			3M		
	Premium	Payoff	Ratio	Premium	Payoff	Ratio	Premium	Payoff	Ratio
USDINR				0.99%	1.01%	102.6%	1.81%	1.97%	109.1%
USDJPY	0.66%	0.54%	81.8%	1.28%	1.11%	86.3%	2.24%	1.94%	86.6%
USDKRW	0.65%	0.54%	83.3%	1.20%	1.17%	97.6%	2.12%	2.10%	98.8%
USDMXN	0.67%	0.55%	81.1%	1.29%	1.15%	89.4%	2.33%	2.32%	99.7%
USDNOK	0.72%	0.68%	94.5%	1.40%	1.40%	100.3%	2.45%	2.70%	109.9%
USDPHP				1.23%	0.86%	70.2%	2.31%	1.89%	81.7%
USDPLN				1.70%	1.93%	113.5%	2.99%	3.74%	125.3%
USDSEK	0.72%	0.65%	90.9%	1.42%	1.39%	98.0%	2.48%	2.50%	100.7%
USDSGD	0.36%	0.30%	82.3%	0.67%	0.67%	100.6%	1.21%	1.29%	106.1%
USDTRY	0.72%	0.78%	107.5%	1.57%	1.87%	119.1%	2.82%	3.66%	129.4%
USDTWD	0.33%	0.21%	62.8%	0.57%	0.48%	84.0%	1.07%	0.93%	87.0%
USDZAR	1.01%	0.91%	89.4%	1.98%	2.01%	101.3%	3.41%	3.74%	109.7%

TABLE A.11 Payoff/premium for ATMF puts, 31/12/1995–31/12/2013 (full period) (6M–3Y tenors)

	6M			12M			2Y			3Y		
	Premium	Payoff	Ratio	Premium	Payoff	Ratio	Premium	Payoff	Ratio	Premium	Payoff	Ratio
AUDUSD	3.19%	3.15%	98.6%	4.44%	4.50%	101.4%	6.21%	2.24%	36.1%	6.88%	0.85%	12.3%
EURAUD	3.06%	4.55%	148.7%	4.37%	7.98%	182.4%	6.09%	15.42%	253.1%	6.63%	22.78%	343.6%
EURCHF	1.47%	1.40%	95.0%	2.07%	2.35%	113.6%	3.23%	7.15%	221.5%	3.11%	10.63%	341.2%
EURCZK	2.01%	2.30%	114.2%	2.82%	3.87%	137.5%						
EURGBP	2.37%	1.87%	79.1%	3.37%	2.46%	73.1%	5.03%	2.12%	42.1%	5.83%	2.42%	41.5%
EURHUF	3.15%	3.51%	111.6%	4.45%	4.58%	102.9%						
EURJPY	3.51%	3.15%	89.8%	4.90%	4.42%	90.2%	7.17%	9.34%	130.3%	8.98%	14.79%	164.7%
EURNOK	2.03%	2.17%	107.0%	2.83%	3.66%	129.5%	4.17%	5.01%	120.2%	4.82%	6.61%	137.2%
EURPLN	3.02%	3.35%	110.9%	4.26%	5.36%	125.9%						
EURUSD	3.08%	2.93%	95.0%	4.37%	3.94%	90.0%	6.09%	3.06%	50.3%	6.75%	3.38%	50.1%
GBPUSD	2.65%	2.24%	84.5%	3.75%	2.96%	79.0%	5.86%	6.94%	118.5%	6.81%	8.83%	129.7%
USDARS	4.82%	4.79%	99.3%	8.00%	8.16%	101.9%						
USDBRL	4.30%	8.97%	208.9%	6.33%	16.37%	258.8%						
USDCAD	2.53%	3.05%	120.9%	3.60%	4.90%	136.3%	5.97%	5.90%	98.9%	7.26%	5.35%	73.7%
USDCHF	3.11%	3.15%	101.4%	4.36%	4.38%	100.5%	5.91%	7.41%	125.3%	6.47%	9.42%	145.7%

(continued)

TABLE A.11 (Continued)

	6M			12M			2Y			3Y		
	Premium	Payoff	Ratio	Premium	Payoff	Ratio	Premium	Payoff	Ratio	Premium	Payoff	Ratio
USDCLP	3.57%	4.23%	118.4%	5.15%	6.29%	122.3%						
USDCOP	4.24%	5.68%	134.1%	6.45%	7.38%	114.5%						
USDCZK	3.85%	4.62%	120.2%	5.43%	6.25%	115.2%						
USDDKK	3.17%	3.21%	101.1%	4.54%	4.10%	90.1%	6.18%	4.04%	65.4%	6.77%	3.20%	47.2%
USDHKD	0.32%	0.06%	18.7%	0.63%	0.09%	14.7%						
USDIDR	4.16%	4.58%	110.1%	6.39%	7.75%	121.3%						
USDILS	2.35%	3.76%	160.1%	3.29%	6.09%	185.1%						
USDINR	2.61%	2.80%	107.2%	5.15%	3.43%	66.7%						
USDJPY	3.15%	2.68%	85.1%	4.39%	3.46%	78.8%	5.97%	7.68%	128.6%	6.70%	9.74%	145.2%
USDKRW	3.00%	3.36%	111.9%	4.25%	5.18%	122.0%						
USDMXN	3.36%	3.50%	104.1%	4.91%	5.73%	116.7%						
USDNOK	3.47%	4.21%	121.4%	4.88%	6.66%	136.5%	7.18%	6.83%	95.2%	8.08%	6.36%	78.8%
USDPHP	3.48%	3.15%	90.5%	5.12%	5.75%	112.3%						
USDPLN	4.22%	5.85%	138.7%	5.95%	8.94%	150.3%						
USDSEK	3.50%	3.94%	112.6%	4.91%	6.21%	126.6%	7.28%	7.34%	100.8%	8.36%	5.82%	69.6%
USDSGD	1.77%	1.99%	112.5%	2.57%	3.06%	119.2%						
USDTRY	4.18%	6.15%	147.1%	6.29%	10.51%	167.1%						
USDTWD	1.60%	1.27%	79.5%	2.42%	1.51%	62.7%						
USDZAR	4.81%	6.22%	129.4%	6.79%	10.47%	154.2%						

TABLE A.12 Payoff/premium for ATMF puts, 31/12/1995–31/12/2013 (full period) averaged over all currency pairs

Tenor	Ratio
1W	86.1%
1M	94.5%
3M	101.5%
6M	110.8%
12M	117.6%
2Y	113.3%
3Y	127.2%

TABLE A.13 Payoff/premium for ATMF puts, 31/12/1995–31/12/2001 (1W–3M tenors)

	1W			1M			3M		
	Premium	Payoff	Ratio	Premium	Payoff	Ratio	Premium	Payoff	Ratio
AUDUSD	0.76%	0.72%	94.2%	1.25%	1.49%	118.9%	2.08%	2.73%	131.4%
EURAUD									
EURCHF	0.25%	0.20%	81.3%	0.50%	0.40%	80.8%	0.80%	0.75%	93.5%
EURCZK	0.35%	0.34%	99.6%	0.69%	0.79%	114.2%	1.29%	1.78%	138.2%
EURGBP	0.55%	0.56%	101.7%	1.06%	1.12%	105.5%	1.86%	2.19%	117.5%
EURHUF									
EURJPY	0.83%	0.83%	100.6%	1.64%	1.60%	97.5%	2.83%	2.94%	104.0%
EURNOK	0.38%	0.35%	92.1%	0.72%	0.84%	117.2%	1.25%	1.75%	139.8%
EURPLN									
EURUSD	0.67%	0.74%	110.0%	1.34%	1.66%	124.1%	2.34%	3.59%	153.9%
GBPUSD	0.51%	0.44%	85.5%	0.98%	0.84%	85.9%	1.74%	1.32%	75.9%
USDARS									
USDBRL									
USDCAD	0.37%	0.25%	67.2%	0.74%	0.53%	72.2%	1.26%	0.54%	42.7%
USDCHF	0.67%	0.56%	84.2%	1.25%	0.94%	75.1%	2.22%	1.27%	57.0%
USDCLP				1.13%	0.75%	66.0%	2.14%	1.11%	51.8%
USDCOP									
USDCZK									
USDDKK									
USDHKD				0.09%	0.01%	6.6%	0.18%	0.01%	6.6%
USDIDR									
USDILS									
USDINR									
USDJPY	0.76%	0.58%	76.5%	1.43%	1.09%	76.6%	2.51%	1.70%	67.8%
USDKRW				1.02%	0.82%	80.4%	1.90%	1.06%	55.9%
USDMXN	0.36%	0.52%	144.1%	1.12%	1.42%	126.5%	2.29%	3.37%	147.7%
USDNOK	0.67%	0.52%	77.1%	1.32%	0.83%	62.8%	2.30%	1.26%	54.9%
USDPHP				1.89%	0.95%	50.3%	3.40%	1.74%	51.3%
USDPLN				1.60%	1.99%	124.6%	2.71%	3.08%	113.9%
USDSEK	0.70%	0.56%	80.1%	1.37%	0.77%	55.9%	2.36%	0.72%	30.4%
USDSGD				0.62%	0.45%	72.7%	1.14%	0.60%	52.3%
USDTRY									
USDTWD				0.46%	0.41%	87.8%	0.87%	0.82%	93.8%
USDZAR	0.67%	0.42%	62.3%	1.36%	0.68%	50.3%	2.31%	0.78%	33.7%

TABLE A.14 Payoff/premium for ATMF puts, 31/12/1995–12/12/2001 (6M–3Y tenors)

	6M			12M			2Y			3Y		
	Premium	Payoff	Ratio	Premium	Payoff	Ratio	Premium	Payoff	Ratio	Premium	Payoff	Ratio
AUDUSD	2.78%	4.51%	162.3%	3.82%	8.22%	214.9%	5.59%	6.78%	121.3%	6.21%	2.51%	40.3%
EURAUD												
EURCHF	1.13%	1.18%	104.6%	1.57%	1.86%	118.1%						
EURCZK	1.95%	3.75%	192.7%	2.84%	7.22%	254.5%						
EURGBP	2.60%	2.76%	106.1%	3.59%	3.89%	108.5%						
EURHUF												
EURJPY	4.01%	4.37%	108.8%	5.49%	5.62%	102.3%						
EURNOK	1.75%	2.93%	167.6%	2.41%	5.89%	244.2%						
EURPLN												
EURUSD	3.26%	4.98%	152.8%	4.50%	8.36%	185.7%						
GBPUSD	2.45%	1.71%	69.6%	3.40%	2.48%	72.9%						
USDARS												
USDBRL												
USDCAD	1.74%	0.47%	27.2%	2.37%	0.31%	13.1%						
USDCHF	3.13%	1.23%	39.3%	4.33%	1.85%	42.7%						
USDCLP	3.20%	1.62%	50.5%	4.65%	0.21%	4.5%						

USDCOP					
USDCZK					
USDDKK					
USDHKD	0.37%	0.05%	14.5%	0.80%	0.21%	26.0%
USDIDR					
USDILS					
USDINR					
USDJPY	3.53%	2.15%	61.0%	4.88%	2.14%	43.9%
USDKRW	2.78%	1.86%	67.0%	3.97%	3.70%	93.1%
USDMXN	3.49%	5.68%	162.8%	5.42%	9.30%	171.7%
USDNOK	3.18%	2.11%	66.3%	4.36%	6.34%	145.6%
USDPHP	5.01%	2.52%	50.3%	7.03%	4.24%	60.2%
USDPLN	3.87%	6.21%	160.4%	5.12%	11.58%	226.3%
USDSEK	3.25%	0.78%	23.9%	4.45%	2.68%	60.3%
USDSGD	1.70%	0.35%	20.4%	2.48%	0.87%	35.2%
USDTRY					
USDTWD	1.38%	1.08%	78.1%	2.25%	1.29%	57.2%
USDZAR	3.27%	1.22%	37.4%	4.58%	1.45%	31.7%

TABLE A.15 Payoff/premium for ATMF puts, 31/12/1995–12/12/2001 averaged over all currency pairs

Tenor	Ratio
1W	90.4%
1M	84.2%
3M	82.4%
6M	87.4%
12M	105.1%
2Y	121.3%
3Y	40.3%

TABLE A.16 Payoff/premium for ATMF puts, 31/12/2001–12/12/2007 (1W–3M tenors)

	1W			1M			3M		
	Premium	Payoff	Ratio	Premium	Payoff	Ratio	Premium	Payoff	Ratio
AUDUSD	0.58%	0.45%	77.3%	1.14%	0.78%	68.1%	1.99%	0.66%	32.9%
EURAUD	0.51%	0.46%	90.5%	0.90%	0.88%	98.4%	1.58%	1.55%	98.0%
EURCHF	0.23%	0.16%	67.5%	0.42%	0.26%	60.6%	0.75%	0.29%	39.4%
EURCZK	0.38%	0.31%	81.6%	0.73%	0.73%	100.4%	1.23%	1.47%	119.6%
EURGBP	0.35%	0.30%	86.3%	0.69%	0.59%	86.3%	1.23%	0.91%	74.4%
EURHUF	0.50%	0.44%	88.2%	0.98%	1.04%	106.4%	1.76%	2.22%	126.0%
EURJPY	0.52%	0.40%	75.4%	1.03%	0.65%	63.8%	1.79%	0.64%	35.9%
EURNOK	0.39%	0.33%	84.4%	0.74%	0.77%	104.6%	1.27%	1.38%	108.5%
EURPLN				1.12%	1.06%	94.5%	1.93%	2.13%	110.4%
EURUSD	0.51%	0.38%	74.3%	1.01%	0.69%	68.1%	1.81%	0.83%	45.7%
GBPUSD	0.46%	0.36%	78.1%	0.91%	0.70%	77.1%	1.61%	0.73%	45.4%
USDARS				0.56%	0.39%	69.1%	1.11%	1.01%	91.1%
USDBRL	0.80%	0.91%	114.6%	1.54%	2.54%	165.2%	2.72%	6.30%	231.8%
USDCAD	0.47%	0.52%	110.1%	0.94%	1.28%	135.6%	1.59%	2.78%	174.8%
USDCHF	0.56%	0.54%	97.2%	1.10%	1.30%	118.3%	1.95%	2.62%	134.1%
USDCLP				1.25%	1.35%	108.4%	2.24%	3.11%	138.5%
USDCOP				1.74%	2.38%	136.8%	2.78%	5.67%	204.2%
USDCZK	0.59%	0.56%	95.4%	1.08%	1.48%	136.7%	1.91%	3.27%	170.9%
USDDKK	0.47%	0.41%	88.3%	0.88%	0.97%	110.0%	1.57%	1.92%	122.6%
USDHKD	0.07%	0.02%	25.5%	0.10%	0.04%	33.9%	0.20%	0.06%	32.6%
USDIDR				0.93%	0.72%	77.4%	1.59%	1.13%	71.0%
USDILS				0.82%	1.12%	137.1%	1.37%	2.50%	182.8%
USDINR				0.60%	0.84%	141.0%	1.07%	1.96%	182.5%
USDJPY	0.54%	0.47%	85.9%	1.05%	1.06%	101.0%	1.79%	1.88%	104.9%
USDKRW	0.42%	0.39%	92.8%	0.81%	1.09%	135.6%	1.47%	2.34%	158.6%
USDMXN	0.51%	0.41%	81.6%	1.01%	0.84%	82.9%	1.84%	1.58%	85.8%
USDNOK	0.62%	0.68%	109.6%	1.18%	1.68%	141.9%	2.08%	3.51%	168.7%
USDPHP				1.12%	0.92%	82.4%	2.18%	2.40%	110.0%
USDPLN				1.32%	1.85%	139.9%	2.29%	3.88%	169.3%
USDSEK	0.60%	0.63%	104.0%	1.18%	1.56%	131.9%	2.08%	3.27%	157.0%
USDSGD	0.30%	0.25%	83.2%	0.53%	0.60%	111.9%	0.96%	1.23%	128.0%
USDTRY	0.67%	0.87%	128.9%	1.59%	2.44%	154.0%	2.91%	5.60%	192.3%
USDTWD	0.21%	0.11%	52.5%	0.49%	0.46%	93.6%	0.89%	0.94%	105.7%
USDZAR	1.11%	1.06%	95.4%	2.13%	2.81%	131.7%	3.58%	5.54%	155.1%

TABLE A.17 Payoff/premium for ATMF puts, 31/12/2001–12/12/2007 (6M–3Y tenors)

	6M			12M			2Y			3Y		
	Premium	Payoff	Ratio	Premium	Payoff	Ratio	Premium	Payoff	Ratio	Premium	Payoff	Ratio
AUDUSD	2.78%	0.58%	20.7%	3.83%	1.38%	35.9%	5.11%	1.28%	25.0%	5.94%	0.63%	10.7%
EURAUD	2.23%	2.27%	101.6%	3.12%	2.40%	77.0%	4.27%	3.35%	78.5%	4.88%	9.54%	195.6%
EURCHF	1.06%	0.27%	25.3%	1.49%	0.37%	25.0%	1.72%	2.04%	118.5%	2.08%	4.60%	221.2%
EURCZK	1.71%	2.42%	141.4%	2.36%	4.19%	177.2%						
EURGBP	1.75%	1.27%	72.2%	2.48%	1.75%	70.5%	2.90%	0.61%	21.1%	3.60%	0.00%	0.0%
EURHUF	2.52%	3.81%	151.2%	3.56%	6.14%	172.6%						
EURJPY	2.52%	0.32%	12.5%	3.52%	1.00%	28.5%	4.32%	6.43%	148.8%	4.94%	17.90%	362.6%
EURNOK	1.77%	1.66%	93.6%	2.46%	1.88%	76.4%	2.99%	0.43%	14.5%	3.61%	1.39%	38.5%
EURPLN	2.69%	3.62%	134.4%	3.74%	6.64%	177.7%						
EURUSD	2.59%	1.00%	38.5%	3.65%	1.34%	36.7%	4.37%	0.54%	12.4%	5.17%	1.88%	36.4%
GBPUSD	2.29%	0.82%	36.0%	3.19%	1.92%	60.2%	4.03%	10.37%	257.2%	4.80%	14.86%	309.9%
USDARS	1.80%	1.90%	105.6%	3.19%	3.60%	112.8%						
USDBRL	3.95%	12.76%	322.7%	5.80%	25.30%	436.1%						
USDCAD	2.20%	4.67%	212.4%	3.13%	7.90%	252.9%	4.08%	5.86%	143.4%	4.72%	2.41%	51.1%
USDCHF	2.76%	4.25%	154.0%	3.88%	6.04%	155.7%	4.55%	5.97%	131.1%	5.34%	6.35%	118.9%
USDCLP	3.21%	4.88%	152.1%	4.58%	7.71%	168.6%						
USDCOP	3.73%	10.89%	291.6%									

(continued)

TABLE A.17 (Continued)

	6M			12M			2Y			3Y		
	Premium	Payoff	Ratio	Premium	Payoff	Ratio	Premium	Payoff	Ratio	Premium	Payoff	Ratio
USDCZK	2.70%	6.57%	242.8%	3.79%	11.70%	308.5%						
USDDKK	2.23%	3.95%	177.6%	3.13%	6.57%	209.6%	4.28%	7.87%	183.8%	5.02%	5.53%	110.2%
USDHKD	0.33%	0.07%	22.0%	0.69%	0.09%	13.7%						
USDIDR	2.12%	1.38%	65.1%	3.14%	1.29%	41.1%						
USDILS	1.92%	4.58%	238.6%	2.69%	7.96%	295.2%						
USDINR	1.53%	3.20%	208.8%									
USDJPY	2.49%	2.68%	107.8%	3.43%	3.60%	104.9%	4.16%	6.95%	167.0%	4.85%	10.27%	211.6%
USDKRW	2.05%	3.69%	179.7%	2.92%	6.04%	206.9%						
USDMXN	2.68%	2.39%	89.1%	3.90%	4.17%	106.8%						
USDNOK	2.93%	5.73%	195.4%	4.11%	8.58%	209.1%	5.13%	7.05%	137.5%	6.01%	5.04%	83.8%
USDPHP	3.32%	4.19%	126.2%	4.86%	7.50%	154.5%						
USDPLN	3.21%	6.88%	214.0%	4.48%	12.53%	279.8%						
USDSEK	2.95%	5.74%	194.8%	4.13%	9.09%	219.8%	5.12%	6.31%	123.3%	5.78%	0.09%	1.6%
USDSGD	1.39%	2.03%	146.4%	1.98%	2.96%	149.2%						
USDTRY	4.35%	10.06%	231.5%	6.46%	17.98%	278.3%						
USDTWD	1.32%	1.41%	106.7%	1.95%	1.51%	77.5%						
USDZAR	4.95%	9.40%	190.0%	6.91%	16.10%	233.2%						

TABLE A.18 Payoff/premium for ATMF puts, 31/12/2001–12/12/2007 averaged over all currency pairs

Tenor	Ratio
1W	86.8%
1M	106.0%
3M	120.8%
6M	141.2%
12M	154.7%
2Y	111.6%
3Y	125.2%

TABLE A.19 Payoff/premium for ATMF puts, 31/12/2007–12/12/2013 (1W–3M tenors)

	1W			1M			3M		
	Premium	Payoff	Ratio	Premium	Payoff	Ratio	Premium	Payoff	Ratio
AUDUSD	0.81%	0.72%	88.6%	1.60%	1.53%	95.1%	2.83%	2.94%	103.7%
EURAUD	0.68%	0.66%	96.9%	1.34%	1.54%	114.6%	2.40%	3.23%	134.6%
EURCHF	0.44%	0.41%	93.8%	0.82%	0.93%	112.8%	1.44%	1.69%	117.6%
EURCZK	0.52%	0.41%	78.6%	1.00%	0.78%	78.3%	1.70%	1.30%	76.5%
EURGBP	0.55%	0.44%	80.2%	1.10%	0.90%	82.5%	1.97%	1.48%	75.0%
EURHUF	0.74%	0.64%	86.8%	1.44%	1.21%	83.7%	2.53%	2.41%	95.1%
EURJPY	0.86%	0.78%	91.0%	1.71%	1.66%	97.6%	2.99%	3.35%	112.0%
EURNOK	0.52%	0.44%	84.0%	1.00%	0.83%	83.1%	1.73%	1.42%	82.0%
EURPLN				1.37%	1.12%	81.3%	2.37%	2.20%	92.8%
EURUSD	0.66%	0.61%	91.3%	1.34%	1.36%	101.3%	2.41%	2.44%	101.4%
GBPUSD	0.61%	0.59%	96.0%	1.22%	1.20%	98.1%	2.21%	2.45%	110.8%
USDARS				1.46%	1.00%	68.2%	3.22%	2.90%	89.9%
USDBRL	0.94%	0.84%	89.3%	1.83%	1.90%	103.9%	3.17%	3.96%	125.0%
USDCAD	0.63%	0.58%	93.4%	1.27%	1.01%	79.9%	2.23%	1.59%	71.2%
USDCHF	0.67%	0.69%	102.6%	1.36%	1.56%	114.9%	2.40%	2.70%	112.4%
USDCLP				1.59%	1.48%	93.0%	2.80%	2.93%	104.7%
USDCOP				1.70%	1.61%	94.4%	3.01%	3.14%	104.3%
USDCZK	0.90%	0.85%	94.7%	1.78%	1.81%	101.4%	3.09%	3.01%	97.4%
USDDKK	0.72%	0.59%	83.1%	1.42%	1.30%	91.8%	2.50%	2.07%	82.8%
USDHKD	0.05%	0.02%	40.3%	0.09%	0.04%	42.6%	0.17%	0.05%	29.1%
USDIDR				1.51%	1.21%	80.3%	2.88%	2.53%	88.1%
USDILS				1.15%	1.18%	102.2%	1.97%	2.03%	103.1%
USDINR				1.26%	1.13%	89.7%	2.32%	1.97%	85.0%
USDJPY	0.70%	0.59%	84.0%	1.38%	1.19%	86.1%	2.41%	2.26%	93.6%
USDKRW	0.85%	0.67%	79.3%	1.66%	1.39%	83.7%	2.88%	2.33%	80.7%
USDMXN	0.84%	0.68%	80.4%	1.62%	1.37%	84.4%	2.83%	2.70%	95.4%
USDNOK	0.83%	0.76%	91.5%	1.65%	1.40%	85.1%	2.90%	2.60%	89.4%
USDPHP				1.04%	0.77%	73.7%	1.94%	1.43%	74.0%
USDPLN				2.11%	1.98%	93.7%	3.72%	3.69%	99.2%
USDSEK	0.85%	0.75%	88.7%	1.68%	1.57%	93.5%	2.95%	2.75%	93.2%
USDSGD	0.42%	0.34%	82.3%	0.81%	0.79%	96.9%	1.49%	1.47%	99.2%
USDTRY	0.76%	0.72%	94.9%	1.56%	1.48%	95.2%	2.76%	2.33%	84.3%
USDTWD	0.35%	0.22%	63.8%	0.71%	0.54%	76.2%	1.33%	0.98%	73.8%
USDZAR	1.08%	0.98%	90.9%	2.13%	1.84%	86.2%	3.77%	3.32%	88.0%

TABLE A.20 Payoff/premium for ATMF puts, 31/12/2007–12/12/2013 (6M–3Y tenors)

	6M			12M			2Y			3Y		
	Premium	Payoff	Ratio	Premium	Payoff	Ratio	Premium	Payoff	Ratio	Premium	Payoff	Ratio
AUDUSD	4.06%	4.43%	109.1%	5.85%	3.94%	67.3%	8.13%	1.08%	13.3%	9.13%	0.02%	0.3%
EURAUD	3.47%	5.67%	163.5%	5.06%	10.99%	217.5%	7.28%	23.26%	319.6%	8.12%	34.20%	421.3%
EURCHF	2.08%	2.70%	130.0%	3.03%	4.94%	163.4%	4.21%	10.49%	249.4%	4.00%	15.86%	397.0%
EURCZK	2.36%	1.52%	64.2%	3.32%	1.71%	51.6%						
EURGBP	2.90%	2.05%	70.8%	4.27%	2.47%	57.8%	6.33%	3.04%	48.0%	7.62%	4.36%	57.1%
EURHUF	3.62%	3.31%	91.5%	5.17%	3.28%	63.4%						
EURJPY	4.30%	5.51%	128.1%	6.16%	7.75%	125.9%	9.03%	11.28%	125.0%	10.76%	13.53%	125.8%
EURNOK	2.44%	2.34%	95.8%	3.49%	4.48%	128.6%	4.93%	7.98%	161.7%	5.84%	11.07%	189.5%
EURPLN	3.36%	3.08%	91.6%	4.85%	3.86%	79.5%						
EURUSD	3.51%	3.87%	110.4%	5.13%	4.39%	85.5%	7.20%	4.70%	65.3%	8.05%	4.66%	57.9%
GBPUSD	3.23%	4.24%	131.3%	4.77%	4.79%	100.4%	7.04%	4.76%	67.6%	8.53%	3.74%	43.9%
USDARS	5.30%	5.25%	99.2%	8.84%	8.94%	101.1%						
USDBRL	4.53%	6.33%	139.6%	6.73%	9.41%	140.0%						
USDCAD	3.26%	2.63%	80.5%	4.81%	3.91%	81.2%	7.19%	5.90%	82.1%	8.84%	7.15%	80.9%
USDCHF	3.44%	3.92%	113.9%	4.95%	5.24%	105.9%	6.80%	8.35%	122.9%	7.42%	12.07%	162.7%

	C1	C2	C3	C4	C5	C6	C7	C8	C9	C10	C11	C12
USDCLP	4.03%	4.17%	103.2%	5.93%	6.27%	105.8%						
USDCOP	4.35%	4.57%	105.0%	6.45%	7.38%	114.5%						
USDCZK	4.39%	3.74%	85.1%	6.28%	3.35%	53.4%						
USDDKK	3.63%	2.87%	78.9%	5.28%	2.78%	52.5%	7.41%	1.53%	20.6%	8.26%	1.18%	14.3%
USDHKD	0.27%	0.05%	17.2%	0.48%	0.03%	6.6%						
USDIDR	4.33%	4.85%	112.1%	6.69%	8.35%	124.7%						
USDILS	2.77%	3.00%	108.2%	3.93%	4.06%	103.3%						
USDINR	3.41%	2.50%	73.4%	5.15%	3.43%	66.7%						
USDJPY	3.45%	3.25%	94.3%	4.93%	4.86%	98.7%	7.14%	8.19%	114.7%	8.28%	9.36%	113.0%
USDKRW	4.12%	3.76%	91.3%	5.93%	4.98%	84.1%						
USDMXN	4.04%	3.89%	96.1%	5.87%	6.07%	103.5%						
USDNOK	4.17%	3.74%	89.8%	6.06%	4.68%	77.2%	8.55%	6.65%	77.8%	9.89%	7.49%	75.8%
USDPHP	2.92%	2.37%	81.1%	4.42%	4.52%	102.2%						
USDPLN	5.31%	4.75%	89.3%	7.66%	4.66%	60.8%						
USDSEK	4.22%	3.95%	93.8%	6.09%	5.20%	85.3%	8.72%	7.99%	91.7%	9.96%	9.35%	93.9%
USDSGD	2.19%	2.26%	103.2%	3.26%	3.60%	110.4%						
USDTRY	4.07%	3.39%	83.4%	6.16%	4.85%	78.7%						
USDTWD	2.00%	1.25%	62.4%	3.03%	1.63%	53.8%						
USDZAR	5.43%	5.37%	98.9%	7.87%	8.96%	113.9%						

TABLE A.21   Payoff/premium for ATMF
puts, 31/12/2007–12/12/2013 averaged over
all currency pairs

Tenor	Ratio
1W	85.8%
1M	89.6%
3M	93.1%
6M	96.7%
12M	93.1%
2Y	111.4%
3Y	130.9%

Payoff/Premium Ratios for ATMF Calls, by Time Period

TABLE A.22   Payoff/premium for ATMF calls, 31/12/1995–12/12/2013 (full period)
(1W–3M tenors)

	1W			1M			3M		
	Premium	Payoff	Ratio	Premium	Payoff	Ratio	Premium	Payoff	Ratio
AUDUSD	0.71%	0.69%	96.1%	1.33%	1.47%	110.6%	2.30%	2.64%	114.7%
EURAUD	0.64%	0.53%	82.7%	1.21%	1.01%	83.6%	2.14%	1.42%	66.2%
EURCHF	0.32%	0.25%	80.0%	0.60%	0.52%	86.5%	1.04%	0.80%	77.2%
EURCZK	0.43%	0.31%	72.2%	0.84%	0.56%	67.0%	1.44%	0.83%	57.6%
EURGBP	0.47%	0.41%	87.3%	0.93%	0.80%	86.1%	1.65%	1.40%	84.5%
EURHUF	0.64%	0.48%	74.6%	1.26%	0.83%	66.4%	2.22%	1.36%	61.3%
EURJPY	0.72%	0.68%	94.3%	1.42%	1.44%	101.2%	2.48%	2.65%	107.0%
EURNOK	0.44%	0.34%	76.5%	0.84%	0.64%	76.1%	1.45%	0.99%	68.0%
EURPLN				1.25%	0.95%	76.3%	2.16%	1.66%	77.1%
EURUSD	0.60%	0.55%	91.0%	1.21%	1.21%	99.5%	2.16%	2.18%	100.7%
GBPUSD	0.53%	0.47%	89.2%	1.04%	1.02%	98.1%	1.86%	1.71%	92.2%
USDARS				1.34%	0.15%	11.1%	2.92%	0.29%	10.1%
USDBRL	0.88%	0.63%	71.5%	1.71%	1.19%	69.5%	3.00%	1.82%	60.9%
USDCAD	0.52%	0.45%	85.9%	1.04%	0.76%	73.3%	1.79%	1.17%	65.2%
USDCHF	0.63%	0.56%	89.1%	1.24%	1.21%	97.9%	2.20%	2.12%	96.3%
USDCLP				1.39%	1.08%	77.9%	2.49%	1.96%	78.8%
USDCOP				1.72%	1.14%	66.1%	3.00%	1.85%	61.7%
USDCZK	0.80%	0.71%	88.9%	1.57%	1.46%	93.3%	2.73%	2.41%	88.2%
USDDKK	0.64%	0.52%	80.9%	1.25%	1.11%	88.5%	2.22%	1.79%	80.6%
USDHKD	0.06%	0.03%	51.2%	0.09%	0.06%	64.8%	0.18%	0.14%	74.5%
USDIDR				1.46%	0.84%	57.9%	2.77%	1.47%	53.3%
USDILS				0.99%	0.74%	74.9%	1.68%	1.11%	66.2%

TABLE A.22 (*Continued*)

	1W			1M			3M		
	Premium	**Payoff**	**Ratio**	**Premium**	**Payoff**	**Ratio**	**Premium**	**Payoff**	**Ratio**
USDINR				0.99%	0.81%	82.0%	1.79%	1.56%	86.9%
USDJPY	0.66%	0.55%	83.6%	1.29%	1.29%	100.6%	2.24%	2.44%	109.2%
USDKRW	0.65%	0.47%	72.2%	1.20%	0.92%	76.7%	2.13%	1.52%	71.1%
USDMXN	0.67%	0.51%	75.8%	1.29%	0.92%	71.2%	2.32%	1.47%	63.3%
USDNOK	0.72%	0.61%	84.8%	1.40%	1.08%	77.4%	2.46%	1.78%	72.5%
USDPHP				1.23%	0.55%	44.8%	2.32%	1.00%	43.1%
USDPLN				1.70%	1.28%	75.2%	3.00%	2.11%	70.6%
USDSEK	0.72%	0.61%	84.6%	1.42%	1.21%	85.3%	2.49%	2.00%	80.5%
USDSGD	0.36%	0.25%	69.6%	0.67%	0.52%	77.8%	1.22%	0.82%	67.8%
USDTRY	0.72%	0.63%	86.5%	1.57%	1.17%	74.6%	2.84%	1.94%	68.4%
USDTWD	0.33%	0.22%	64.9%	0.57%	0.54%	93.7%	1.07%	1.14%	106.7%
USDZAR	1.01%	0.82%	81.2%	1.98%	1.60%	80.8%	3.41%	2.66%	78.0%

TABLE A.23 Payoff/premium for ATMF calls, 31/12/1995–12/12/2013 (full period) (6M–3Y tenors)

	6M			12M			2Y			3Y		
	Premium	Payoff	Ratio	Premium	Payoff	Ratio	Premium	Payoff	Ratio	Premium	Payoff	Ratio
AUDUSD	3.19%	4.15%	130.0%	4.45%	6.54%	146.9%	6.19%	12.59%	203.4%	6.85%	16.56%	241.6%
EURAUD	3.06%	2.06%	67.5%	4.39%	2.18%	49.7%	6.06%	1.19%	19.7%	6.59%	0.98%	14.9%
EURCHF	1.47%	1.12%	76.5%	2.07%	1.68%	81.1%	3.17%	1.91%	60.2%	3.00%	0.72%	23.9%
EURCZK	2.02%	0.97%	48.3%	2.82%	1.21%	42.8%						
EURGBP	2.37%	1.97%	82.9%	3.37%	2.89%	85.8%	5.01%	5.58%	111.3%	5.77%	8.15%	141.2%
EURHUF	3.15%	1.69%	53.7%	4.45%	1.64%	36.8%						
EURJPY	3.51%	4.04%	115.1%	4.89%	6.58%	134.4%	7.13%	6.12%	85.8%	8.88%	2.95%	33.2%
EURNOK	2.03%	1.25%	61.9%	2.83%	1.64%	57.9%	4.15%	1.33%	32.0%	4.80%	1.52%	31.7%
EURPLN	3.03%	2.31%	76.4%	4.27%	3.12%	73.0%						
EURUSD	3.09%	3.26%	105.6%	4.38%	4.69%	107.1%	6.05%	3.43%	56.7%	6.70%	2.72%	40.6%
GBPUSD	2.65%	2.52%	94.9%	3.75%	3.36%	89.4%	5.85%	3.13%	53.4%	6.77%	1.55%	22.8%
USDARS	4.73%	0.49%	10.3%	7.98%	0.97%	12.2%						
USDBRL	4.30%	2.58%	60.0%	6.37%	2.86%	44.9%						
USDCAD	2.53%	1.58%	62.3%	3.61%	1.85%	51.2%	5.96%	1.70%	28.5%	7.26%	0.88%	12.1%
USDCHF	3.11%	2.92%	94.0%	4.37%	3.57%	81.7%	5.87%	1.52%	25.9%	6.43%	0.02%	0.4%
USDCLP	3.57%	2.52%	70.7%	5.16%	2.54%	49.2%						
USDCOP	4.27%	2.27%	53.2%	6.54%	1.83%	28.0%						
USDCZK	3.86%	3.22%	83.4%	5.44%	3.51%	64.6%						

USDDKK	3.19%	2.65%	83.0%	4.56%	2.95%	64.6%	6.14%	2.69%	43.8%	6.70%	2.84%	42.4%
USDHKD	0.32%	0.20%	64.2%	0.63%	0.30%	46.8%						
USDIDR	4.14%	2.64%	63.6%	6.47%	3.17%	49.0%						
USDILS	2.35%	1.48%	63.1%	3.29%	1.59%	48.4%						
USDINR	2.59%	2.29%	88.5%	5.18%	3.58%	69.0%						
USDJPY	3.14%	3.65%	116.0%	4.39%	5.20%	118.5%	5.95%	4.24%	71.3%	6.62%	2.89%	43.6%
USDKRW	3.01%	2.20%	73.3%	4.26%	3.24%	76.1%						
USDMXN	3.36%	1.78%	53.0%	4.92%	2.25%	45.8%						
USDNOK	3.47%	2.39%	68.9%	4.89%	2.78%	56.9%	7.15%	2.31%	32.3%	8.01%	1.45%	18.1%
USDPHP	3.50%	1.31%	37.3%	5.16%	1.78%	34.6%						
USDPLN	4.22%	2.55%	60.5%	5.95%	3.17%	53.3%						
USDSEK	3.50%	2.92%	83.5%	4.91%	3.90%	79.3%	7.24%	3.46%	47.8%	8.28%	2.74%	33.0%
USDSGD	1.77%	1.02%	57.4%	2.57%	0.96%	37.5%						
USDTRY	4.19%	2.48%	59.2%	6.35%	2.66%	41.9%						
USDTWD	1.61%	1.73%	108.0%	2.42%	2.45%	101.2%						
USDZAR	4.81%	4.10%	85.2%	6.80%	5.73%	84.4%						

TABLE A.24 Payoff/premium for ATMF calls, 31/12/1995–12/12/2013 (full period) averaged over all currency pairs

Tenor	Ratio
1W	80.6%
1M	78.4%
3M	75.3%
6M	73.9%
12M	66.0%
2Y	62.3%
3Y	50.0%

TABLE A.25 Payoff/premium for ATMF calls, 31/12/1995–12/12/2001 (1W–3M tenors)

	1W			1M			3M		
	Premium	Payoff	Ratio	Premium	Payoff	Ratio	Premium	Payoff	Ratio
AUDUSD	0.76%	0.59%	76.9%	1.25%	0.99%	78.8%	2.08%	1.03%	49.4%
EURAUD									
EURCHF	0.25%	0.18%	72.5%	0.50%	0.31%	62.6%	0.80%	0.42%	52.7%
EURCZK	0.35%	0.21%	61.2%	0.69%	0.25%	36.0%	1.29%	0.14%	10.8%
EURGBP	0.55%	0.48%	87.0%	1.06%	0.64%	60.0%	1.86%	0.90%	48.5%
EURHUF									
EURJPY	0.83%	0.86%	103.8%	1.64%	1.48%	90.2%	2.83%	2.69%	95.2%
EURNOK	0.38%	0.24%	63.2%	0.72%	0.31%	43.1%	1.25%	0.27%	21.9%
EURPLN									
EURUSD	0.67%	0.54%	80.1%	1.34%	0.81%	60.9%	2.34%	1.12%	47.8%
GBPUSD	0.51%	0.36%	70.1%	0.98%	0.81%	82.6%	1.74%	1.12%	64.1%
USDARS									
USDBRL									
USDCAD	0.37%	0.31%	83.8%	0.74%	0.66%	89.5%	1.26%	1.18%	93.8%
USDCHF	0.67%	0.68%	102.5%	1.25%	1.56%	124.3%	2.22%	3.31%	148.8%
USDCLP				1.13%	1.58%	139.5%	2.14%	3.25%	151.8%
USDCOP									
USDCZK									
USDDKK									
USDHKD				0.09%	0.03%	32.3%	0.18%	0.06%	34.1%
USDIDR									
USDILS									
USDINR									
USDJPY	0.76%	0.67%	87.6%	1.43%	1.72%	120.6%	2.51%	3.61%	144.0%
USDKRW				1.02%	0.91%	88.9%	1.90%	1.63%	85.9%
USDMXN	0.36%	0.03%	8.7%	1.12%	0.51%	45.3%	2.29%	0.29%	12.8%
USDNOK	0.67%	0.58%	86.8%	1.32%	0.98%	74.2%	2.30%	1.88%	82.0%
USDPHP				1.89%	0.84%	44.7%	3.40%	1.99%	58.7%
USDPLN				1.60%	0.76%	47.6%	2.71%	0.80%	29.4%
USDSEK	0.70%	0.70%	99.5%	1.37%	1.47%	107.1%	2.36%	2.91%	123.3%
USDSGD				0.62%	1.01%	162.3%	1.14%	2.14%	187.6%
USDTRY									
USDTWD				0.46%	0.49%	104.6%	0.87%	1.22%	139.9%
USDZAR	0.67%	0.74%	111.4%	1.36%	1.84%	136.0%	2.31%	4.40%	190.4%

TABLE A.26 Payoff/premium for ATMF calls, 31/12/1995–12/12/2001 (6M–3Y tenors)

	6M			12M			2Y			3Y		
	Premium	Payoff	Ratio	Premium	Payoff	Ratio	Premium	Payoff	Ratio	Premium	Payoff	Ratio
AUDUSD	2.78%	1.23%	44.1%	3.82%	1.80%	47.1%	5.59%	8.60%	153.9%	6.21%	15.09%	242.8%
EURAUD												
EURCHF	1.13%	0.43%	37.8%	1.57%	0.19%	12.0%						
EURCZK	1.95%	0.01%	0.5%	2.84%	0.00%	0.0%						
EURGBP	2.60%	0.70%	26.8%	3.59%	0.92%	25.7%						
EURHUF												
EURJPY	4.01%	4.09%	101.9%	5.49%	7.87%	143.3%						
EURNOK	1.75%	0.08%	4.4%	2.41%	0.01%	0.2%						
EURPLN												
EURUSD	3.26%	0.91%	28.0%	4.50%	2.40%	53.3%						
GBPUSD	2.45%	1.23%	50.1%	3.40%	1.82%	53.4%						
USDARS												
USDBRL												
USDCAD	1.74%	1.60%	91.9%	2.37%	2.60%	109.5%						
USDCHF	3.13%	4.89%	156.4%	4.33%	6.84%	158.1%						
USDCLP	3.20%	4.99%	155.8%	4.65%	7.30%	157.0%						

(continued)

TABLE A.26 (Continued)

	6M			12M			2Y			3Y		
	Premium	Payoff	Ratio	Premium	Payoff	Ratio	Premium	Payoff	Ratio	Premium	Payoff	Ratio
USDCOP												
USDCZK												
USDDKK												
USDHKD	0.37%	0.07%	19.0%	0.80%	0.06%	7.4%						
USDIDR												
USDILS												
USDINR												
USDJPY	3.53%	5.72%	161.9%	4.88%	8.20%	168.1%						
USDKRW	2.78%	2.64%	95.2%	3.97%	4.48%	113.0%						
USDMXN	3.49%	0.08%	2.4%	5.42%	0.13%	2.4%						
USDNOK	3.18%	2.68%	84.2%	4.36%	4.56%	104.6%						
USDPHP	5.01%	2.72%	54.3%	7.03%	5.01%	71.3%						
USDPLN	3.87%	0.00%	0.0%	5.12%	0.00%	0.0%						
USDSEK	3.25%	4.76%	146.3%	4.45%	7.83%	175.9%						
USDSGD	1.70%	2.14%	126.1%	2.48%	2.22%	89.4%						
USDTRY												
USDTWD	1.38%	2.01%	145.4%	2.25%	3.75%	166.8%						
USDZAR	3.27%	7.72%	236.3%	4.58%	12.58%	274.4%						

TABLE A.27 Payoff/premium for ATMF calls, 31/12/1995–12/12/2001 averaged over all currency pairs

Tenor	Ratio
1W	79.7%
1M	83.2%
3M	85.1%
6M	80.4%
12M	87.9%
2Y	153.9%
3Y	242.8%

TABLE A.28 Payoff/premium for ATMF calls, 31/12/2001–12/12/2007 (1W–3M tenors)

	1W			1M			3M		
	Premium	Payoff	Ratio	Premium	Payoff	Ratio	Premium	Payoff	Ratio
AUDUSD	0.58%	0.67%	114.8%	1.14%	1.65%	145.2%	1.99%	3.42%	171.8%
EURAUD	0.51%	0.45%	88.3%	0.90%	0.80%	89.4%	1.58%	0.76%	47.8%
EURCHF	0.23%	0.22%	96.8%	0.42%	0.53%	125.3%	0.75%	1.05%	141.1%
EURCZK	0.38%	0.26%	66.7%	0.73%	0.44%	60.2%	1.23%	0.57%	46.5%
EURGBP	0.35%	0.33%	94.4%	0.69%	0.70%	102.1%	1.23%	1.31%	107.1%
EURHUF	0.50%	0.33%	64.8%	0.98%	0.57%	57.8%	1.76%	0.76%	43.2%
EURJPY	0.52%	0.55%	104.7%	1.03%	1.26%	122.8%	1.79%	2.47%	138.0%
EURNOK	0.39%	0.31%	78.6%	0.74%	0.66%	89.2%	1.27%	1.17%	92.4%
EURPLN				1.12%	0.81%	72.3%	1.93%	1.29%	66.7%
EURUSD	0.51%	0.53%	104.4%	1.01%	1.33%	131.5%	1.81%	2.87%	158.4%
GBPUSD	0.46%	0.48%	104.7%	0.91%	1.23%	135.3%	1.61%	2.36%	146.7%
USDARS				0.56%	0.27%	47.5%	1.11%	0.47%	41.8%
USDBRL	0.80%	0.44%	55.1%	1.54%	0.73%	47.5%	2.72%	0.31%	11.3%
USDCAD	0.47%	0.36%	76.5%	0.94%	0.56%	59.7%	1.59%	0.73%	45.8%
USDCHF	0.56%	0.44%	78.7%	1.10%	0.86%	78.4%	1.95%	1.11%	57.2%
USDCLP				1.25%	0.82%	66.1%	2.24%	1.21%	54.1%
USDCOP				1.74%	0.93%	53.4%	2.78%	0.97%	35.1%
USDCZK	0.59%	0.42%	71.1%	1.08%	0.76%	70.4%	1.91%	0.63%	32.9%
USDDKK	0.47%	0.35%	74.4%	0.88%	0.71%	80.8%	1.57%	0.73%	46.9%
USDHKD	0.07%	0.04%	59.4%	0.10%	0.08%	81.5%	0.20%	0.20%	103.0%
USDIDR				0.93%	1.08%	115.3%	1.59%	0.74%	46.5%
USDILS				0.82%	0.53%	64.4%	1.37%	0.63%	46.3%
USDINR				0.60%	0.33%	56.0%	1.07%	0.66%	61.6%
USDJPY	0.54%	0.46%	84.6%	1.05%	0.98%	93.8%	1.79%	1.55%	86.4%
USDKRW	0.42%	0.26%	62.7%	0.81%	0.47%	58.7%	1.47%	0.63%	42.7%
USDMXN	0.51%	0.38%	74.2%	1.01%	0.71%	70.1%	1.84%	1.09%	59.3%
USDNOK	0.62%	0.49%	78.3%	1.18%	0.85%	71.8%	2.08%	1.03%	49.7%
USDPHP				1.12%	0.29%	25.5%	2.18%	0.41%	18.9%
USDPLN				1.32%	0.90%	68.4%	2.29%	0.81%	35.4%
USDSEK	0.60%	0.45%	75.2%	1.18%	0.89%	75.7%	2.08%	1.07%	51.4%
USDSGD	0.30%	0.20%	65.9%	0.53%	0.36%	67.4%	0.96%	0.44%	45.7%
USDTRY	0.67%	0.48%	70.9%	1.58%	0.80%	50.3%	2.91%	1.17%	40.0%
USDTWD	0.21%	0.12%	59.2%	0.49%	0.50%	103.2%	0.89%	0.99%	110.4%
USDZAR	1.11%	0.74%	66.4%	2.13%	1.39%	65.1%	3.58%	1.73%	48.5%

TABLE A.29 Payoff/premium for ATMF calls, 31/12/2001–12/12/2007 (6M–3Y tenors)

	6M			12M			2Y			3Y		
	Premium	Payoff	Ratio	Premium	Payoff	Ratio	Premium	Payoff	Ratio	Premium	Payoff	Ratio
AUDUSD	2.78%	5.90%	212.1%	3.83%	9.61%	250.9%	5.11%	12.90%	252.2%	5.94%	15.35%	258.3%
EURAUD	2.23%	1.09%	48.9%	3.12%	1.91%	61.1%	4.27%	2.51%	58.7%	4.88%	2.00%	41.0%
EURCHF	1.06%	1.81%	170.8%	1.49%	3.13%	210.0%	1.72%	3.58%	207.9%	2.08%	1.49%	71.8%
EURCZK	1.71%	0.71%	41.5%	2.36%	0.81%	34.2%						
EURGBP	1.75%	2.13%	121.4%	2.48%	3.64%	146.6%	2.90%	11.72%	403.8%	3.60%	15.08%	419.3%
EURHUF	2.52%	0.77%	30.6%	3.56%	0.75%	21.0%						
EURJPY	2.52%	4.14%	164.6%	3.52%	7.25%	206.0%	4.32%	8.94%	207.0%	4.94%	0.01%	0.3%
EURNOK	1.77%	1.42%	80.5%	2.46%	2.21%	90.0%	2.99%	2.94%	98.2%	3.61%	3.12%	86.3%
EURPLN	2.69%	1.63%	60.7%	3.74%	2.06%	55.2%						
EURUSD	2.59%	5.02%	194.0%	3.65%	7.62%	208.6%	4.37%	6.86%	157.0%	5.17%	4.66%	90.1%
GBPUSD	2.29%	3.96%	173.1%	3.19%	6.09%	190.9%	4.03%	4.43%	109.9%	4.80%	1.10%	22.9%
USDARS	1.80%	0.53%	29.4%	3.19%	0.37%	11.7%						
USDBRL	3.95%	0.01%	0.3%	5.80%	1.01%	17.5%						
USDCAD	2.20%	0.69%	31.5%	3.13%	0.90%	28.7%	4.08%	2.74%	67.0%	4.72%	2.07%	43.8%
USDCHF	2.76%	1.29%	46.8%	3.88%	1.52%	39.2%	4.55%	0.66%	14.5%	5.34%	0.05%	0.9%

USDCLP	3.21%	1.22%	38.2%	4.58%	1.49%	32.5%						
USDCOP	3.73%	0.37%	9.8%									
USDCZK	2.70%	0.48%	17.7%	3.79%	0.46%	12.2%						
USDDKK	2.23%	0.84%	37.7%	3.13%	0.97%	31.0%	4.28%	0.46%	10.7%	5.02%	1.56%	31.1%
USDHKD	0.33%	0.33%	97.8%	0.69%	0.48%	69.5%						
USDIDR	2.12%	0.56%	26.5%	3.14%	6.43%	204.6%						
USDILS	1.92%	0.60%	31.1%	2.69%	0.46%	16.9%						
USDINR	1.53%	0.94%	61.4%									
USDJPY	2.49%	2.19%	88.0%	3.43%	3.10%	90.3%	4.16%	3.21%	77.2%	4.85%	1.35%	27.8%
USDKRW	2.05%	0.74%	36.3%	2.92%	2.29%	78.5%						
USDMXN	2.68%	1.06%	39.6%	3.90%	1.48%	37.9%						
USDNOK	2.93%	0.97%	33.1%	4.11%	1.41%	34.2%	5.13%	2.54%	49.5%	6.01%	2.78%	46.2%
USDPHP	3.32%	0.39%	11.6%	4.86%	0.49%	10.0%						
USDPLN	3.21%	0.44%	13.7%	4.48%	0.55%	12.4%						
USDSEK	2.95%	1.29%	43.8%	4.13%	1.96%	47.3%	5.12%	4.92%	96.1%	5.78%	6.54%	113.3%
USDSGD	1.39%	0.39%	28.0%	1.98%	0.36%	18.3%						
USDTRY	4.35%	1.10%	25.2%	6.46%	1.11%	17.1%						
USDTWD	1.32%	1.40%	105.6%	1.95%	1.82%	93.2%						
USDZAR	4.95%	2.31%	46.7%	6.91%	3.18%	46.1%						

TABLE A.30 Payoff/premium for ATMF calls, 31/12/2001–12/12/2007 averaged over all currency pairs

Tenor	Ratio
1W	78.8%
1M	79.5%
3M	68.5%
6M	64.6%
12M	75.7%
2Y	129.3%
3Y	89.5%

TABLE A.31 Payoff/premium for ATMF calls, 31/12/2007–12/12/2013 (1W–3M tenors)

	1W			1M			3M		
	Premium	Payoff	Ratio	Premium	Payoff	Ratio	Premium	Payoff	Ratio
AUDUSD	0.81%	0.77%	95.3%	1.61%	1.78%	110.5%	2.86%	3.50%	122.4%
EURAUD	0.68%	0.55%	81.5%	1.35%	1.10%	81.8%	2.41%	1.75%	72.3%
EURCHF	0.44%	0.32%	73.1%	0.83%	0.61%	73.2%	1.46%	0.72%	49.6%
EURCZK	0.52%	0.41%	79.0%	1.00%	0.81%	80.7%	1.72%	1.39%	80.9%
EURGBP	0.56%	0.47%	85.3%	1.10%	0.98%	88.9%	2.00%	1.76%	88.0%
EURHUF	0.74%	0.58%	79.2%	1.45%	1.03%	70.8%	2.56%	1.80%	70.4%
EURJPY	0.86%	0.74%	85.2%	1.71%	1.59%	92.9%	3.01%	2.81%	93.2%
EURNOK	0.52%	0.42%	79.6%	1.00%	0.78%	77.7%	1.74%	1.14%	65.9%
EURPLN				1.38%	1.10%	79.4%	2.39%	2.05%	85.7%
EURUSD	0.66%	0.58%	87.6%	1.35%	1.27%	94.2%	2.44%	2.02%	83.0%
GBPUSD	0.61%	0.53%	86.0%	1.23%	1.00%	81.3%	2.23%	1.61%	72.0%
USDARS				1.45%	0.13%	9.0%	3.19%	0.27%	8.3%
USDBRL	0.94%	0.76%	80.6%	1.83%	1.50%	81.7%	3.19%	2.87%	90.1%
USDCAD	0.63%	0.59%	93.8%	1.28%	1.01%	79.4%	2.26%	1.62%	71.8%
USDCHF	0.68%	0.61%	89.8%	1.36%	1.23%	90.6%	2.43%	1.99%	82.1%
USDCLP				1.60%	1.23%	76.9%	2.82%	2.40%	85.1%
USDCOP				1.71%	1.18%	68.6%	3.05%	2.03%	66.7%
USDCZK	0.90%	0.85%	94.0%	1.79%	1.78%	99.5%	3.12%	3.25%	104.1%
USDDKK	0.72%	0.59%	82.6%	1.43%	1.29%	90.5%	2.53%	2.29%	90.3%
USDHKD	0.05%	0.02%	47.8%	0.09%	0.05%	60.1%	0.17%	0.10%	59.8%
USDIDR				1.50%	0.82%	54.8%	2.87%	1.53%	53.5%
USDILS				1.16%	0.95%	81.6%	1.99%	1.57%	79.2%
USDINR				1.26%	1.14%	90.6%	2.31%	2.21%	95.5%
USDJPY	0.70%	0.56%	79.9%	1.38%	1.18%	85.1%	2.42%	2.17%	89.4%
USDKRW	0.85%	0.65%	76.0%	1.68%	1.38%	82.1%	2.93%	2.39%	81.8%
USDMXN	0.84%	0.65%	77.2%	1.63%	1.27%	78.0%	2.84%	2.29%	80.6%
USDNOK	0.83%	0.73%	88.6%	1.65%	1.36%	82.4%	2.93%	2.50%	85.3%
USDPHP				1.04%	0.68%	65.4%	1.96%	1.14%	58.2%
USDPLN				2.12%	1.86%	87.4%	3.75%	3.61%	96.2%
USDSEK	0.85%	0.71%	83.9%	1.68%	1.38%	81.7%	2.98%	2.43%	81.6%
USDSGD	0.42%	0.30%	71.7%	0.82%	0.60%	73.5%	1.50%	1.00%	66.5%
USDTRY	0.76%	0.72%	95.5%	1.56%	1.42%	91.0%	2.78%	2.48%	89.3%
USDTWD	0.35%	0.23%	65.3%	0.71%	0.59%	83.6%	1.34%	1.26%	93.7%
USDZAR	1.08%	0.95%	87.8%	2.14%	1.69%	78.9%	3.79%	2.80%	73.7%

TABLE A.32 Payoff/premium for ATMF calls, 31/12/2007–12/12/2013 (6M–3Y tenors)

	6M			12M			2Y			3Y		
	Premium	Payoff	Ratio	Premium	Payoff	Ratio	Premium	Payoff	Ratio	Premium	Payoff	Ratio
AUDUSD	4.08%	5.41%	132.5%	5.92%	8.42%	142.2%	8.14%	14.49%	178.0%	9.16%	20.20%	220.5%
EURAUD	3.48%	2.56%	73.5%	5.10%	2.39%	46.8%	7.28%	0.29%	4.0%	8.13%	0.05%	0.7%
EURCHF	2.09%	0.74%	35.3%	3.05%	0.80%	26.1%	4.15%	0.76%	18.3%	3.84%	0.01%	0.4%
EURCZK	2.38%	1.74%	73.0%	3.34%	2.33%	69.8%						
EURGBP	2.92%	2.49%	85.1%	4.31%	3.22%	74.8%	6.36%	1.67%	26.3%	7.62%	2.25%	29.5%
EURHUF	3.64%	2.40%	66.0%	5.21%	2.40%	46.0%						
EURJPY	4.32%	3.90%	90.2%	6.19%	5.01%	81.0%	9.02%	4.17%	46.3%	10.71%	4.31%	40.3%
EURNOK	2.45%	1.68%	68.8%	3.52%	1.97%	55.9%	4.93%	0.23%	4.7%	5.87%	0.07%	1.2%
EURPLN	3.39%	3.04%	89.8%	4.89%	4.40%	90.0%						
EURUSD	3.54%	2.66%	75.0%	5.18%	2.57%	49.7%	7.19%	1.08%	15.0%	8.03%	1.00%	12.4%
GBPUSD	3.26%	2.26%	69.3%	4.82%	1.81%	37.5%	7.08%	2.22%	31.4%	8.55%	1.94%	22.7%
USDARS	5.21%	0.48%	9.2%	8.85%	1.09%	12.3%						
USDBRL	4.55%	4.43%	97.5%	6.81%	4.39%	64.5%						
USDCAD	3.29%	2.53%	76.8%	4.88%	2.62%	53.6%	7.24%	1.00%	13.9%	8.92%	0.09%	1.1%
USDCHF	3.46%	2.68%	77.5%	4.99%	2.36%	47.3%	6.77%	2.10%	31.0%	7.42%	0.00%	0.0%
USDCLP	4.06%	3.30%	81.5%	5.99%	2.51%	42.0%						
USDCOP	4.39%	2.69%	61.2%	6.54%	1.83%	28.0%						
USDCZK	4.43%	4.57%	103.2%	6.33%	5.18%	81.7%						

(continued)

TABLE A.32 (Continued)

	6M			12M			2Y			3Y		
	Premium	Payoff	Ratio	Premium	Payoff	Ratio	Premium	Payoff	Ratio	Premium	Payoff	Ratio
USDDKK	3.66%	3.54%	96.6%	5.34%	4.03%	75.4%	7.40%	4.20%	56.8%	8.21%	4.02%	49.0%
USDHKD	0.27%	0.14%	51.9%	0.48%	0.21%	44.2%						
USDIDR	4.32%	2.81%	65.1%	6.79%	2.89%	42.5%						
USDILS	2.78%	2.37%	85.2%	3.94%	2.85%	72.3%						
USDINR	3.38%	3.33%	98.3%	5.18%	3.58%	69.0%						
USDJPY	3.44%	2.99%	86.9%	4.95%	4.12%	83.3%	7.15%	4.92%	68.8%	8.21%	4.26%	51.9%
USDKRW	4.15%	3.60%	86.6%	6.01%	3.78%	62.8%						
USDMXN	4.05%	3.21%	79.4%	5.92%	4.12%	69.6%						
USDNOK	4.20%	3.77%	89.7%	6.13%	3.47%	56.6%	8.56%	2.15%	25.1%	9.86%	0.23%	2.3%
USDPHP	2.94%	1.62%	55.1%	4.49%	1.59%	35.4%						
USDPLN	5.35%	5.14%	96.2%	7.73%	6.44%	83.3%						
USDSEK	4.25%	3.56%	83.8%	6.15%	3.64%	59.1%	8.72%	2.46%	28.3%	9.92%	0.23%	2.4%
USDSGD	2.20%	1.49%	67.7%	3.30%	1.43%	43.5%						
USDTRY	4.08%	3.48%	85.2%	6.26%	3.91%	62.5%						
USDTWD	2.02%	1.96%	96.8%	3.07%	2.51%	81.7%						
USDZAR	5.45%	4.19%	76.8%	7.92%	4.97%	62.7%						

TABLE A.33 Payoff/premium for ATMF
calls, 31/12/2007–12/12/2013 averaged over
all currency pairs

Tenor	Ratio
1W	81.8%
1M	79.5%
3M	78.4%
6M	78.4%
12M	60.4%
2Y	39.1%
3Y	31.0%

CHAPTER 5

Out-of-the-Money versus At-the-Money-Forward Options

Recall that the Chapter 5 dataset was limited to a 10-year history – the period for which high quality volatility skew data were available.

TABLE A.34 Payoff/premium ratio for ATMF straddles (1W–3M tenors)

	1W			1M			3M		
	Premium	Payoff	Ratio	Premium	Payoff	Ratio	Premium	Payoff	Ratio
AUDUSD	1.43%	1.30%	91.4%	2.67%	2.74%	102.7%	4.61%	4.72%	102.4%
EURAUD	1.29%	1.15%	89.4%	2.42%	2.37%	97.8%	4.28%	4.16%	97.2%
EURCHF	0.64%	0.52%	82.0%	1.20%	1.07%	89.4%	2.07%	1.74%	84.0%
EURCZK	0.87%	0.67%	77.1%	1.67%	1.32%	79.2%	2.88%	2.29%	79.8%
EURGBP	0.95%	0.83%	87.1%	1.85%	1.62%	87.4%	3.31%	2.78%	84.0%
EURHUF	1.28%	1.04%	81.0%	2.51%	1.98%	78.8%	4.44%	3.73%	84.1%
EURJPY	1.43%	1.31%	91.1%	2.84%	2.68%	94.4%	4.95%	4.85%	97.8%
EURNOK	0.88%	0.71%	80.9%	1.68%	1.45%	86.3%	2.90%	2.47%	85.2%
EURPLN				2.50%	2.05%	81.8%	4.32%	3.84%	89.1%
EURUSD	1.21%	1.09%	90.5%	2.42%	2.36%	97.4%	4.33%	4.23%	97.8%
GBPUSD	1.06%	0.94%	88.6%	2.08%	1.94%	93.2%	3.72%	3.23%	86.9%
USDARS				2.67%	1.07%	40.2%	5.84%	3.02%	51.8%
USDBRL	1.77%	1.50%	85.2%	3.42%	3.36%	98.2%	5.99%	6.81%	113.7%
USDCAD	1.04%	0.95%	91.3%	2.08%	1.80%	86.6%	3.58%	3.06%	85.6%
USDCHF	1.25%	1.16%	92.4%	2.48%	2.49%	100.5%	4.39%	4.33%	98.6%
USDCLP				2.78%	2.43%	87.3%	4.97%	4.80%	96.6%
USDCOP				3.43%	2.89%	84.3%	6.00%	5.50%	91.7%
USDCZK	1.61%	1.47%	91.6%	3.14%	3.18%	101.3%	5.47%	5.53%	101.2%

(continued)

TABLE A.34 (*Continued*)

	1W			1M			3M		
	Premium	Payoff	Ratio	Premium	Payoff	Ratio	Premium	Payoff	Ratio
USDDKK	1.28%	1.05%	82.3%	2.51%	2.32%	92.3%	4.44%	3.82%	86.2%
USDHKD	0.11%	0.05%	43.6%	0.19%	0.09%	48.6%	0.37%	0.18%	50.6%
USDIDR				2.92%	2.03%	69.6%	5.54%	3.95%	71.3%
USDILS				1.99%	1.89%	95.2%	3.37%	3.38%	100.3%
USDINR				1.97%	1.83%	92.7%	3.58%	3.52%	98.3%
USDJPY	1.31%	1.09%	82.7%	2.57%	2.40%	93.5%	4.47%	4.39%	98.2%
USDKRW	1.31%	1.02%	77.6%	2.40%	2.09%	87.2%	4.26%	3.63%	85.2%
USDMXN	1.35%	1.06%	78.6%	2.58%	2.08%	80.5%	4.65%	3.82%	82.1%
USDNOK	1.43%	1.28%	89.6%	2.79%	2.49%	89.1%	4.91%	4.50%	91.7%
USDPHP				2.47%	1.42%	57.6%	4.64%	2.91%	62.7%
USDPLN				3.40%	3.22%	94.5%	5.99%	5.89%	98.3%
USDSEK	1.44%	1.26%	87.6%	2.84%	2.60%	91.7%	4.97%	4.52%	90.9%
USDSGD	0.73%	0.55%	75.9%	1.34%	1.20%	89.4%	2.43%	2.13%	87.5%
USDTRY	1.45%	1.41%	97.1%	3.14%	3.05%	97.2%	5.67%	5.66%	99.8%
USDTWD	0.66%	0.42%	63.8%	1.15%	1.02%	89.1%	2.14%	2.08%	97.2%
USDZAR	2.03%	1.73%	85.4%	3.96%	3.62%	91.2%	6.83%	6.44%	94.4%

TABLE A.35 Payoff/premium ratio for ATMF straddles (6M–3Y tenors)

	6M			12M			2Y			3Y		
	Premium	Payoff	Ratio	Premium	Payoff	Ratio	Premium	Payoff	Ratio	Premium	Payoff	Ratio
AUDUSD	6.39%	7.32%	114.6%	8.90%	10.94%	123.0%	12.38%	14.73%	119.0%	13.71%	17.41%	127.0%
EURAUD	6.11%	6.71%	109.7%	8.78%	10.34%	117.7%	12.12%	17.00%	140.3%	13.18%	24.45%	185.5%
EURCHF	2.94%	2.53%	86.1%	4.14%	4.06%	98.0%	6.34%	9.24%	145.8%	6.01%	11.62%	193.4%
EURCZK	4.03%	3.30%	81.9%	5.63%	5.13%	91.0%						
EURGBP	4.74%	3.81%	80.3%	6.74%	5.34%	79.2%	10.02%	7.68%	76.7%	11.54%	10.54%	91.3%
EURHUF	6.31%	5.27%	83.6%	8.91%	6.30%	70.7%						
EURJPY	7.02%	7.23%	102.9%	9.79%	11.05%	112.9%	14.25%	15.67%	110.0%	17.76%	18.32%	103.2%
EURNOK	4.05%	3.45%	85.2%	5.67%	5.35%	94.5%	8.30%	6.47%	77.9%	9.60%	8.33%	86.8%
EURPLN	6.05%	5.66%	93.6%	8.53%	8.52%	99.8%						
EURUSD	6.18%	6.22%	100.8%	8.76%	8.68%	99.0%	12.11%	6.57%	54.3%	13.40%	6.20%	46.3%
GBPUSD	5.31%	4.78%	90.1%	7.51%	6.35%	84.6%	11.70%	10.24%	87.6%	13.54%	10.64%	78.6%
USDARS	9.47%	5.40%	57.0%	15.97%	9.37%	58.7%						
USDBRL	8.60%	11.70%	136.1%	12.73%	19.54%	153.4%						
USDCAD	5.06%	4.67%	92.3%	7.21%	6.81%	94.4%	11.93%	7.75%	65.0%	14.51%	6.42%	44.2%
USDCHF	6.22%	6.06%	97.6%	8.73%	7.97%	91.3%	11.75%	9.10%	77.4%	12.87%	9.64%	74.9%
USDCLP	7.15%	6.81%	95.4%	10.32%	8.92%	86.5%						
USDCOP	8.54%	8.10%	94.8%	13.08%	9.47%	72.4%						
USDCZK	7.72%	7.94%	102.9%	10.88%	9.90%	91.0%						

(continued)

TABLE A.35 (Continued)

	6M			12M			2Y			3Y		
	Premium	Payoff	Ratio	Premium	Payoff	Ratio	Premium	Payoff	Ratio	Premium	Payoff	Ratio
USDDKK	6.37%	5.86%	91.9%	9.13%	7.09%	77.7%	12.28%	6.76%	55.0%	13.39%	6.08%	45.4%
USDHKD	0.63%	0.26%	41.5%	1.27%	0.39%	30.8%						
USDIDR	8.29%	7.32%	88.4%	12.94%	11.17%	86.3%						
USDILS	4.70%	5.26%	111.9%	6.57%	7.66%	116.5%						
USDINR	5.17%	5.08%	98.2%	10.36%	7.13%	68.8%						
USDJPY	6.29%	6.35%	101.0%	8.77%	8.69%	99.0%	11.89%	12.09%	101.6%	13.24%	12.91%	97.5%
USDKRW	6.01%	5.53%	92.0%	8.52%	8.46%	99.3%						
USDMXN	6.72%	5.32%	79.2%	9.84%	8.06%	82.0%						
USDNOK	6.94%	6.65%	95.8%	9.78%	9.53%	97.4%	14.30%	9.31%	65.1%	16.02%	8.00%	49.9%
USDPHP	7.00%	4.50%	64.3%	10.31%	7.61%	73.8%						
USDPLN	8.44%	8.39%	99.5%	11.90%	12.17%	102.3%						
USDSEK	7.00%	6.89%	98.4%	9.83%	10.18%	103.6%	14.48%	10.83%	74.8%	16.56%	8.56%	51.7%
USDSGD	3.54%	3.03%	85.6%	5.14%	4.07%	79.1%						
USDTRY	8.39%	8.75%	104.3%	12.70%	13.37%	105.3%						
USDTWD	3.21%	3.02%	94.1%	4.85%	3.99%	82.2%						
USDZAR	9.62%	10.41%	108.3%	13.59%	16.34%	120.2%						

TABLE A.36 Payoff/premium ratio for ATMF straddles averaged over all currency pairs

Tenor	Ratio
1W	83.3%
1M	86.7%
3M	88.9%
6M	92.9%
12M	92.4%
2Y	89.3%
3Y	91.1%

TABLE A.37 Payoff/premium ratio for 25-delta straddles (1W–3M tenors)

	1W			1M			3M		
	Premium	Payoff	Ratio	Premium	Payoff	Ratio	Premium	Payoff	Ratio
AUDUSD	0.58%	0.48%	81.8%	1.05%	1.05%	100.0%	1.84%	2.01%	108.8%
EURAUD	0.56%	0.42%	73.6%	0.99%	0.90%	90.6%	1.75%	1.57%	89.9%
EURCHF	0.29%	0.18%	61.7%	0.51%	0.38%	75.0%	0.87%	0.60%	69.3%
EURCZK	0.39%	0.21%	55.0%	0.71%	0.38%	54.0%	1.23%	0.70%	57.0%
EURGBP	0.40%	0.28%	69.7%	0.74%	0.52%	70.9%	1.33%	0.85%	64.0%
EURHUF	0.57%	0.33%	57.6%	1.08%	0.59%	54.8%	1.90%	1.10%	57.9%
EURJPY	0.60%	0.47%	78.4%	1.14%	0.96%	84.6%	1.99%	1.85%	93.3%
EURNOK	0.38%	0.24%	62.1%	0.69%	0.49%	70.7%	1.19%	0.82%	69.3%
EURPLN				1.05%	0.61%	57.6%	1.80%	1.33%	73.5%
EURUSD	0.49%	0.37%	75.5%	0.95%	0.85%	89.6%	1.71%	1.58%	92.5%
GBPUSD	0.44%	0.32%	73.5%	0.83%	0.69%	83.4%	1.49%	1.14%	77.0%
USDARS				1.41%	0.16%	11.5%	2.97%	0.52%	17.5%
USDBRL	0.78%	0.52%	66.1%	1.39%	1.28%	91.9%	2.43%	2.97%	122.0%
USDCAD	0.43%	0.32%	73.6%	0.82%	0.59%	71.8%	1.43%	1.06%	74.4%
USDCHF	0.52%	0.42%	80.6%	0.97%	0.94%	96.8%	1.74%	1.64%	94.2%
USDCLP				1.20%	0.84%	70.2%	2.15%	1.78%	82.8%
USDCOP				1.57%	0.99%	63.2%	2.73%	2.20%	80.7%
USDCZK	0.77%	0.54%	70.1%	1.41%	1.28%	90.7%	2.42%	2.10%	86.8%
USDDKK	0.57%	0.34%	59.7%	1.05%	0.80%	76.0%	1.83%	1.24%	67.9%
USDHKD	0.07%	0.01%	14.9%	0.10%	0.02%	23.7%	0.20%	0.06%	28.1%
USDIDR				1.48%	0.67%	44.8%	2.80%	1.34%	48.0%
USDILS				0.85%	0.67%	79.1%	1.43%	1.25%	87.3%
USDINR				0.86%	0.71%	82.4%	1.57%	1.45%	92.6%
USDJPY	0.54%	0.35%	65.1%	1.03%	0.84%	82.0%	1.79%	1.69%	94.1%
USDKRW	0.59%	0.31%	52.6%	1.00%	0.73%	73.1%	1.81%	1.39%	77.0%
USDMXN	0.61%	0.32%	53.4%	1.09%	0.65%	59.4%	1.97%	1.15%	58.6%
USDNOK	0.61%	0.46%	74.6%	1.12%	0.89%	79.1%	1.97%	1.59%	81.1%
USDPHP				1.19%	0.42%	35.3%	2.24%	0.84%	37.4%
USDPLN				1.41%	1.19%	84.5%	2.49%	2.16%	86.7%
USDSEK	0.61%	0.43%	70.9%	1.13%	0.90%	79.8%	1.99%	1.61%	81.0%
USDSGD	0.33%	0.17%	50.2%	0.57%	0.41%	72.7%	1.03%	0.68%	66.5%
USDTRY	0.62%	0.51%	82.5%	1.29%	1.12%	87.1%	2.33%	2.21%	94.8%
USDTWD	0.32%	0.12%	37.4%	0.49%	0.39%	78.8%	0.92%	0.83%	90.7%
USDZAR	0.87%	0.59%	67.6%	1.64%	1.26%	77.1%	2.81%	2.51%	89.2%

TABLE A.38 Payoff/premium ratio for 25-delta straddles (6M–3Y tenors)

	6M			12M			2Y			3Y		
	Premium	Payoff	Ratio	Premium	Payoff	Ratio	Premium	Payoff	Ratio	Premium	Payoff	Ratio
AUDUSD	2.61%	3.41%	130.8%	3.82%	5.40%	141.6%	5.67%	7.46%	131.7%	6.82%	9.40%	137.9%
EURAUD	2.49%	2.46%	98.9%	3.57%	4.09%	114.5%	4.96%	7.80%	157.1%	5.55%	13.03%	234.8%
EURCHF	1.24%	0.87%	70.1%	1.74%	1.63%	93.5%	2.72%	4.54%	166.9%	2.64%	6.67%	252.6%
EURCZK	1.73%	1.10%	63.9%	2.41%	1.69%	70.2%						
EURGBP	1.92%	1.17%	61.2%	2.78%	1.81%	65.1%	4.32%	3.66%	84.6%	5.32%	4.97%	93.4%
EURHUF	2.70%	1.73%	64.3%	3.80%	1.57%	41.4%						
EURJPY	2.86%	2.97%	103.7%	4.04%	4.51%	111.7%	6.29%	6.13%	97.5%	8.39%	5.93%	70.7%
EURNOK	1.66%	1.12%	67.4%	2.32%	1.66%	71.2%	3.51%	1.52%	43.4%	4.18%	2.27%	54.3%
EURPLN	2.53%	2.12%	83.7%	3.57%	3.28%	91.8%						
EURUSD	2.46%	2.23%	90.7%	3.57%	3.32%	93.2%	5.17%	1.60%	31.0%	6.01%	0.88%	14.7%
GBPUSD	2.15%	1.72%	79.9%	3.13%	2.48%	79.2%	5.10%	4.98%	97.7%	6.31%	5.37%	85.0%
USDARS	4.69%	0.93%	19.9%	7.79%	1.74%	22.4%						
USDBRL	3.50%	5.48%	156.7%	5.20%	9.47%	182.1%						
USDCAD	2.04%	1.71%	84.0%	3.01%	2.61%	86.9%	5.10%	1.73%	33.8%	6.56%	0.54%	8.2%
USDCHF	2.49%	2.27%	91.2%	3.58%	3.09%	86.4%	5.08%	2.11%	41.6%	5.94%	1.98%	33.3%
USDCLP	3.09%	2.60%	84.4%	4.47%	3.37%	75.5%						
USDCOP	3.89%	3.29%	84.6%	6.02%	2.82%	46.8%						
USDCZK	3.42%	3.36%	98.1%	4.89%	4.04%	82.7%						

USDDKK	2.64%	1.82%	69.1%	3.83%	1.97%	51.5%	5.34%	1.70%	31.9%	6.21%	0.87%	14.1%
USDHKD	0.34%	0.07%	19.9%	0.68%	0.07%	9.7%						
USDIDR	4.19%	2.95%	70.3%	6.45%	4.09%	63.4%						
USDILS	1.99%	2.23%	111.9%	2.79%	3.24%	116.3%						
USDINR	2.28%	1.97%	86.6%	4.62%	1.23%	26.7%						
USDJPY	2.53%	2.42%	95.6%	3.59%	3.35%	93.2%	5.12%	3.77%	73.6%	6.07%	3.66%	60.3%
USDKRW	2.52%	2.28%	90.3%	3.58%	3.49%	97.6%						
USDMXN	2.84%	1.69%	59.5%	4.17%	2.29%	55.0%						
USDNOK	2.80%	2.42%	86.4%	4.02%	3.84%	95.6%	6.24%	1.89%	30.3%	7.44%	0.89%	12.0%
USDPHP	3.34%	1.43%	42.7%	5.05%	2.53%	50.2%						
USDPLN	3.50%	3.46%	99.1%	4.94%	5.07%	102.5%						
USDSEK	2.82%	2.63%	93.2%	4.04%	4.18%	103.5%	6.34%	3.03%	47.8%	7.68%	0.75%	9.8%
USDSGD	1.49%	0.94%	62.9%	2.16%	1.17%	53.9%						
USDTRY	3.44%	3.28%	95.5%	5.18%	4.83%	93.4%						
USDTWD	1.37%	1.22%	89.1%	2.05%	1.20%	58.8%						
USDZAR	3.95%	4.17%	105.6%	5.58%	7.16%	128.3%						

TABLE A.39 Payoff/premium ratio for 25-delta straddles averaged over all currency pairs

Tenor	Ratio
1W	64.3%
1M	71.8%
3M	76.2%
6M	82.7%
12M	81.1%
2Y	76.4%
3Y	77.2%

TABLE A.40 Payoff/premium ratio for 10-delta straddles (1W–3M tenors)

	1W			1M			3M		
	Premium	Payoff	Ratio	Premium	Payoff	Ratio	Premium	Payoff	Ratio
AUDUSD	0.21%	0.14%	65.8%	0.36%	0.33%	93.2%	0.64%	0.81%	127.5%
EURAUD	0.22%	0.13%	60.1%	0.35%	0.29%	81.7%	0.62%	0.55%	88.3%
EURCHF	0.12%	0.05%	41.8%	0.20%	0.09%	48.2%	0.33%	0.17%	50.5%
EURCZK	0.16%	0.07%	40.9%	0.27%	0.10%	35.3%	0.47%	0.16%	34.9%
EURGBP	0.15%	0.07%	49.4%	0.26%	0.12%	46.5%	0.46%	0.24%	51.3%
EURHUF	0.23%	0.08%	33.5%	0.41%	0.13%	30.9%	0.73%	0.20%	27.0%
EURJPY	0.22%	0.14%	63.4%	0.40%	0.30%	73.8%	0.70%	0.65%	92.5%
EURNOK	0.15%	0.07%	47.8%	0.25%	0.12%	49.8%	0.43%	0.25%	58.2%
EURPLN				0.39%	0.13%	31.9%	0.67%	0.38%	57.2%
EURUSD	0.18%	0.10%	57.4%	0.32%	0.24%	74.4%	0.58%	0.44%	74.8%
GBPUSD	0.16%	0.09%	53.1%	0.28%	0.21%	72.9%	0.51%	0.41%	80.2%
USDARS				0.73%	0.04%	5.3%	1.49%	0.10%	6.4%
USDBRL	0.31%	0.16%	50.5%	0.47%	0.44%	92.6%	0.85%	1.05%	124.2%
USDCAD	0.16%	0.07%	46.1%	0.28%	0.17%	60.2%	0.50%	0.40%	79.7%
USDCHF	0.19%	0.12%	63.6%	0.33%	0.30%	89.6%	0.59%	0.49%	82.1%
USDCLP				0.47%	0.27%	57.9%	0.86%	0.61%	71.4%
USDCOP				0.68%	0.26%	38.4%	1.16%	0.80%	69.4%
USDCZK	0.35%	0.14%	39.4%	0.58%	0.40%	69.2%	0.97%	0.60%	62.1%
USDDKK	0.24%	0.09%	37.4%	0.39%	0.21%	54.0%	0.67%	0.32%	47.6%
USDHKD	0.04%	0.00%	2.6%	0.06%	0.01%	12.9%	0.11%	0.02%	21.5%
USDIDR				0.73%	0.20%	27.7%	1.37%	0.57%	41.5%
USDILS				0.34%	0.18%	54.2%	0.56%	0.34%	61.5%
USDINR				0.34%	0.28%	82.6%	0.62%	0.50%	80.0%
USDJPY	0.19%	0.10%	49.4%	0.37%	0.25%	68.3%	0.64%	0.54%	84.4%
USDKRW	0.25%	0.09%	34.7%	0.38%	0.24%	64.3%	0.70%	0.60%	85.6%
USDMXN	0.24%	0.09%	36.4%	0.41%	0.19%	47.4%	0.73%	0.42%	58.0%
USDNOK	0.25%	0.14%	55.8%	0.39%	0.29%	73.8%	0.68%	0.59%	87.1%
USDPHP				0.54%	0.13%	24.5%	1.01%	0.25%	24.4%
USDPLN				0.52%	0.37%	72.0%	0.92%	0.71%	77.1%
USDSEK	0.24%	0.13%	53.6%	0.39%	0.26%	66.8%	0.69%	0.50%	72.9%
USDSGD	0.14%	0.04%	28.1%	0.21%	0.12%	58.2%	0.39%	0.16%	40.3%
USDTRY	0.24%	0.15%	61.4%	0.47%	0.39%	81.6%	0.86%	0.70%	81.8%
USDTWD	0.14%	0.03%	18.6%	0.19%	0.14%	70.4%	0.36%	0.29%	82.7%
USDZAR	0.34%	0.18%	51.4%	0.60%	0.36%	60.6%	1.02%	0.94%	92.0%

TABLE A.41 Payoff/premium ratio for 10-delta straddles (6M–3Y tenors)

	6M			12M			2Y			3Y		
	Premium	Payoff	Ratio	Premium	Payoff	Ratio	Premium	Payoff	Ratio	Premium	Payoff	Ratio
AUDUSD	0.90%	1.36%	150.1%	1.36%	2.31%	170.5%	1.97%	2.84%	144.4%	2.35%	2.70%	114.7%
EURAUD	0.89%	0.55%	61.9%	1.28%	0.91%	70.8%	1.78%	2.31%	129.6%	2.02%	5.69%	282.3%
EURCHF	0.47%	0.24%	50.9%	0.66%	0.54%	80.7%	1.05%	1.47%	139.7%	1.07%	2.26%	210.3%
EURCZK	0.66%	0.47%	71.8%	0.92%	0.64%	70.0%						
EURGBP	0.67%	0.38%	56.8%	0.97%	0.71%	73.8%	1.53%	2.26%	147.9%	1.95%	2.65%	136.1%
EURHUF	1.03%	0.42%	40.3%	1.46%	0.15%	10.4%						
EURJPY	1.02%	1.08%	105.6%	1.44%	1.18%	81.8%	2.38%	1.42%	59.6%	3.34%	0.46%	13.7%
EURNOK	0.61%	0.33%	54.3%	0.85%	0.37%	43.8%	1.33%	0.07%	5.1%	1.63%	0.13%	8.3%
EURPLN	0.94%	0.77%	81.9%	1.33%	1.25%	94.1%						
EURUSD	0.84%	0.61%	71.9%	1.22%	1.04%	84.8%	1.83%	0.14%	7.8%	2.15%	0.01%	0.3%
GBPUSD	0.74%	0.66%	88.6%	1.08%	0.89%	82.2%	1.83%	2.10%	114.7%	2.27%	1.53%	67.2%
USDARS	2.24%	0.15%	6.7%	3.67%	0.12%	3.2%						
USDBRL	1.22%	2.16%	177.1%	1.80%	3.85%	213.6%						
USDCAD	0.71%	0.73%	102.5%	1.08%	0.91%	84.1%	1.80%	0.10%	5.5%	2.35%	0.00%	0.0%
USDCHF	0.85%	0.63%	73.8%	1.22%	1.02%	83.5%	1.82%	0.10%	5.4%	2.14%	0.08%	3.6%
USDCLP	1.24%	1.00%	80.5%	1.83%	0.96%	52.7%						
USDCOP	1.63%	1.26%	77.6%	2.45%	0.38%	15.4%						
USDCZK	1.35%	1.29%	95.5%	1.91%	1.47%	76.8%						

(*continued*)

TABLE A.41 (Continued)

	6M			12M			2Y			3Y		
	Premium	Payoff	Ratio	Premium	Payoff	Ratio	Premium	Payoff	Ratio	Premium	Payoff	Ratio
USDDKK	0.95%	0.45%	46.7%	1.38%	0.37%	27.2%	1.91%	0.21%	11.2%	2.22%	0.04%	1.7%
USDHKD	0.17%	0.03%	18.3%	0.38%	0.03%	7.7%						
USDIDR	2.05%	1.20%	58.3%	3.06%	1.69%	55.3%						
USDILS	0.77%	0.70%	90.9%	1.08%	1.04%	96.2%						
USDINR	0.91%	0.62%	68.6%	1.86%	0.02%	1.3%						
USDJPY	0.89%	0.74%	83.4%	1.24%	0.87%	70.1%	1.89%	0.37%	19.7%	2.28%	0.00%	0.1%
USDKRW	0.95%	1.16%	122.5%	1.35%	1.63%	120.8%						
USDMXN	1.06%	0.68%	64.2%	1.55%	0.59%	37.9%						
USDNOK	0.97%	0.88%	90.9%	1.38%	1.38%	99.5%	2.25%	0.08%	3.7%	2.68%	0.01%	0.5%
USDPHP	1.45%	0.41%	28.0%	2.25%	0.64%	28.3%						
USDPLN	1.28%	1.60%	124.5%	1.82%	2.30%	126.3%						
USDSEK	0.98%	0.82%	83.7%	1.39%	1.34%	96.5%	2.32%	0.36%	15.5%	2.84%	0.00%	0.1%
USDSGD	0.56%	0.19%	32.9%	0.82%	0.26%	31.4%						
USDTRY	1.26%	0.89%	70.7%	1.88%	1.49%	79.0%						
USDTWD	0.53%	0.38%	71.4%	0.78%	0.34%	43.8%						
USDZAR	1.44%	1.42%	99.1%	2.03%	3.21%	158.4%						

TABLE A.42 Payoff/premium ratio for 10-delta straddles averaged over all currency pairs

Tenor	Ratio
1W	45.7%
1M	58.0%
3M	66.9%
6M	76.5%
12M	72.7%
2Y	57.8%
3Y	59.9%

CHAPTER 6

Payoff/Premium Ratios for G10 and EM Straddles (All Data)

TABLE A.43 Payoff/premium ratios for ATMF G10 straddles (1W–3M tenors)

	1W			1M			3M		
	Premium	Payoff	Ratio	Premium	Payoff	Ratio	Premium	Payoff	Ratio
AUDUSD	1.43%	1.30%	91.4%	2.67%	2.74%	102.7%	4.61%	4.72%	102.4%
EURAUD	1.29%	1.15%	89.4%	2.42%	2.37%	97.8%	4.28%	4.16%	97.2%
EURCHF	0.64%	0.52%	82.0%	1.20%	1.07%	89.4%	2.07%	1.74%	84.0%
EURGBP	0.95%	0.83%	87.1%	1.85%	1.62%	87.4%	3.31%	2.78%	84.0%
EURJPY	1.43%	1.31%	91.1%	2.84%	2.68%	94.4%	4.95%	4.85%	97.8%
EURNOK	0.88%	0.71%	80.9%	1.68%	1.45%	86.3%	2.90%	2.47%	85.2%
EURUSD	1.21%	1.09%	90.5%	2.42%	2.36%	97.4%	4.33%	4.23%	97.8%
GBPUSD	1.06%	0.94%	88.6%	2.08%	1.94%	93.2%	3.72%	3.23%	86.9%
USDCAD	1.04%	0.95%	91.3%	2.08%	1.80%	86.6%	3.58%	3.06%	85.6%
USDCHF	1.25%	1.16%	92.4%	2.48%	2.49%	100.5%	4.39%	4.33%	98.6%
USDDKK	1.28%	1.05%	82.3%	2.51%	2.32%	92.3%	4.44%	3.82%	86.2%
USDJPY	1.31%	1.09%	82.7%	2.57%	2.40%	93.5%	4.47%	4.39%	98.2%
USDNOK	1.43%	1.28%	89.6%	2.79%	2.49%	89.1%	4.91%	4.50%	91.7%
USDSEK	1.44%	1.26%	87.6%	2.84%	2.60%	91.7%	4.97%	4.52%	90.9%

TABLE A.44 Payoff/premium ratios for ATMF G10 straddles (6M–3Y tenors)

	6M			12M			2Y			3Y		
	Premium	Payoff	Ratio	Premium	Payoff	Ratio	Premium	Payoff	Ratio	Premium	Payoff	Ratio
AUDUSD	6.39%	7.32%	114.6%	8.90%	10.94%	123.0%	12.38%	14.73%	119.0%	13.71%	17.41%	127.0%
EURAUD	6.11%	6.71%	109.7%	8.78%	10.34%	117.7%	12.12%	17.00%	140.3%	13.18%	24.45%	185.5%
EURCHF	2.94%	2.53%	86.1%	4.14%	4.06%	98.0%	6.34%	9.24%	145.8%	6.01%	11.62%	193.4%
EURGBP	4.74%	3.81%	80.3%	6.74%	5.34%	79.2%	10.02%	7.68%	76.7%	11.54%	10.54%	91.3%
EURJPY	7.02%	7.23%	102.9%	9.79%	11.05%	112.9%	14.25%	15.67%	110.0%	17.76%	18.32%	103.2%
EURNOK	4.05%	3.45%	85.2%	5.67%	5.35%	94.5%	8.30%	6.47%	77.9%	9.60%	8.33%	86.8%
EURUSD	6.18%	6.22%	100.8%	8.76%	8.68%	99.0%	12.11%	6.57%	54.3%	13.40%	6.20%	46.3%
GBPUSD	5.31%	4.78%	90.1%	7.51%	6.35%	84.6%	11.70%	10.24%	87.6%	13.54%	10.64%	78.6%
USDCAD	5.06%	4.67%	92.3%	7.21%	6.81%	94.4%	11.93%	7.75%	65.0%	14.51%	6.42%	44.2%
USDCHF	6.22%	6.06%	97.6%	8.73%	7.97%	91.3%	11.75%	9.10%	77.4%	12.87%	9.64%	74.9%
USDDKK	6.37%	5.86%	91.9%	9.13%	7.09%	77.7%	12.28%	6.76%	55.0%	13.39%	6.08%	45.4%
USDJPY	6.29%	6.35%	101.0%	8.77%	8.69%	99.0%	11.89%	12.09%	101.6%	13.24%	12.91%	97.5%
USDNOK	6.94%	6.65%	95.8%	9.78%	9.53%	97.4%	14.30%	9.31%	65.1%	16.02%	8.00%	49.9%
USDSEK	7.00%	6.89%	98.4%	9.83%	10.18%	103.6%	14.48%	10.83%	74.8%	16.56%	8.56%	51.7%

TABLE A.45 Payoff/premium ratios for ATMF
G10 straddles averaged over all currency pairs

Tenor	Ratio
1W	78.8%
1M	79.5%
3M	68.5%
6M	64.6%
12M	75.7%
2Y	129.3%
3Y	89.5%

TABLE A.46 Payoff/premium ratios for ATMF EM straddles (1W–3M tenors)

	1W			1M			3M		
	Premium	Payoff	Ratio	Premium	Payoff	Ratio	Premium	Payoff	Ratio
EURCZK	0.87%	0.67%	77.1%	1.67%	1.32%	79.2%	2.88%	2.29%	79.8%
EURHUF	1.28%	1.04%	81.0%	2.51%	1.98%	78.8%	4.44%	3.73%	84.1%
EURPLN				2.50%	2.05%	81.8%	4.32%	3.84%	89.1%
USDARS				2.67%	1.07%	40.2%	5.84%	3.02%	51.8%
USDBRL	1.77%	1.50%	85.2%	3.42%	3.36%	98.2%	5.99%	6.81%	113.7%
USDCLP				2.78%	2.43%	87.3%	4.97%	4.80%	96.6%
USDCOP				3.43%	2.89%	84.3%	6.00%	5.50%	91.7%
USDCZK	1.61%	1.47%	91.6%	3.14%	3.18%	101.3%	5.47%	5.53%	101.2%
USDHKD	0.11%	0.05%	43.6%	0.19%	0.09%	48.6%	0.37%	0.18%	50.6%
USDIDR				2.92%	2.03%	69.6%	5.54%	3.95%	71.3%
USDILS				1.99%	1.89%	95.2%	3.37%	3.38%	100.3%
USDINR				1.97%	1.83%	92.7%	3.58%	3.52%	98.3%
USDKRW	1.31%	1.02%	77.6%	2.40%	2.09%	87.2%	4.26%	3.63%	85.2%
USDMXN	1.35%	1.06%	78.6%	2.58%	2.08%	80.5%	4.65%	3.82%	82.1%
USDPHP				2.47%	1.42%	57.6%	4.64%	2.91%	62.7%
USDPLN				3.40%	3.22%	94.5%	5.99%	5.89%	98.3%
USDSGD	0.73%	0.55%	75.9%	1.34%	1.20%	89.4%	2.43%	2.13%	87.5%
USDTRY	1.45%	1.41%	97.1%	3.14%	3.05%	97.2%	5.67%	5.66%	99.8%
USDTWD	0.66%	0.42%	63.8%	1.15%	1.02%	89.1%	2.14%	2.08%	97.2%
USDZAR	2.03%	1.73%	85.4%	3.96%	3.62%	91.2%	6.83%	6.44%	94.4%

TABLE A.47   Payoff/premium ratios for ATMF EM straddles (6M–12M tenors)

	6M			12M		
	Premium	**Payoff**	**Ratio**	**Premium**	**Payoff**	**Ratio**
EURCZK	4.03%	3.30%	81.9%	5.63%	5.13%	91.0%
EURHUF	6.31%	5.27%	83.6%	8.91%	6.30%	70.7%
EURPLN	6.05%	5.66%	93.6%	8.53%	8.52%	99.8%
USDARS	9.47%	5.40%	57.0%	15.97%	9.37%	58.7%
USDBRL	8.60%	11.70%	136.1%	12.73%	19.54%	153.4%
USDCLP	7.15%	6.81%	95.4%	10.32%	8.92%	86.5%
USDCOP	8.54%	8.10%	94.8%	13.08%	9.47%	72.4%
USDCZK	7.72%	7.94%	102.9%	10.88%	9.90%	91.0%
USDHKD	0.63%	0.26%	41.5%	1.27%	0.39%	30.8%
USDIDR	8.29%	7.32%	88.4%	12.94%	11.17%	86.3%
USDILS	4.70%	5.26%	111.9%	6.57%	7.66%	116.5%
USDINR	5.17%	5.08%	98.2%	10.36%	7.13%	68.8%
USDKRW	6.01%	5.53%	92.0%	8.52%	8.46%	99.3%
USDMXN	6.72%	5.32%	79.2%	9.84%	8.06%	82.0%
USDPHP	7.00%	4.50%	64.3%	10.31%	7.61%	73.8%
USDPLN	8.44%	8.39%	99.5%	11.90%	12.17%	102.3%
USDSGD	3.54%	3.03%	85.6%	5.14%	4.07%	79.1%
USDTRY	8.39%	8.75%	104.3%	12.70%	13.37%	105.3%
USDTWD	3.21%	3.02%	94.1%	4.85%	3.99%	82.2%
USDZAR	9.62%	10.41%	108.3%	13.59%	16.34%	120.2%

TABLE A.48   Payoff/premium ratios for ATMF
EM straddles averaged over all currency pairs

Tenor	Ratio
1W	77.9%
1M	82.2%
3M	86.8%
6M	90.6%
12M	88.5%

Payoff/Premium Ratios for G10 and EM ATMF Puts
(All Data)

TABLE A.49 Payoff/premium ratios for ATMF G10 puts (1W–3M tenors)

	1W			1M			3M		
	Premium	Payoff	Ratio	Premium	Payoff	Ratio	Premium	Payoff	Ratio
AUDUSD	0.71%	0.62%	86.8%	1.33%	1.26%	94.9%	2.30%	2.11%	91.5%
EURAUD	0.64%	0.62%	96.0%	1.21%	1.34%	111.2%	2.13%	2.69%	126.1%
EURCHF	0.32%	0.27%	83.9%	0.60%	0.55%	92.0%	1.03%	0.94%	90.4%
EURGBP	0.47%	0.41%	87.1%	0.93%	0.82%	89.0%	1.65%	1.39%	84.4%
EURJPY	0.72%	0.63%	87.8%	1.42%	1.24%	87.6%	2.47%	2.17%	87.9%
EURNOK	0.44%	0.38%	85.4%	0.84%	0.81%	96.3%	1.45%	1.47%	101.0%
EURUSD	0.60%	0.54%	89.9%	1.21%	1.15%	95.2%	2.16%	2.03%	94.1%
GBPUSD	0.53%	0.47%	87.8%	1.04%	0.92%	88.1%	1.85%	1.50%	81.0%
USDCAD	0.52%	0.50%	96.5%	1.04%	1.03%	99.7%	1.78%	1.87%	105.1%
USDCHF	0.63%	0.60%	95.6%	1.24%	1.27%	102.9%	2.19%	2.20%	100.5%
USDDKK	0.64%	0.53%	83.9%	1.25%	1.20%	95.7%	2.21%	2.01%	91.0%
USDJPY	0.66%	0.54%	81.8%	1.28%	1.11%	86.3%	2.24%	1.94%	86.6%
USDNOK	0.72%	0.68%	94.5%	1.40%	1.40%	100.3%	2.45%	2.70%	109.9%
USDSEK	0.72%	0.65%	90.9%	1.42%	1.39%	98.0%	2.48%	2.50%	100.7%

TABLE A.50 Payoff/premium ratios for ATMF G10 puts (6M–3Y tenors)

	6M			12M			2Y			3Y		
	Premium	Payoff	Ratio	Premium	Payoff	Ratio	Premium	Payoff	Ratio	Premium	Payoff	Ratio
AUDUSD	3.19%	3.15%	98.6%	4.44%	4.50%	101.4%	6.21%	2.24%	36.1%	6.88%	0.85%	12.3%
EURAUD	3.06%	4.55%	148.7%	4.37%	7.98%	182.4%	6.09%	15.42%	253.1%	6.63%	22.78%	343.6%
EURCHF	1.47%	1.40%	95.0%	2.07%	2.35%	113.6%	3.23%	7.15%	221.5%	3.11%	10.63%	341.2%
EURGBP	2.37%	1.87%	79.1%	3.37%	2.46%	73.1%	5.03%	2.12%	42.1%	5.83%	2.42%	41.5%
EURJPY	3.51%	3.15%	89.8%	4.90%	4.42%	90.2%	7.17%	9.34%	130.3%	8.98%	14.79%	164.7%
EURNOK	2.03%	2.17%	107.0%	2.83%	3.66%	129.5%	4.17%	5.01%	120.2%	4.82%	6.61%	137.2%
EURUSD	3.08%	2.93%	95.0%	4.37%	3.94%	90.0%	6.09%	3.06%	50.3%	6.75%	3.38%	50.1%
GBPUSD	2.65%	2.24%	84.5%	3.75%	2.96%	79.0%	5.86%	6.94%	118.5%	6.81%	8.83%	129.7%
USDCAD	2.53%	3.05%	120.9%	3.60%	4.90%	136.3%	5.97%	5.90%	98.9%	7.26%	5.35%	73.7%
USDCHF	3.11%	3.15%	101.4%	4.36%	4.38%	100.5%	5.91%	7.41%	125.3%	6.47%	9.42%	145.7%
USDDKK	3.17%	3.21%	101.1%	4.54%	4.10%	90.1%	6.18%	4.04%	65.4%	6.77%	3.20%	47.2%
USDJPY	3.15%	2.68%	85.1%	4.39%	3.46%	78.8%	5.97%	7.68%	128.6%	6.70%	9.74%	145.2%
USDNOK	3.47%	4.21%	121.4%	4.88%	6.66%	136.5%	7.18%	6.83%	95.2%	8.08%	6.36%	78.8%
USDSEK	3.50%	3.94%	112.6%	4.91%	6.21%	126.6%	7.28%	7.34%	100.8%	8.36%	5.82%	69.6%

TABLE A.51 Payoff/premium ratios for ATMF
G10 puts averaged over all currency pairs

Tenor	Ratio
1W	89.1%
1M	95.5%
3M	96.4%
6M	102.9%
12M	109.1%
2Y	113.3%
3Y	127.2%

TABLE A.52 Payoff/premium ratios for ATMF EM puts (1W–3M tenors)

	1W			1M			3M		
	Premium	Payoff	Ratio	Premium	Payoff	Ratio	Premium	Payoff	Ratio
EURCZK	0.43%	0.36%	82.2%	0.83%	0.76%	91.1%	1.43%	1.45%	101.0%
EURHUF	0.64%	0.56%	87.3%	1.25%	1.14%	91.2%	2.21%	2.33%	105.5%
EURPLN				1.25%	1.09%	87.3%	2.15%	2.16%	100.7%
USDARS				1.34%	0.92%	68.3%	2.95%	2.66%	90.1%
USDBRL	0.88%	0.87%	98.6%	1.71%	2.16%	126.2%	2.99%	4.91%	164.1%
USDCLP				1.39%	1.34%	96.4%	2.48%	2.80%	113.0%
USDCOP				1.71%	1.74%	102.0%	2.97%	3.56%	120.0%
USDCZK	0.80%	0.76%	94.5%	1.56%	1.70%	108.7%	2.72%	3.07%	112.8%
USDHKD	0.06%	0.02%	36.0%	0.09%	0.03%	32.4%	0.18%	0.05%	26.5%
USDIDR				1.46%	1.17%	80.1%	2.78%	2.42%	87.2%
USDILS				0.99%	1.14%	115.3%	1.68%	2.24%	133.6%
USDINR				0.99%	1.01%	102.6%	1.81%	1.97%	109.1%
USDKRW	0.65%	0.54%	83.3%	1.20%	1.17%	97.6%	2.12%	2.10%	98.8%
USDMXN	0.67%	0.55%	81.1%	1.29%	1.15%	89.4%	2.33%	2.32%	99.7%
USDPHP				1.23%	0.86%	70.2%	2.31%	1.89%	81.7%
USDPLN				1.70%	1.93%	113.5%	2.99%	3.74%	125.3%
USDSGD	0.36%	0.30%	82.3%	0.67%	0.67%	100.6%	1.21%	1.29%	106.1%
USDTRY	0.72%	0.78%	107.5%	1.57%	1.87%	119.1%	2.82%	3.66%	129.4%
USDTWD	0.33%	0.21%	62.8%	0.57%	0.48%	84.0%	1.07%	0.93%	87.0%
USDZAR	1.01%	0.91%	89.4%	1.98%	2.01%	101.3%	3.41%	3.74%	109.7%

TABLE A.53 Payoff/premium ratios for ATMF EM puts (6M–12M tenors)

	6M			12M		
	Premium	Payoff	Ratio	Premium	Payoff	Ratio
EURCZK	2.01%	2.30%	114.2%	2.82%	3.87%	137.5%
EURHUF	3.15%	3.51%	111.6%	4.45%	4.58%	102.9%
EURPLN	3.02%	3.35%	110.9%	4.26%	5.36%	125.9%
USDARS	4.82%	4.79%	99.3%	8.00%	8.16%	101.9%
USDBRL	4.30%	8.97%	208.9%	6.33%	16.37%	258.8%
USDCLP	3.57%	4.23%	118.4%	5.15%	6.29%	122.3%
USDCOP	4.24%	5.68%	134.1%	6.45%	7.38%	114.5%
USDCZK	3.85%	4.62%	120.2%	5.43%	6.25%	115.2%
USDHKD	0.32%	0.06%	18.7%	0.63%	0.09%	14.7%
USDIDR	4.16%	4.58%	110.1%	6.39%	7.75%	121.3%
USDILS	2.35%	3.76%	160.1%	3.29%	6.09%	185.1%
USDINR	2.61%	2.80%	107.2%	5.15%	3.43%	66.7%
USDKRW	3.00%	3.36%	111.9%	4.25%	5.18%	122.0%
USDMXN	3.36%	3.50%	104.1%	4.91%	5.73%	116.7%
USDPHP	3.48%	3.15%	90.5%	5.12%	5.75%	112.3%
USDPLN	4.22%	5.85%	138.7%	5.95%	8.94%	150.3%
USDSGD	1.77%	1.99%	112.5%	2.57%	3.06%	119.2%
USDTRY	4.18%	6.15%	147.1%	6.29%	10.51%	167.1%
USDTWD	1.60%	1.27%	79.5%	2.42%	1.51%	62.7%
USDZAR	4.81%	6.22%	129.4%	6.79%	10.47%	154.2%

TABLE A.54 Payoff/premium ratios for ATMF
EM puts averaged over all currency pairs

Tenor	Ratio
1W	82.3%
1M	93.9%
3M	105.1%
6M	116.4%
12M	123.6%

Payoff/Premium Ratios for G10 and EM ATMF Calls (All Data)

TABLE A.55 Payoff/premium ratios for ATMF G10 calls (1W–3M tenors)

	1W			1M			3M		
	Premium	Payoff	Ratio	Premium	Payoff	Ratio	Premium	Payoff	Ratio
AUDUSD	0.71%	0.69%	96.1%	1.33%	1.47%	110.6%	2.30%	2.64%	114.7%
EURAUD	0.64%	0.53%	82.7%	1.21%	1.01%	83.6%	2.14%	1.42%	66.2%
EURCHF	0.32%	0.25%	80.0%	0.60%	0.52%	86.5%	1.04%	0.80%	77.2%
EURGBP	0.47%	0.41%	87.3%	0.93%	0.80%	86.1%	1.65%	1.40%	84.5%
EURJPY	0.72%	0.68%	94.3%	1.42%	1.44%	101.2%	2.48%	2.65%	107.0%
EURNOK	0.44%	0.34%	76.5%	0.84%	0.64%	76.1%	1.45%	0.99%	68.0%
EURUSD	0.60%	0.55%	91.0%	1.21%	1.21%	99.5%	2.16%	2.18%	100.7%
GBPUSD	0.53%	0.47%	89.2%	1.04%	1.02%	98.1%	1.86%	1.71%	92.2%
USDCAD	0.52%	0.45%	85.9%	1.04%	0.76%	73.3%	1.79%	1.17%	65.2%
USDCHF	0.63%	0.56%	89.1%	1.24%	1.21%	97.9%	2.20%	2.12%	96.3%
USDDKK	0.64%	0.52%	80.9%	1.25%	1.11%	88.5%	2.22%	1.79%	80.6%
USDJPY	0.66%	0.55%	83.6%	1.29%	1.29%	100.6%	2.24%	2.44%	109.2%
USDNOK	0.72%	0.61%	84.8%	1.40%	1.08%	77.4%	2.46%	1.78%	72.5%
USDSEK	0.72%	0.61%	84.6%	1.42%	1.21%	85.3%	2.49%	2.00%	80.5%

TABLE A.56 Payoff/premium ratios for ATMF G10 calls (6M–3Y tenors)

	6M			12M			2Y			3Y		
	Premium	Payoff	Ratio	Premium	Payoff	Ratio	Premium	Payoff	Ratio	Premium	Payoff	Ratio
AUDUSD	3.19%	4.15%	130.0%	4.45%	6.54%	146.9%	6.19%	12.59%	203.4%	6.85%	16.56%	241.6%
EURAUD	3.06%	2.06%	67.5%	4.39%	2.18%	49.7%	6.06%	1.19%	19.7%	6.59%	0.98%	14.9%
EURCHF	1.47%	1.12%	76.5%	2.07%	1.68%	81.1%	3.17%	1.91%	60.2%	3.00%	0.72%	23.9%
EURGBP	2.37%	1.97%	82.9%	3.37%	2.89%	85.8%	5.01%	5.58%	111.3%	5.77%	8.15%	141.2%
EURJPY	3.51%	4.04%	115.1%	4.89%	6.58%	134.4%	7.13%	6.12%	85.8%	8.88%	2.95%	33.2%
EURNOK	2.03%	1.25%	61.9%	2.83%	1.64%	57.9%	4.15%	1.33%	32.0%	4.80%	1.52%	31.7%
EURUSD	3.09%	3.26%	105.6%	4.38%	4.69%	107.1%	6.05%	3.43%	56.7%	6.70%	2.72%	40.6%
GBPUSD	2.65%	2.52%	94.9%	3.75%	3.36%	89.4%	5.85%	3.13%	53.4%	6.77%	1.55%	22.8%
USDCAD	2.53%	1.58%	62.3%	3.61%	1.85%	51.2%	5.96%	1.70%	28.5%	7.26%	0.88%	12.1%
USDCHF	3.11%	2.92%	94.0%	4.37%	3.57%	81.7%	5.87%	1.52%	25.9%	6.43%	0.02%	0.4%
USDDKK	3.19%	2.65%	83.0%	4.56%	2.95%	64.6%	6.14%	2.69%	43.8%	6.70%	2.84%	42.4%
USDJPY	3.14%	3.65%	116.0%	4.39%	5.20%	118.5%	5.95%	4.24%	71.3%	6.62%	2.89%	43.6%
USDNOK	3.47%	2.39%	68.9%	4.89%	2.78%	56.9%	7.15%	2.31%	32.3%	8.01%	1.45%	18.1%
USDSEK	3.50%	2.92%	83.5%	4.91%	3.90%	79.3%	7.24%	3.46%	47.8%	8.28%	2.74%	33.0%

TABLE A.57 Payoff/premium ratios for ATMF G10 calls averaged over all currency pairs

Tenor	Ratio
1W	86.1%
1M	90.3%
3M	86.8%
6M	88.7%
12M	86.1%
2Y	62.3%
3Y	50.0%

TABLE A.58 Payoff/premium ratios for ATMF EM calls (1W–3M tenors)

	1W			1M			3M		
	Premium	Payoff	Ratio	Premium	Payoff	Ratio	Premium	Payoff	Ratio
EURCZK	0.43%	0.31%	72.2%	0.84%	0.56%	67.0%	1.44%	0.83%	57.6%
EURHUF	0.64%	0.48%	74.6%	1.26%	0.83%	66.4%	2.22%	1.36%	61.3%
EURPLN				1.25%	0.95%	76.3%	2.16%	1.66%	77.1%
USDARS				1.34%	0.15%	11.1%	2.92%	0.29%	10.1%
USDBRL	0.88%	0.63%	71.5%	1.71%	1.19%	69.5%	3.00%	1.82%	60.9%
USDCLP				1.39%	1.08%	77.9%	2.49%	1.96%	78.8%
USDCOP				1.72%	1.14%	66.1%	3.00%	1.85%	61.7%
USDCZK	0.80%	0.71%	88.9%	1.57%	1.46%	93.3%	2.73%	2.41%	88.2%
USDHKD	0.06%	0.03%	51.2%	0.09%	0.06%	64.8%	0.18%	0.14%	74.5%
USDIDR				1.46%	0.84%	57.9%	2.77%	1.47%	53.3%
USDILS				0.99%	0.74%	74.9%	1.68%	1.11%	66.2%
USDINR				0.99%	0.81%	82.0%	1.79%	1.56%	86.9%
USDKRW	0.65%	0.47%	72.2%	1.20%	0.92%	76.7%	2.13%	1.52%	71.1%
USDMXN	0.67%	0.51%	75.8%	1.29%	0.92%	71.2%	2.32%	1.47%	63.3%
USDPHP				1.23%	0.55%	44.8%	2.32%	1.00%	43.1%
USDPLN				1.70%	1.28%	75.2%	3.00%	2.11%	70.6%
USDSGD	0.36%	0.25%	69.6%	0.67%	0.52%	77.8%	1.22%	0.82%	67.8%
USDTRY	0.72%	0.63%	86.5%	1.57%	1.17%	74.6%	2.84%	1.94%	68.4%
USDTWD	0.33%	0.22%	64.9%	0.57%	0.54%	93.7%	1.07%	1.14%	106.7%
USDZAR	1.01%	0.82%	81.2%	1.98%	1.60%	80.8%	3.41%	2.66%	78.0%

TABLE A.59 Payoff/premium ratios for ATMF EM calls (6M–12M tenors)

	6M			12M		
	Premium	**Payoff**	**Ratio**	**Premium**	**Payoff**	**Ratio**
EURCZK	2.02%	0.97%	48.3%	2.82%	1.21%	42.8%
EURHUF	3.15%	1.69%	53.7%	4.45%	1.64%	36.8%
EURPLN	3.03%	2.31%	76.4%	4.27%	3.12%	73.0%
USDARS	4.73%	0.49%	10.3%	7.98%	0.97%	12.2%
USDBRL	4.30%	2.58%	60.0%	6.37%	2.86%	44.9%
USDCLP	3.57%	2.52%	70.7%	5.16%	2.54%	49.2%
USDCOP	4.27%	2.27%	53.2%	6.54%	1.83%	28.0%
USDCZK	3.86%	3.22%	83.4%	5.44%	3.51%	64.6%
USDHKD	0.32%	0.20%	64.2%	0.63%	0.30%	46.8%
USDIDR	4.14%	2.64%	63.6%	6.47%	3.17%	49.0%
USDILS	2.35%	1.48%	63.1%	3.29%	1.59%	48.4%
USDINR	2.59%	2.29%	88.5%	5.18%	3.58%	69.0%
USDKRW	3.01%	2.20%	73.3%	4.26%	3.24%	76.1%
USDMXN	3.36%	1.78%	53.0%	4.92%	2.25%	45.8%
USDPHP	3.50%	1.31%	37.3%	5.16%	1.78%	34.6%
USDPLN	4.22%	2.55%	60.5%	5.95%	3.17%	53.3%
USDSGD	1.77%	1.02%	57.4%	2.57%	0.96%	37.5%
USDTRY	4.19%	2.48%	59.2%	6.35%	2.66%	41.9%
USDTWD	1.61%	1.73%	108.0%	2.42%	2.45%	101.2%
USDZAR	4.81%	4.10%	85.2%	6.80%	5.73%	84.4%

TABLE A.60 Payoff/premium ratios for ATMF
EM calls averaged over all currency pairs

Tenor	Ratio
1W	73.5%
1M	70.1%
3M	67.3%
6M	63.5%
12M	52.0%

Payoff/Premium Ratios for G10 and EM 25-Delta Puts (All Data)

TABLE A.61 Payoff/premium ratios for 25-delta G10 puts (1W–3M tenors)

	1W			1M			3M		
	Premium	Payoff	Ratio	Premium	Payoff	Ratio	Premium	Payoff	Ratio
AUDUSD	0.29%	0.23%	79.2%	0.55%	0.53%	97.2%	0.98%	1.05%	107.2%
EURAUD	0.26%	0.20%	77.1%	0.46%	0.48%	103.9%	0.81%	0.91%	112.9%
EURCHF	0.14%	0.10%	69.3%	0.25%	0.21%	83.1%	0.44%	0.38%	87.2%
EURGBP	0.19%	0.14%	72.5%	0.36%	0.23%	63.5%	0.64%	0.30%	46.1%
EURJPY	0.30%	0.23%	78.2%	0.58%	0.43%	74.8%	1.01%	0.87%	85.7%
EURNOK	0.18%	0.11%	63.0%	0.33%	0.25%	76.0%	0.56%	0.40%	71.4%
EURUSD	0.24%	0.18%	73.9%	0.49%	0.39%	80.3%	0.89%	0.80%	90.4%
GBPUSD	0.22%	0.16%	74.8%	0.42%	0.33%	78.9%	0.77%	0.56%	72.7%
USDCAD	0.21%	0.17%	83.0%	0.40%	0.34%	86.8%	0.68%	0.69%	101.3%
USDCHF	0.25%	0.23%	90.8%	0.48%	0.53%	110.2%	0.84%	0.87%	102.8%
USDDKK	0.27%	0.18%	67.6%	0.49%	0.41%	84.2%	0.85%	0.55%	65.3%
USDJPY	0.27%	0.18%	67.8%	0.52%	0.38%	74.2%	0.90%	0.73%	80.4%
USDNOK	0.30%	0.23%	78.7%	0.54%	0.52%	96.8%	0.93%	0.97%	104.2%
USDSEK	0.29%	0.22%	76.4%	0.55%	0.50%	92.2%	0.95%	0.88%	93.3%

TABLE A.62 Payoff/premium ratios for 25-delta G10 puts (6M–3Y tenors)

	6M			12M			2Y			3Y		
	Premium	Payoff	Ratio	Premium	Payoff	Ratio	Premium	Payoff	Ratio	Premium	Payoff	Ratio
AUDUSD	1.41%	1.72%	122.0%	2.10%	2.53%	120.7%	3.19%	1.07%	33.6%	3.85%	0.33%	8.6%
EURAUD	1.13%	1.47%	129.4%	1.60%	3.23%	202.4%	2.18%	7.44%	340.6%	2.40%	12.83%	534.1%
EURCHF	0.63%	0.53%	83.6%	0.91%	0.95%	105.1%	1.43%	3.67%	257.3%	1.35%	6.39%	471.9%
EURGBP	0.92%	0.36%	39.5%	1.32%	0.46%	34.7%	1.97%	0.01%	0.7%	2.38%	0.02%	1.0%
EURJPY	1.46%	1.34%	91.8%	2.06%	1.61%	78.3%	3.21%	3.06%	95.2%	4.18%	5.52%	132.2%
EURNOK	0.78%	0.53%	68.4%	1.08%	0.95%	88.4%	1.58%	1.17%	74.2%	1.86%	1.72%	92.8%
EURUSD	1.30%	1.18%	91.1%	1.91%	1.58%	82.7%	2.84%	0.62%	21.7%	3.30%	0.48%	14.7%
GBPUSD	1.13%	0.99%	87.6%	1.67%	1.40%	83.6%	2.83%	4.43%	156.7%	3.52%	5.32%	151.0%
USDCAD	0.96%	1.16%	119.8%	1.41%	1.90%	134.7%	2.33%	1.44%	62.0%	2.97%	0.42%	14.1%
USDCHF	1.20%	1.14%	94.7%	1.72%	1.63%	94.5%	2.41%	1.94%	80.7%	2.80%	1.98%	70.7%
USDDKK	1.21%	0.84%	69.4%	1.74%	1.29%	74.0%	2.42%	1.27%	52.6%	2.82%	0.68%	24.0%
USDJPY	1.28%	0.86%	67.6%	1.81%	0.64%	35.1%	2.69%	1.71%	63.5%	3.20%	3.08%	96.2%
USDNOK	1.32%	1.51%	114.5%	1.87%	2.68%	143.4%	2.81%	1.47%	52.5%	3.35%	0.86%	25.9%
USDSEK	1.33%	1.37%	103.1%	1.88%	2.30%	122.6%	2.85%	1.58%	55.6%	3.41%	0.20%	5.9%

TABLE A.63 Payoff/premium ratios for 25-delta
G10 puts averaged over all currency pairs

Tenor	Ratio
1W	75.1%
1M	85.9%
3M	87.2%
6M	91.6%
12M	100.0%
2Y	96.2%
3Y	117.4%

TABLE A.64 Payoff/premium ratios for 25-delta EM puts (1W–3M tenors)

	1W			1M			3M		
	Premium	Payoff	Ratio	Premium	Payoff	Ratio	Premium	Payoff	Ratio
EURCZK	0.18%	0.12%	68.6%	0.33%	0.23%	69.9%	0.57%	0.47%	83.8%
EURHUF	0.25%	0.18%	74.4%	0.46%	0.33%	71.2%	0.79%	0.67%	85.0%
EURPLN				0.48%	0.31%	65.9%	0.80%	0.64%	80.8%
USDARS				0.63%	0.13%	21.3%	1.31%	0.46%	35.5%
USDBRL	0.34%	0.28%	83.0%	0.61%	0.76%	124.3%	1.10%	1.96%	178.8%
USDCLP				0.57%	0.46%	80.4%	1.00%	1.03%	103.0%
USDCOP				0.72%	0.62%	86.0%	1.26%	1.50%	119.4%
USDCZK	0.36%	0.29%	80.6%	0.67%	0.70%	105.1%	1.16%	1.25%	108.1%
USDHKD	0.03%	0.00%	11.0%	0.05%	0.01%	14.8%	0.11%	0.01%	11.0%
USDIDR				0.62%	0.39%	63.3%	1.13%	0.69%	61.1%
USDILS				0.40%	0.44%	108.5%	0.66%	0.92%	139.7%
USDINR				0.39%	0.39%	99.5%	0.69%	0.71%	102.2%
USDKRW	0.27%	0.17%	62.0%	0.46%	0.38%	82.4%	0.81%	0.68%	84.3%
USDMXN	0.27%	0.16%	57.8%	0.49%	0.35%	72.4%	0.87%	0.55%	63.7%
USDPHP				0.58%	0.28%	49.1%	1.09%	0.56%	51.3%
USDPLN				0.65%	0.71%	109.7%	1.11%	1.33%	119.8%
USDSGD	0.16%	0.09%	57.6%	0.27%	0.23%	85.9%	0.48%	0.38%	78.1%
USDTRY	0.28%	0.28%	99.0%	0.57%	0.66%	114.5%	1.01%	1.29%	127.1%
USDTWD	0.15%	0.07%	45.2%	0.24%	0.18%	76.9%	0.44%	0.36%	80.5%
USDZAR	0.40%	0.28%	68.6%	0.75%	0.65%	86.4%	1.25%	1.30%	104.1%

TABLE A.65   Payoff/premium ratios for 25-delta EM puts (6M–12M tenors)

	6M			12M		
	Premium	**Payoff**	**Ratio**	**Premium**	**Payoff**	**Ratio**
EURCZK	0.79%	0.81%	102.6%	1.09%	1.47%	135.4%
EURHUF	1.10%	1.05%	95.3%	1.52%	1.32%	86.9%
EURPLN	1.10%	1.06%	96.1%	1.53%	1.84%	120.6%
USDARS	2.12%	0.90%	42.4%	3.69%	1.73%	46.8%
USDBRL	1.55%	4.23%	273.2%	2.26%	8.72%	385.4%
USDCLP	1.44%	1.62%	112.1%	2.12%	2.30%	108.4%
USDCOP	1.81%	2.35%	129.9%	2.83%	2.31%	81.7%
USDCZK	1.66%	2.10%	126.5%	2.42%	2.97%	122.9%
USDHKD	0.19%	0.01%	4.6%	0.38%	0.00%	0.2%
USDIDR	1.65%	1.59%	96.3%	2.44%	2.87%	117.7%
USDILS	0.91%	1.70%	187.6%	1.26%	2.76%	219.4%
USDINR	0.98%	0.97%	99.2%	1.85%	0.39%	21.1%
USDKRW	1.11%	0.96%	86.1%	1.55%	1.26%	81.6%
USDMXN	1.24%	0.74%	60.1%	1.78%	1.18%	66.4%
USDPHP	1.64%	0.94%	57.2%	2.51%	1.92%	76.6%
USDPLN	1.54%	2.13%	138.4%	2.12%	3.51%	165.9%
USDSGD	0.69%	0.60%	86.4%	1.00%	0.88%	88.2%
USDTRY	1.46%	2.32%	158.8%	2.16%	4.36%	202.3%
USDTWD	0.66%	0.48%	72.5%	0.98%	0.29%	29.9%
USDZAR	1.73%	2.44%	141.2%	2.38%	5.09%	214.2%

TABLE A.66   Payoff/premium ratios for 25-delta EM puts averaged over all currency pairs

Tenor	Ratio
1W	64.4%
1M	79.4%
3M	90.9%
6M	108.3%
12M	118.6%

Payoff/Premium Ratios for G10 and EM 25-Delta Calls (All Data)

TABLE A.67   Payoff/premium ratios for 25-delta G10 calls (1W–3M tenors)

	1W			1M			3M		
	Premium	Payoff	Ratio	Premium	Payoff	Ratio	Premium	Payoff	Ratio
AUDUSD	0.29%	0.24%	84.4%	0.50%	0.52%	103.1%	0.86%	0.96%	110.6%
EURAUD	0.30%	0.21%	70.6%	0.53%	0.42%	78.9%	0.94%	0.66%	70.2%
EURCHF	0.15%	0.08%	54.7%	0.26%	0.17%	67.1%	0.43%	0.22%	51.3%
EURGBP	0.21%	0.14%	67.2%	0.38%	0.30%	77.8%	0.69%	0.55%	80.8%
EURJPY	0.30%	0.24%	78.5%	0.56%	0.53%	94.8%	0.97%	0.98%	101.2%
EURNOK	0.20%	0.12%	61.4%	0.36%	0.24%	65.9%	0.63%	0.42%	67.4%
EURUSD	0.25%	0.19%	77.1%	0.46%	0.46%	99.2%	0.82%	0.78%	94.8%
GBPUSD	0.22%	0.16%	72.2%	0.40%	0.36%	88.2%	0.72%	0.58%	81.6%
USDCAD	0.23%	0.15%	64.9%	0.43%	0.25%	57.9%	0.75%	0.37%	50.0%
USDCHF	0.26%	0.19%	71.0%	0.50%	0.42%	83.8%	0.89%	0.77%	86.1%
USDDKK	0.30%	0.16%	52.8%	0.56%	0.39%	68.8%	0.98%	0.69%	70.1%
USDJPY	0.27%	0.17%	62.5%	0.51%	0.46%	89.9%	0.89%	0.96%	108.2%
USDNOK	0.32%	0.23%	70.9%	0.58%	0.36%	62.8%	1.03%	0.62%	60.2%
USDSEK	0.32%	0.21%	65.9%	0.59%	0.40%	68.3%	1.05%	0.73%	70.0%

TABLE A.68 Payoff/premium ratios for 25-delta G10 calls (6M–3Y tenors)

	6M			12M			2Y			3Y		
	Premium	Payoff	Ratio	Premium	Payoff	Ratio	Premium	Payoff	Ratio	Premium	Payoff	Ratio
AUDUSD	1.20%	1.69%	141.2%	1.72%	2.87%	167.2%	2.48%	6.39%	257.8%	2.97%	9.07%	305.1%
EURAUD	1.36%	1.00%	73.4%	1.97%	0.86%	43.5%	2.78%	0.36%	12.9%	3.15%	0.20%	6.3%
EURCHF	0.61%	0.34%	55.9%	0.84%	0.68%	81.0%	1.29%	0.87%	67.3%	1.29%	0.28%	21.7%
EURGBP	1.00%	0.81%	81.3%	1.46%	1.35%	92.8%	2.35%	3.65%	155.2%	2.93%	4.94%	168.5%
EURJPY	1.40%	1.63%	116.1%	1.98%	2.90%	146.4%	3.07%	3.07%	99.9%	4.21%	0.40%	9.6%
EURNOK	0.88%	0.59%	66.5%	1.24%	0.70%	56.3%	1.93%	0.35%	18.2%	2.32%	0.55%	23.6%
EURUSD	1.16%	1.05%	90.3%	1.65%	1.74%	105.3%	2.32%	0.98%	42.3%	2.71%	0.40%	14.8%
GBPUSD	1.02%	0.73%	71.3%	1.46%	1.08%	74.2%	2.28%	0.55%	24.3%	2.79%	0.05%	1.7%
USDCAD	1.08%	0.56%	51.9%	1.60%	0.71%	44.7%	2.77%	0.28%	10.1%	3.59%	0.12%	3.2%
USDCHF	1.28%	1.13%	88.0%	1.86%	1.46%	78.8%	2.67%	0.17%	6.3%	3.15%	0.00%	0.0%
USDDKK	1.43%	0.98%	68.8%	2.09%	0.68%	32.6%	2.92%	0.43%	14.8%	3.39%	0.20%	5.8%
USDJPY	1.25%	1.55%	124.1%	1.78%	2.71%	152.2%	2.43%	2.06%	84.8%	2.87%	0.58%	20.3%
USDNOK	1.48%	0.91%	61.5%	2.15%	1.16%	54.1%	3.43%	0.42%	12.1%	4.09%	0.03%	0.6%
USDSEK	1.49%	1.26%	84.4%	2.16%	1.88%	87.0%	3.50%	1.45%	41.5%	4.27%	0.55%	12.8%

TABLE A.69   Payoff/premium ratios for 25-delta G10 calls averaged over all currency pairs

Tenor	Ratio
1W	68.2%
1M	79.0%
3M	78.7%
6M	83.9%
12M	86.9%
2Y	60.5%
3Y	42.4%

TABLE A.70   Payoff/premium ratios for 25-delta EM calls (1W–3M tenors)

	1W			1M			3M		
	Premium	Payoff	Ratio	Premium	Payoff	Ratio	Premium	Payoff	Ratio
EURCZK	0.21%	0.09%	43.3%	0.38%	0.15%	40.1%	0.67%	0.23%	34.3%
EURHUF	0.32%	0.15%	44.9%	0.61%	0.26%	42.5%	1.11%	0.43%	38.5%
EURPLN				0.57%	0.29%	50.8%	1.01%	0.68%	67.8%
USDARS				0.78%	0.03%	3.6%	1.66%	0.05%	3.2%
USDBRL	0.44%	0.24%	53.2%	0.78%	0.52%	66.6%	1.34%	1.01%	75.5%
USDCLP				0.63%	0.39%	61.1%	1.15%	0.75%	65.2%
USDCOP				0.85%	0.37%	43.8%	1.47%	0.70%	47.7%
USDCZK	0.41%	0.25%	61.0%	0.75%	0.58%	77.7%	1.26%	0.85%	67.3%
USDHKD	0.04%	0.01%	18.3%	0.05%	0.02%	33.0%	0.09%	0.04%	48.1%
USDIDR				0.86%	0.27%	31.6%	1.67%	0.65%	39.1%
USDILS				0.45%	0.24%	52.8%	0.77%	0.33%	42.9%
USDINR				0.47%	0.32%	68.1%	0.88%	0.74%	85.0%
USDKRW	0.33%	0.15%	44.9%	0.55%	0.36%	65.2%	1.00%	0.71%	71.2%
USDMXN	0.33%	0.17%	49.8%	0.61%	0.30%	49.1%	1.09%	0.60%	54.6%
USDPHP				0.61%	0.14%	22.5%	1.15%	0.28%	24.3%
USDPLN				0.76%	0.48%	63.0%	1.37%	0.83%	60.0%
USDSGD	0.18%	0.08%	43.7%	0.30%	0.18%	60.9%	0.55%	0.31%	56.3%
USDTRY	0.34%	0.23%	68.7%	0.72%	0.47%	65.2%	1.32%	0.92%	70.0%
USDTWD	0.17%	0.05%	30.5%	0.26%	0.21%	80.7%	0.47%	0.47%	100.3%
USDZAR	0.47%	0.31%	66.8%	0.89%	0.62%	69.3%	1.56%	1.20%	77.3%

TABLE A.71   Payoff/premium ratios for 25-delta EM calls (6M–12M tenors)

	6M			12M		
	Premium	**Payoff**	**Ratio**	**Premium**	**Payoff**	**Ratio**
EURCZK	0.94%	0.30%	31.5%	1.32%	0.22%	16.6%
EURHUF	1.59%	0.68%	42.8%	2.28%	0.26%	11.3%
EURPLN	1.43%	1.06%	74.2%	2.04%	1.43%	70.3%
USDARS	2.56%	0.03%	1.2%	4.09%	0.02%	0.4%
USDBRL	1.95%	1.26%	64.4%	2.94%	0.76%	25.7%
USDCLP	1.64%	0.98%	60.0%	2.35%	1.07%	45.7%
USDCOP	2.08%	0.94%	45.3%	3.19%	0.51%	15.9%
USDCZK	1.77%	1.26%	71.4%	2.48%	1.07%	43.4%
USDHKD	0.15%	0.06%	38.8%	0.30%	0.06%	21.5%
USDIDR	2.54%	1.36%	53.5%	4.01%	1.22%	30.4%
USDILS	1.08%	0.53%	48.6%	1.53%	0.48%	31.4%
USDINR	1.30%	1.00%	77.0%	2.78%	0.84%	30.4%
USDKRW	1.41%	1.32%	93.6%	2.03%	2.23%	109.8%
USDMXN	1.61%	0.95%	59.0%	2.39%	1.11%	46.5%
USDPHP	1.70%	0.49%	28.8%	2.54%	0.61%	24.2%
USDPLN	1.96%	1.34%	68.3%	2.83%	1.56%	55.1%
USDSGD	0.80%	0.34%	42.5%	1.16%	0.29%	24.5%
USDTRY	1.97%	0.96%	48.5%	3.02%	0.47%	15.7%
USDTWD	0.71%	0.74%	104.7%	1.06%	0.91%	85.4%
USDZAR	2.22%	1.73%	77.9%	3.20%	2.07%	64.6%

TABLE A.72   Payoff/premium ratios for 25-delta EM calls averaged over all currency pairs

Tenor	Ratio
1W	47.7%
1M	52.4%
3M	56.4%
6M	56.6%
12M	38.4%

Payoff/Premium Ratios for G10 and EM 10-Delta Puts (All Data)

TABLE A.73   Payoff/premium ratios for 10-delta G10 puts (1W–3M tenors)

	1W			1M			3M		
	Premium	**Payoff**	**Ratio**	**Premium**	**Payoff**	**Ratio**	**Premium**	**Payoff**	**Ratio**
AUDUSD	0.10%	0.08%	76.3%	0.19%	0.19%	104.3%	0.34%	0.53%	156.8%
EURAUD	0.10%	0.05%	55.7%	0.16%	0.11%	69.4%	0.28%	0.22%	79.1%
EURCHF	0.05%	0.03%	54.8%	0.09%	0.06%	59.1%	0.16%	0.11%	67.9%
EURGBP	0.07%	0.04%	55.7%	0.12%	0.03%	27.8%	0.22%	0.03%	14.2%
EURJPY	0.10%	0.07%	69.7%	0.20%	0.13%	62.5%	0.36%	0.33%	90.5%
EURNOK	0.06%	0.03%	39.2%	0.11%	0.05%	42.0%	0.19%	0.07%	36.4%
EURUSD	0.08%	0.05%	60.1%	0.16%	0.10%	63.1%	0.30%	0.23%	77.0%
GBPUSD	0.08%	0.04%	53.4%	0.14%	0.11%	73.8%	0.26%	0.23%	87.3%
USDCAD	0.07%	0.04%	54.1%	0.13%	0.09%	70.4%	0.23%	0.25%	109.3%
USDCHF	0.09%	0.07%	79.2%	0.16%	0.19%	119.7%	0.29%	0.28%	96.6%
USDDKK	0.10%	0.05%	47.3%	0.17%	0.11%	62.4%	0.29%	0.09%	29.6%
USDJPY	0.09%	0.05%	57.8%	0.19%	0.13%	70.7%	0.33%	0.22%	68.6%
USDNOK	0.11%	0.07%	58.2%	0.18%	0.18%	99.4%	0.32%	0.33%	106.0%
USDSEK	0.11%	0.07%	63.3%	0.18%	0.15%	83.0%	0.32%	0.20%	63.6%

TABLE A.74 Payoff/premium ratios for 10-delta G10 puts (6M–3Y tenors)

	6M			12M			2Y			3Y		
	Premium	Payoff	Ratio	Premium	Payoff	Ratio	Premium	Payoff	Ratio	Premium	Payoff	Ratio
AUDUSD	0.50%	0.83%	167.7%	0.76%	1.18%	156.7%	1.12%	0.38%	34.0%	1.32%	0.02%	1.1%
EURAUD	0.39%	0.21%	53.8%	0.55%	0.74%	134.2%	0.76%	2.25%	294.2%	0.83%	5.69%	682.8%
EURCHF	0.24%	0.12%	51.1%	0.35%	0.26%	72.7%	0.57%	1.13%	199.3%	0.56%	2.25%	403.5%
EURGBP	0.31%	0.04%	11.3%	0.46%	0.10%	23.0%	0.69%	0.00%	0.0%	0.85%	0.00%	0.0%
EURJPY	0.54%	0.52%	97.7%	0.76%	0.27%	35.2%	1.27%	0.41%	32.5%	1.69%	0.46%	27.1%
EURNOK	0.27%	0.10%	35.8%	0.38%	0.21%	55.8%	0.56%	0.01%	1.7%	0.68%	0.07%	10.4%
EURUSD	0.44%	0.34%	76.6%	0.66%	0.43%	65.4%	1.01%	0.04%	4.0%	1.16%	0.01%	0.4%
GBPUSD	0.39%	0.48%	122.8%	0.58%	0.63%	109.9%	1.01%	2.08%	205.8%	1.25%	1.53%	122.0%
USDCAD	0.33%	0.47%	144.5%	0.50%	0.71%	142.6%	0.81%	0.10%	12.1%	1.05%	0.00%	0.0%
USDCHF	0.41%	0.29%	70.2%	0.59%	0.58%	98.5%	0.87%	0.10%	11.2%	1.02%	0.08%	7.5%
USDDKK	0.42%	0.14%	32.5%	0.60%	0.34%	56.4%	0.84%	0.20%	24.2%	0.99%	0.04%	3.7%
USDJPY	0.46%	0.16%	35.7%	0.65%	0.01%	1.7%	1.06%	0.10%	9.6%	1.30%	0.00%	0.2%
USDNOK	0.45%	0.45%	102.0%	0.63%	1.06%	167.7%	0.99%	0.08%	8.5%	1.19%	0.01%	1.2%
USDSEK	0.45%	0.27%	59.9%	0.64%	0.69%	107.3%	1.01%	0.08%	7.7%	1.22%	0.00%	0.0%

TABLE A.75   Payoff/premium ratios for 10-delta
G10 puts averaged over all currency pairs

Tenor	Ratio
1W	58.9%
1M	72.0%
3M	77.3%
6M	75.8%
12M	87.7%
2Y	60.3%
3Y	90.0%

TABLE A.76   Payoff/premium ratios for 10-delta EM puts (1W–3M tenors)

	1W			1M			3M		
	Premium	Payoff	Ratio	Premium	Payoff	Ratio	Premium	Payoff	Ratio
EURCZK	0.07%	0.04%	62.5%	0.12%	0.06%	52.6%	0.20%	0.13%	64.9%
EURHUF	0.09%	0.04%	49.1%	0.16%	0.06%	38.2%	0.27%	0.13%	47.2%
EURPLN				0.16%	0.05%	32.8%	0.27%	0.12%	45.9%
USDARS				0.30%	0.03%	11.6%	0.60%	0.09%	15.5%
USDBRL	0.12%	0.08%	66.5%	0.17%	0.23%	136.1%	0.37%	0.54%	144.7%
USDCLP				0.21%	0.13%	61.8%	0.37%	0.32%	87.9%
USDCOP				0.28%	0.18%	62.6%	0.48%	0.52%	108.2%
USDCZK	0.15%	0.08%	53.1%	0.25%	0.22%	89.9%	0.42%	0.33%	79.3%
USDHKD	0.02%	0.00%	0.7%	0.03%	0.00%	13.6%	0.06%	0.01%	10.5%
USDIDR				0.28%	0.15%	55.7%	0.50%	0.25%	50.6%
USDILS				0.15%	0.12%	79.0%	0.24%	0.29%	119.4%
USDINR				0.14%	0.17%	116.1%	0.25%	0.24%	94.6%
USDKRW	0.10%	0.04%	36.0%	0.16%	0.10%	62.6%	0.29%	0.23%	80.7%
USDMXN	0.10%	0.04%	39.4%	0.17%	0.07%	38.9%	0.30%	0.08%	26.3%
USDPHP				0.25%	0.09%	37.2%	0.47%	0.18%	38.9%
USDPLN				0.22%	0.21%	95.1%	0.38%	0.37%	98.5%
USDSGD	0.06%	0.02%	32.9%	0.10%	0.06%	65.6%	0.17%	0.07%	39.6%
USDTRY	0.10%	0.07%	70.7%	0.20%	0.20%	99.4%	0.35%	0.38%	109.2%
USDTWD	0.06%	0.02%	25.4%	0.09%	0.06%	72.4%	0.17%	0.12%	74.1%
USDZAR	0.15%	0.06%	40.0%	0.25%	0.15%	59.3%	0.43%	0.41%	96.1%

TABLE A.77 Payoff/premium ratios for 10-delta EM puts (6M–12M tenors)

	6M			12M		
	Premium	**Payoff**	**Ratio**	**Premium**	**Payoff**	**Ratio**
EURCZK	0.28%	0.35%	125.6%	0.39%	0.60%	156.2%
EURHUF	0.37%	0.21%	57.1%	0.51%	0.15%	29.8%
EURPLN	0.38%	0.22%	59.2%	0.52%	0.48%	92.3%
USDARS	0.91%	0.15%	16.5%	1.59%	0.12%	7.4%
USDBRL	0.53%	1.54%	292.5%	0.76%	3.84%	502.6%
USDCLP	0.53%	0.51%	96.8%	0.78%	0.53%	67.0%
USDCOP				1.00%	0.37%	36.8%
USDCZK	0.59%	0.75%	125.7%	0.86%	1.25%	145.4%
USDHKD	0.10%	0.00%	2.7%	0.21%	0.00%	0.0%
USDIDR	0.73%	0.73%	100.4%	1.01%	1.23%	121.9%
USDILS	0.33%	0.60%	180.5%	0.46%	1.02%	221.1%
USDINR	0.35%	0.42%	117.3%	0.64%	0.00%	0.0%
USDKRW	0.38%	0.31%	81.6%	0.53%	0.14%	25.5%
USDMXN	0.42%	0.08%	18.7%	0.61%	0.06%	10.0%
USDPHP	0.67%	0.26%	37.9%	1.05%	0.55%	52.0%
USDPLN	0.53%	0.81%	154.4%	0.72%	1.40%	192.4%
USDSGD	0.25%	0.10%	39.3%	0.36%	0.22%	60.4%
USDTRY	0.50%	0.76%	152.6%	0.73%	1.49%	204.7%
USDTWD	0.24%	0.13%	51.7%	0.36%	0.00%	0.8%
USDZAR	0.59%	0.83%	140.7%	0.84%	2.38%	283.1%

TABLE A.78 Payoff/premium ratios for 10-delta EM puts averaged over all currency pairs

Tenor	Ratio
1W	43.3%
1M	64.0%
3M	71.6%
6M	97.4%
12M	110.5%

Payoff/Premium Ratios for G10 and EM 10-Delta Calls
(All Data)

TABLE A.79   Payoff/premium ratios for 10-delta G10 calls (1W–3M tenors)

	1W			1M			3M		
	Premium	Payoff	Ratio	Premium	Payoff	Ratio	Premium	Payoff	Ratio
AUDUSD	0.11%	0.06%	55.9%	0.17%	0.14%	81.2%	0.29%	0.28%	93.6%
EURAUD	0.13%	0.08%	63.5%	0.20%	0.18%	91.7%	0.35%	0.33%	95.5%
EURCHF	0.07%	0.02%	31.6%	0.10%	0.04%	38.1%	0.17%	0.06%	33.3%
EURGBP	0.08%	0.04%	44.3%	0.14%	0.09%	63.3%	0.24%	0.21%	84.5%
EURJPY	0.12%	0.07%	57.8%	0.20%	0.17%	85.3%	0.34%	0.32%	94.7%
EURNOK	0.09%	0.05%	54.2%	0.14%	0.08%	56.1%	0.24%	0.18%	76.0%
EURUSD	0.09%	0.05%	54.9%	0.16%	0.14%	86.1%	0.28%	0.20%	72.5%
GBPUSD	0.09%	0.05%	52.9%	0.14%	0.10%	71.9%	0.25%	0.18%	72.6%
USDCAD	0.09%	0.03%	39.5%	0.15%	0.08%	51.3%	0.27%	0.14%	54.3%
USDCHF	0.10%	0.05%	49.9%	0.17%	0.11%	61.4%	0.31%	0.21%	68.6%
USDDKK	0.14%	0.04%	30.1%	0.22%	0.11%	47.6%	0.37%	0.23%	61.7%
USDJPY	0.10%	0.04%	41.7%	0.18%	0.12%	65.8%	0.31%	0.32%	101.1%
USDNOK	0.13%	0.07%	53.8%	0.21%	0.11%	51.7%	0.37%	0.26%	70.7%
USDSEK	0.13%	0.06%	45.5%	0.21%	0.11%	52.6%	0.37%	0.30%	80.8%

TABLE A.80 Payoff/premium ratios for 10-delta G10 calls (6M–3Y tenors)

	6M			12M			2Y			3Y		
	Premium	Payoff	Ratio	Premium	Payoff	Ratio	Premium	Payoff	Ratio	Premium	Payoff	Ratio
AUDUSD	0.41%	0.53%	128.8%	0.60%	1.13%	187.9%	0.85%	2.46%	289.4%	1.03%	2.68%	260.9%
EURAUD	0.50%	0.34%	68.3%	0.73%	0.16%	22.4%	1.02%	0.06%	6.3%	1.18%	0.00%	0.0%
EURCHF	0.23%	0.12%	50.7%	0.31%	0.28%	89.7%	0.48%	0.34%	69.7%	0.52%	0.01%	2.4%
EURGBP	0.35%	0.34%	97.7%	0.51%	0.61%	119.2%	0.84%	2.26%	268.8%	1.10%	2.65%	241.6%
EURJPY	0.49%	0.56%	114.4%	0.68%	0.91%	134.4%	1.11%	1.00%	90.7%	1.65%	0.00%	0.0%
EURNOK	0.33%	0.23%	69.3%	0.47%	0.16%	34.2%	0.76%	0.06%	7.5%	0.95%	0.06%	6.8%
EURUSD	0.40%	0.27%	66.8%	0.57%	0.61%	107.2%	0.83%	0.10%	12.5%	0.99%	0.00%	0.2%
GBPUSD	0.35%	0.18%	51.2%	0.51%	0.26%	50.8%	0.82%	0.02%	2.0%	1.02%	0.00%	0.0%
USDCAD	0.38%	0.26%	66.6%	0.59%	0.20%	34.3%	0.99%	0.00%	0.2%	1.31%	0.00%	0.0%
USDCHF	0.44%	0.34%	77.3%	0.63%	0.44%	69.5%	0.95%	0.00%	0.0%	1.12%	0.00%	0.0%
USDDKK	0.54%	0.31%	57.9%	0.77%	0.03%	4.3%	1.07%	0.01%	0.9%	1.23%	0.00%	0.1%
USDJPY	0.43%	0.58%	134.5%	0.59%	0.86%	145.7%	0.83%	0.27%	32.8%	0.98%	0.00%	0.0%
USDNOK	0.52%	0.42%	81.4%	0.75%	0.31%	41.8%	1.26%	0.00%	0.0%	1.49%	0.00%	0.0%
USDSEK	0.53%	0.55%	104.1%	0.75%	0.66%	87.3%	1.30%	0.28%	21.5%	1.62%	0.00%	0.2%

TABLE A.81 Payoff/premium ratios for 10-delta G10 calls averaged over all currency pairs

Tenor	Ratio
1W	48.3%
1M	64.6%
3M	75.7%
6M	83.5%
12M	80.6%
2Y	57.3%
3Y	36.6%

TABLE A.82 Payoff/premium ratios for 10-delta EM calls (1W–3M tenors)

	1W			1M			3M		
	Premium	Payoff	Ratio	Premium	Payoff	Ratio	Premium	Payoff	Ratio
EURCZK	0.09%	0.02%	25.3%	0.15%	0.03%	21.9%	0.27%	0.03%	12.3%
EURHUF	0.15%	0.04%	24.5%	0.25%	0.07%	26.4%	0.46%	0.07%	15.2%
EURPLN				0.23%	0.07%	31.2%	0.40%	0.26%	65.0%
USDARS				0.43%	0.00%	1.0%	0.89%	0.00%	0.4%
USDBRL	0.19%	0.08%	40.8%	0.30%	0.21%	68.3%	0.48%	0.52%	108.2%
USDCLP				0.26%	0.14%	54.8%	0.49%	0.29%	58.9%
USDCOP				0.39%	0.08%	20.9%	0.68%	0.28%	41.7%
USDCZK	0.20%	0.06%	29.4%	0.34%	0.18%	53.9%	0.55%	0.27%	49.0%
USDHKD	0.02%	0.00%	4.0%	0.03%	0.00%	12.3%	0.05%	0.02%	33.9%
USDIDR				0.46%	0.05%	10.7%	0.87%	0.32%	36.2%
USDILS				0.19%	0.06%	34.4%	0.32%	0.06%	17.6%
USDINR				0.20%	0.12%	58.6%	0.37%	0.26%	70.1%
USDKRW	0.15%	0.05%	33.9%	0.22%	0.14%	65.6%	0.41%	0.36%	89.0%
USDMXN	0.14%	0.05%	34.4%	0.24%	0.13%	53.3%	0.43%	0.34%	79.9%
USDPHP				0.29%	0.04%	13.6%	0.54%	0.06%	11.7%
USDPLN				0.29%	0.16%	54.4%	0.54%	0.33%	61.8%
USDSGD	0.08%	0.02%	24.6%	0.12%	0.06%	52.3%	0.22%	0.09%	40.9%
USDTRY	0.14%	0.08%	54.7%	0.28%	0.19%	68.9%	0.51%	0.32%	63.2%
USDTWD	0.08%	0.01%	13.8%	0.10%	0.07%	68.7%	0.19%	0.17%	90.1%
USDZAR	0.19%	0.12%	60.1%	0.35%	0.21%	61.6%	0.59%	0.53%	89.0%

TABLE A.83 Payoff/premium ratios for 10-delta EM calls (6M–12M tenors)

	6M			12M		
	Premium	**Payoff**	**Ratio**	**Premium**	**Payoff**	**Ratio**
EURCZK	0.38%	0.12%	31.9%	0.53%	0.04%	7.1%
EURHUF	0.66%	0.21%	30.9%	0.95%	0.00%	0.0%
EURPLN	0.57%	0.55%	97.0%	0.81%	0.77%	95.3%
USDARS	1.33%	0.00%	0.0%	2.08%	0.00%	0.0%
USDBRL	0.70%	0.62%	89.9%	1.04%	0.01%	0.9%
USDCLP	0.71%	0.48%	68.4%	1.04%	0.44%	42.0%
USDCOP				1.45%	0.01%	0.6%
USDCZK	0.75%	0.54%	71.7%	1.05%	0.22%	20.6%
USDHKD	0.08%	0.03%	37.1%	0.17%	0.03%	16.8%
USDIDR	1.32%	0.47%	35.3%	2.05%	0.46%	22.4%
USDILS	0.44%	0.11%	23.9%	0.62%	0.02%	3.6%
USDINR	0.55%	0.21%	37.4%	1.22%	0.02%	2.0%
USDKRW	0.56%	0.85%	150.4%	0.82%	1.50%	182.7%
USDMXN	0.63%	0.60%	94.7%	0.93%	0.53%	56.2%
USDPHP	0.77%	0.15%	19.4%	1.20%	0.09%	7.4%
USDPLN	0.76%	0.79%	103.9%	1.10%	0.90%	82.6%
USDSGD	0.32%	0.09%	27.9%	0.46%	0.04%	8.7%
USDTRY	0.76%	0.13%	17.3%	1.16%	0.00%	0.0%
USDTWD	0.28%	0.25%	88.5%	0.42%	0.34%	81.3%
USDZAR	0.85%	0.60%	70.4%	1.19%	0.83%	70.2%

TABLE A.84 Payoff/premium ratios for 10-delta EM calls averaged over all currency pairs

Tenor	Ratio
1W	31.4%
1M	41.6%
3M	51.7%
6M	57.7%
12M	35.0%

Hedging with Forwards vs Hedging with Options

TABLE A.85   Average cash flow in percent of notional for 1W hedges

	Long forward	ATMF call	25-delta call	Short forward	ATMF put	25-delta put
AUDUSD	0.07%	–0.03%	–0.04%	–0.07%	–0.10%	–0.06%
EURAUD	–0.09%	–0.11%	–0.09%	0.09%	–0.02%	–0.06%
EURCHF	–0.01%	–0.06%	–0.07%	0.01%	–0.05%	–0.04%
EURCZK	–0.04%	–0.12%	–0.12%	0.04%	–0.08%	–0.06%
EURGBP	0.00%	–0.06%	–0.07%	0.00%	–0.06%	–0.05%
EURHUF	–0.08%	–0.16%	–0.18%	0.08%	–0.09%	–0.06%
EURJPY	0.05%	–0.04%	–0.06%	–0.05%	–0.08%	–0.06%
EURNOK	–0.04%	–0.10%	–0.08%	0.04%	–0.06%	–0.07%
EURPLN						
EURUSD	0.01%	–0.05%	–0.06%	–0.01%	–0.06%	–0.06%
GBPUSD	0.01%	–0.06%	–0.06%	–0.01%	–0.06%	–0.06%
USDARS						
USDBRL	–0.24%	–0.25%	–0.21%	0.24%	–0.01%	–0.06%
USDCAD	–0.06%	–0.07%	–0.08%	0.06%	–0.02%	–0.03%
USDCHF	–0.04%	–0.07%	–0.08%	0.04%	–0.03%	–0.02%
USDCLP						
USDCOP						
USDCZK	–0.04%	–0.09%	–0.16%	0.04%	–0.05%	–0.07%
USDDKK	–0.02%	–0.12%	–0.14%	0.02%	–0.10%	–0.09%
USDHKD	0.01%	–0.03%	–0.03%	–0.01%	–0.04%	–0.03%
USDIDR						
USDILS						
USDINR						
USDJPY	0.01%	–0.11%	–0.10%	–0.01%	–0.12%	–0.09%
USDKRW	–0.07%	–0.18%	–0.18%	0.07%	–0.11%	–0.10%
USDMXN	–0.04%	–0.16%	–0.17%	0.04%	–0.13%	–0.12%
USDNOK	–0.07%	–0.11%	–0.09%	0.07%	–0.04%	–0.06%
USDPHP						
USDPLN						
USDSEK	–0.04%	–0.11%	–0.11%	0.04%	–0.07%	–0.07%
USDSGD	–0.05%	–0.11%	–0.10%	0.05%	–0.06%	–0.07%
USDTRY	–0.15%	–0.10%	–0.11%	0.15%	0.05%	0.00%
USDTWD	0.01%	–0.12%	–0.12%	–0.01%	–0.13%	–0.08%
USDZAR	–0.09%	–0.19%	–0.16%	0.09%	–0.11%	–0.13%
G10 average	–0.01%	–0.08%	–0.08%	0.01%	–0.06%	–0.06%
EM average	–0.07%	–0.14%	–0.14%	0.07%	–0.07%	–0.07%

TABLE A.86 Average cash flow in percent of notional for 1M hedges

	Long forward	ATMF call	25-delta call	Short forward	ATMF put	25-delta put
AUDUSD	0.21%	0.14%	0.02%	−0.21%	−0.07%	−0.02%
EURAUD	−0.34%	−0.20%	−0.11%	0.34%	0.13%	0.02%
EURCHF	−0.03%	−0.08%	−0.08%	0.03%	−0.05%	−0.04%
EURCZK	−0.20%	−0.28%	−0.23%	0.20%	−0.08%	−0.10%
EURGBP	−0.02%	−0.13%	−0.08%	0.02%	−0.10%	−0.13%
EURHUF	−0.31%	−0.42%	−0.35%	0.31%	−0.12%	−0.13%
EURJPY	0.19%	0.02%	−0.03%	−0.19%	−0.17%	−0.15%
EURNOK	−0.17%	−0.20%	−0.12%	0.17%	−0.03%	−0.08%
EURPLN	−0.14%	−0.30%	−0.28%	0.14%	−0.16%	−0.16%
EURUSD	0.05%	−0.01%	0.00%	−0.05%	−0.06%	−0.10%
GBPUSD	0.10%	−0.02%	−0.05%	−0.10%	−0.13%	−0.09%
USDARS	−0.78%	−1.19%	−0.76%	0.78%	−0.42%	−0.50%
USDBRL	−0.98%	−0.52%	−0.26%	0.98%	0.44%	0.15%
USDCAD	−0.28%	−0.28%	−0.18%	0.28%	−0.01%	−0.05%
USDCHF	−0.07%	−0.03%	−0.08%	0.07%	0.04%	0.05%
USDCLP	−0.26%	−0.31%	−0.25%	0.26%	−0.06%	−0.11%
USDCOP	−0.62%	−0.58%	−0.48%	0.62%	0.02%	−0.10%
USDCZK	−0.25%	−0.10%	−0.17%	0.25%	0.13%	0.03%
USDDKK	−0.10%	−0.14%	−0.17%	0.10%	−0.06%	−0.08%
USDHKD	0.03%	−0.03%	−0.03%	−0.03%	−0.06%	−0.05%
USDIDR	−0.34%	−0.61%	−0.59%	0.34%	−0.28%	−0.23%
USDILS	−0.40%	−0.25%	−0.21%	0.40%	0.14%	0.03%
USDINR	−0.21%	−0.18%	−0.15%	0.21%	0.02%	0.00%
USDJPY	0.18%	0.01%	−0.05%	−0.18%	−0.17%	−0.13%
USDKRW	−0.26%	−0.28%	−0.19%	0.26%	−0.03%	−0.08%
USDMXN	−0.24%	−0.37%	−0.31%	0.24%	−0.14%	−0.13%
USDNOK	−0.33%	−0.32%	−0.22%	0.33%	0.00%	−0.02%
USDPHP	−0.32%	−0.68%	−0.48%	0.32%	−0.36%	−0.29%
USDPLN	−0.66%	−0.42%	−0.28%	0.66%	0.23%	0.06%
USDSEK	−0.18%	−0.21%	−0.19%	0.18%	−0.03%	−0.04%
USDSGD	−0.16%	−0.15%	−0.12%	0.16%	0.01%	−0.04%
USDTRY	−0.71%	−0.40%	−0.25%	0.71%	0.30%	0.08%
USDTWD	0.05%	−0.04%	−0.05%	−0.05%	−0.09%	−0.06%
USDZAR	−0.42%	−0.38%	−0.27%	0.42%	0.02%	−0.10%
G10 average	−0.05%	−0.10%	−0.09%	0.05%	−0.05%	−0.06%
EM average	−0.31%	−0.27%	−0.20%	0.31%	0.03%	−0.04%

TABLE A.87 Average cash flow in percent of notional for 3M hedges

	Long forward	ATMF call	25-delta call	Short forward	ATMF put	25-delta put
AUDUSD	0.57%	0.34%	0.09%	−0.57%	−0.19%	0.07%
EURAUD	−1.33%	−0.72%	−0.28%	1.33%	0.56%	0.10%
EURCHF	−0.14%	−0.24%	−0.21%	0.14%	−0.10%	−0.06%
EURCZK	−0.64%	−0.61%	−0.44%	0.64%	0.01%	−0.09%
EURGBP	0.02%	−0.26%	−0.13%	−0.02%	−0.26%	−0.35%
EURHUF	−1.01%	−0.86%	−0.68%	1.01%	0.12%	−0.12%
EURJPY	0.46%	0.17%	0.01%	−0.46%	−0.30%	−0.15%
EURNOK	−0.50%	−0.46%	−0.20%	0.50%	0.01%	−0.16%
EURPLN	−0.52%	−0.49%	−0.32%	0.52%	0.01%	−0.15%
EURUSD	0.13%	0.02%	−0.04%	−0.13%	−0.13%	−0.09%
GBPUSD	0.20%	−0.15%	−0.13%	−0.20%	−0.35%	−0.21%
USDARS	−2.43%	−2.62%	−1.60%	2.43%	−0.29%	−0.85%
USDBRL	−3.17%	−1.17%	−0.33%	3.17%	1.92%	0.86%
USDCAD	−0.73%	−0.62%	−0.37%	0.73%	0.09%	0.01%
USDCHF	−0.11%	−0.08%	−0.12%	0.11%	0.01%	0.02%
USDCLP	−0.89%	−0.53%	−0.40%	0.89%	0.32%	0.03%
USDCOP	−1.80%	−1.15%	−0.77%	1.80%	0.59%	0.24%
USDCZK	−0.71%	−0.32%	−0.41%	0.71%	0.35%	0.09%
USDDKK	−0.25%	−0.43%	−0.29%	0.25%	−0.20%	−0.29%
USDHKD	0.09%	−0.05%	−0.05%	−0.09%	−0.13%	−0.10%
USDIDR	−1.00%	−1.29%	−1.02%	1.00%	−0.36%	−0.44%
USDILS	−1.15%	−0.57%	−0.44%	1.15%	0.56%	0.26%
USDINR	−0.41%	−0.23%	−0.13%	0.41%	0.16%	0.02%
USDJPY	0.49%	0.21%	0.07%	−0.49%	−0.30%	−0.18%
USDKRW	−0.63%	−0.62%	−0.29%	0.63%	−0.02%	−0.13%
USDMXN	−0.87%	−0.85%	−0.50%	0.87%	−0.01%	−0.32%
USDNOK	−0.94%	−0.68%	−0.41%	0.94%	0.24%	0.04%
USDPHP	−0.91%	−1.32%	−0.87%	0.91%	−0.42%	−0.53%
USDPLN	−1.66%	−0.88%	−0.55%	1.66%	0.76%	0.22%
USDSEK	−0.52%	−0.49%	−0.31%	0.52%	0.02%	−0.06%
USDSGD	−0.48%	−0.39%	−0.24%	0.48%	0.07%	−0.11%
USDTRY	−1.78%	−0.90%	−0.40%	1.78%	0.83%	0.27%
USDTWD	0.20%	0.07%	0.00%	−0.20%	−0.14%	−0.09%
USDZAR	−1.12%	−0.75%	−0.35%	1.12%	0.33%	0.05%
G10 average	−0.17%	−0.22%	−0.16%	0.17%	−0.07%	−0.09%
EM average	−0.92%	−0.59%	−0.33%	0.92%	0.30%	0.03%

TABLE A.88   Average cash flow in percent of notional for 6M hedges

	Long forward	ATMF call	25-delta call	Short forward	ATMF put	25-delta put
AUDUSD	0.98%	0.96%	0.49%	–0.98%	–0.05%	0.31%
EURAUD	–2.58%	–0.99%	–0.36%	2.58%	1.49%	0.33%
EURCHF	–0.28%	–0.34%	–0.27%	0.28%	–0.07%	–0.10%
EURCZK	–1.36%	–1.04%	–0.64%	1.36%	0.29%	0.02%
EURGBP	0.12%	–0.41%	–0.19%	–0.12%	–0.49%	–0.56%
EURHUF	–1.88%	–1.46%	–0.91%	1.88%	0.37%	–0.05%
EURJPY	0.85%	0.53%	0.23%	–0.85%	–0.36%	–0.12%
EURNOK	–0.93%	–0.77%	–0.30%	0.93%	0.14%	–0.25%
EURPLN	–1.04%	–0.71%	–0.37%	1.04%	0.33%	–0.04%
EURUSD	0.30%	0.17%	–0.11%	–0.30%	–0.15%	–0.12%
GBPUSD	0.26%	–0.14%	–0.29%	–0.26%	–0.41%	–0.14%
USDARS	–4.42%	–4.24%	–2.53%	4.42%	–0.03%	–1.22%
USDBRL	–6.54%	–1.72%	–0.70%	6.54%	4.68%	2.68%
USDCAD	–1.51%	–0.95%	–0.52%	1.51%	0.53%	0.19%
USDCHF	–0.22%	–0.19%	–0.15%	0.22%	0.04%	–0.06%
USDCLP	–1.77%	–1.05%	–0.66%	1.77%	0.66%	0.17%
USDCOP	–3.55%	–2.00%	–1.14%	3.55%	1.44%	0.54%
USDCZK	–1.50%	–0.64%	–0.51%	1.50%	0.78%	0.44%
USDDKK	–0.57%	–0.54%	–0.45%	0.57%	0.03%	–0.37%
USDHKD	0.14%	–0.11%	–0.09%	–0.14%	–0.26%	–0.18%
USDIDR	–2.05%	–1.51%	–1.18%	2.05%	0.42%	–0.06%
USDILS	–2.29%	–0.87%	–0.56%	2.29%	1.41%	0.79%
USDINR	–0.50%	–0.30%	–0.30%	0.50%	0.19%	–0.01%
USDJPY	0.94%	0.50%	0.30%	–0.94%	–0.47%	–0.41%
USDKRW	–1.15%	–0.80%	–0.09%	1.15%	0.36%	–0.15%
USDMXN	–1.76%	–1.58%	–0.66%	1.76%	0.14%	–0.49%
USDNOK	–1.87%	–1.08%	–0.57%	1.87%	0.74%	0.19%
USDPHP	–1.88%	–2.19%	–1.21%	1.88%	–0.33%	–0.70%
USDPLN	–3.29%	–1.67%	–0.62%	3.29%	1.63%	0.59%
USDSEK	–1.04%	–0.58%	–0.23%	1.04%	0.44%	0.04%
USDSGD	–1.00%	–0.75%	–0.46%	1.00%	0.22%	–0.09%
USDTRY	–3.78%	–1.71%	–1.01%	3.78%	1.97%	0.86%
USDTWD	0.44%	0.13%	0.03%	–0.44%	–0.33%	–0.18%
USDZAR	–2.23%	–0.71%	–0.49%	2.23%	1.41%	0.71%
G10 average	–0.35%	–0.23%	–0.16%	0.35%	0.10%	–0.06%
EM average	–1.87%	–0.95%	–0.50%	1.87%	0.87%	0.32%

TABLE A.89 Average cash flow in percent of notional for 12M hedges

	Long forward	ATMF call	25-delta call	Short forward	ATMF put	25-delta put
AUDUSD	2.13%	2.09%	1.15%	–2.13%	0.06%	0.44%
EURAUD	–5.97%	–2.21%	–1.12%	5.97%	3.61%	1.63%
EURCHF	–0.70%	–0.39%	–0.16%	0.70%	0.28%	0.05%
EURCZK	–2.72%	–1.61%	–1.10%	2.72%	1.06%	0.38%
EURGBP	0.44%	–0.48%	–0.11%	–0.44%	–0.91%	–0.86%
EURHUF	–3.02%	–2.82%	–2.03%	3.02%	0.13%	–0.20%
EURJPY	2.11%	1.69%	0.92%	–2.11%	–0.48%	–0.45%
EURNOK	–2.06%	–1.19%	–0.54%	2.06%	0.84%	–0.13%
EURPLN	–2.29%	–1.15%	–0.61%	2.29%	1.10%	0.31%
EURUSD	0.71%	0.31%	0.09%	–0.71%	–0.44%	–0.33%
GBPUSD	0.36%	–0.40%	–0.38%	–0.36%	–0.79%	–0.27%
USDARS	–7.42%	–7.01%	–4.08%	7.42%	0.16%	–1.97%
USDBRL	–13.82%	–3.51%	–2.19%	13.82%	10.04%	6.46%
USDCAD	–3.12%	–1.76%	–0.88%	3.12%	1.30%	0.49%
USDCHF	–0.84%	–0.80%	–0.39%	0.84%	0.02%	–0.09%
USDCLP	–3.84%	–2.62%	–1.27%	3.84%	1.15%	0.18%
USDCOP	–5.81%	–4.71%	–2.68%	5.81%	0.93%	–0.52%
USDCZK	–2.87%	–1.93%	–1.40%	2.87%	0.82%	0.55%
USDDKK	–1.19%	–1.61%	–1.41%	1.19%	–0.45%	–0.45%
USDHKD	0.19%	–0.34%	–0.24%	–0.19%	–0.54%	–0.38%
USDIDR	–4.83%	–3.30%	–2.79%	4.83%	1.36%	0.43%
USDILS	–4.48%	–1.69%	–1.05%	4.48%	2.80%	1.50%
USDINR	0.02%	–1.61%	–1.93%	–0.02%	–1.71%	–1.46%
USDJPY	1.71%	0.81%	0.93%	–1.71%	–0.93%	–1.18%
USDKRW	–2.04%	–1.02%	0.20%	2.04%	0.93%	–0.29%
USDMXN	–3.55%	–2.66%	–1.28%	3.55%	0.82%	–0.60%
USDNOK	–3.96%	–2.11%	–0.99%	3.96%	1.78%	0.81%
USDPHP	–4.04%	–3.37%	–1.93%	4.04%	0.63%	–0.59%
USDPLN	–5.84%	–2.78%	–1.27%	5.84%	2.99%	1.40%
USDSEK	–2.38%	–1.02%	–0.28%	2.38%	1.31%	0.42%
USDSGD	–2.14%	–1.61%	–0.88%	2.14%	0.49%	–0.12%
USDTRY	–8.05%	–3.69%	–2.55%	8.05%	4.22%	2.20%
USDTWD	0.92%	0.03%	–0.15%	–0.92%	–0.90%	–0.69%
USDZAR	–4.87%	–1.06%	–1.13%	4.87%	3.68%	2.72%
G10 average	–0.82%	–0.45%	–0.20%	0.82%	0.34%	0.02%
EM average	–3.82%	–1.84%	–1.16%	3.82%	1.89%	0.91%

Glossary

American option   An option that can be exercised at any point in its life up to and including the expiry date for delivery spot value, i.e. the value of the option will be delivered to the owner shortly after the point of exercise. To have any value to exercise early the option must be deep in-the-money and there must be a positive funding value of the currency balances sitting on account.

Arbitrage   The possibility of making a risk-free profit after transaction costs. For example, by taking advantage of mispricing across financial markets. In FX, simple examples would be the triangulation of spot rates or forward rates, making a synthetic EURJPY rate from EURUSD and USDJPY to trade against the actual market. But this does not extend to FX options due to the asymmetric payoff.

ATM option/at-the-money delta neutral straddle option   An option whose strike rate gives a delta neutral straddle. ATM may be confused with ATMF or ATMS (see ATMF option).

ATMF option/at-the-money-forward option   An option whose strike rate is the forward rate for that expiry date. Sometimes referred to as an ATM option but this is ambiguous as it may be confused with an at-the-money delta neutral straddle option (see ATM option) or even an at-the-money-spot option (see ATMS option).

ATMS option/at-the-money-spot option   An option whose strike rate is the current spot rate. Sometimes referred to as an ATM option but this is ambiguous as it may be confused with an at-the-money delta neutral straddle option or even an at-the-money-spot option (see ATMF option).

Balance sheet   A major financial statement that presents a company's financial position at some point in time. The major components of the balance sheet report are assets, liabilities and shareholders' equity.

Base currency   The first currency listed in a currency exchange rate. For example, EUR is the base currency in the EURUSD exchange rate. The exchange rate states the number of units of the quote currency that can be exchanged for one unit of base currency.

Bid-offer or bid-ask costs   The cost of trading arising from the spread between the offer (ask) price of a currency and the bid price. The difference reflects the profit that a trading desk can make from matching client trades. Bid-offer spreads tend to be wider for less liquid currencies.

Break-even point   For a purchased option, the break-even point refers to the spot rate at maturity that ensures that the payout of the option exactly compensates for the initial premium (cost) of the contract.

Brownian motion   The origin of the term Brownian motion is the observation of random motion of particles suspended in a fluid resulting from their collision with the moving atoms or molecules in the fluid. It is named after Robert Brown, who observed the jittery motion of pollen particles in liquid under a microscope in 1827. These days it is often used to refer to the mathematical process which describes such movements, and is also one of the underlying models used to describe asset price movements. The theory, which explains the movements and how far a particle is likely to move away from its starting point in a given time, was published by Einstein in 1905, though, interestingly, a similar model appeared in the PhD thesis of Louis Bachelier in 1901 to explain the stock market.

Butterfly/butterfly spread   A butterfly option strategy involves buying an ATM straddle and selling call and put options of equal delta. A long butterfly strategy stands to make a limited profit if the spot rate at expiry is close to the straddle strike. The butterfly spread is sometimes used to gauge the curvature of the volatility smile.

Call option   A financial contract between a buyer and a seller. The buyer of the option has the right, but not the obligation, to buy an agreed quantity of an underlying asset at a certain time for a pre-agreed price. The buyer pays a fee to obtain this right (see premium).

Contingent claim   A claim that can be made only if some pre-specified outcome arises.

Correlation risk   When hedging option positions in less liquid currency pairs, a trader may use a highly correlated currency pair in order to reduce hedging costs. The risk of course is that correlations change suddenly and unexpectedly, leaving the derivative position unhedged.

Covered option   A combination of option and underlying positions. The option notional is offset by an equal and opposite position in the underlying security. For example, the writer of a call option may hold the underlying and sell an OTM option in an effort to enhance returns. In the case of the option being exercised the underlying can be delivered.

Credit   From the Latin *credere*, 'to believe'. In entering a derivative transaction, one runs the risk that the counterparty will default on future payments. This risk is described as credit risk and must be priced accordingly.

Delta   Delta is the rate of change of an option's value with respect to changes in the underlying asset's price. For currency options, the underlying is an exchange rate and thus the price of one unit of a currency in another currency.

Delta-neutral   A portfolio consisting of positions with offsetting positive and negative deltas so that the overall delta is zero. A delta-neutral straddle consists of long/short put and call option positions with equal and opposite deltas.

Derivative   A financial product whose value is derived from, but not the same as, the value of an underlying market rate which it references. The relationship between the two can be simple or complex.

Desk position   When a trading desk has a 'position', it has an overall sensitivity to market moves, i.e. it is not neutral. There is a consensus on the desk that the market will move in a certain way, so the aggregated desk portfolio has a sensitivity which will mean that the desk will make money if this happens, or conversely could lose money if the market moves in a different way. The position can be made of many small aggregated trades or a single large one.

Developed markets   For the purpose of investing, a country that has an advanced economy and capital markets. The country will usually have a high GDP per capita and should allow foreign ownership of assets and the free movement of capital.

Domestic currency   See quote currency.

Drawdown   The decline in a financial time series from a local maximum to a subsequent minimum. If the entire history of the series is considered then the greatest drawdown observed may be described as the maximum drawdown.

Emerging markets (EM)   See also developed markets. For investment purposes an emerging market is usually considered to have an economy or financial markets that are less advanced than developed markets. Capital controls may exist and market institutions may be inefficient. Various colleagues of the authors are unanimous in saying that the one sure-fire identifier of an emerging market is the style of driving: EM countries treat junctions as a big game of 'chicken', even in sophisticated cities.

European option   An option that can only be exercised at expiry (see American option).

Exercise (of option)   To put into effect the right to buy (call option) or sell (put option) the underlying. The specifics will depend on the contract, but exercise may be automatic at expiry for in-the-money options.

Expiry   The final date of a trade, when conditions which may determine the final payoff may be met.

Foreign currency   See base currency.

Forward points   Relating to foreign exchange forward contracts, forward points are added to a spot rate in order to arrive at a forward rate. The forward points are determined based on the prevailing interest rates for the two currencies in question. Forward points are often specified in fractions of 1/10,000, so that +20 points would mean a forward rate 0.002 higher than the spot rate. However, this is not always true and one must know the market convention in order to scale the forward points correctly before adding to a spot rate.

Forward premium   Instead of paying for an option at the start of the contract, the premium settlement date is the same as the maturity of the contract. See spot premium.

Forward rate   The rate at which parties agree to exchange currencies at some future date. The rate is determined by the relative deposit rates for the two currencies in order to ensure that arbitrage opportunities are eliminated.

FX   Foreign exchange. The foreign exchange market is the market in which currencies are traded.

FX option   An option on a foreign exchange rate.

FX rate   The rate at which one currency may be exchanged for another.

FX spot rate   The rate at which a spot FX transaction settles. Spot contracts generally settle two business days after the trade date, though there are exceptions.

G10   A group originally of ten, now eleven, industrial nations (Belgium, Canada, France, Germany, Italy, Japan, the Netherlands, Sweden, Switzerland, the United Kingdom and the United States). In foreign exchange G10 is more generally used to refer to the currencies of these countries plus those of some other advanced nations, often Australia, New Zealand, Denmark and Norway.

Gamma   The rate of change of delta with respect to the underlying asset's price. A large gamma value will mean that a delta hedge will need to be adjusted more frequently as the price of the underlying moves.

Gamma trader   An options trader that trades volatility rather than directional or macro views. If the volatility looks low, options will be purchased and the trader will trade the positive gamma (adjust the delta as the market moves) so the profit outstrips the premium. If the volatility is too high, options will be sold and the trader will manage the negative gamma (adjust the delta as little as possible) to try to capture the premium.

Hedge   A trade which is done to cancel or reduce overall variation in value of another trade or set of trades or exposures. Thus, on a trading desk, a trade is 'hedged' when an opposing trade is done which means that the combination of both have little or no sensitivity to market movements. Ideally, a profit is also locked in. When a portfolio of options is considered, the situation can become more complex, with certain types of market movement being better hedged than others.

The concept extends to different institutions, who may want to do trades which hedge away their exposure to various market movements. In FX, a common situation arises where companies have income in currencies other than their home currency. In this case they may want to do trades to hedge away this exposure.

Hedge fund   An institution whose sole purpose is to solicit investments and use the money to place trades which garner a good return for their investors. Profit is the dominant driver for these firms, as they are usually paid as a percentage of the return delivered to their investors.

Hedger   An individual or institution whose motivation in placing a trade is preservation of value or reduction of overall volatility.

Inception   The start date of a trade.

Investor   An individual or institution whose motivation in placing a trade is generation of profit.

ITM (in-the-money) option   See also OTM option. An option that has a positive intrinsic value. For vanilla options:

Intrinsic value (call) = Max(0, Underlying price – Strike price)

Intrinsic value (put) = Max(0, Strike price – Underlying price)

Liquidity   The degree to which an asset or security can be bought or sold in the market. Liquid assets are characterised by a high level of trading activity.

Long   To be long of a financial instrument is to have bought it, to own it. Hence the phrases 'go long', 'I'm long of that', etc., and an awful lot of bad jokes. See also short.

LTCM (Long-Term Capital Management)   An American hedge fund which collapsed in 1998 with losses of about 4.6 billion USD. The loss followed several very successful years which led the fund to increase market leverage. Containing the subsequent crisis required intervention by the Federal Reserve.

Mark-to-market   To value a portfolio based on the current market prices of the constituents.

NDF (non-deliverable forward)   For currencies that are not freely convertible due to restrictions imposed by governing authorities, an offshore foreign exchange market often operates. A non-deliverable forward will be settled in a hard currency (e.g. USD or EUR). For example, an offshore investor may enter a non-deliverable forward in order to take a long position in Brazilian real versus the US dollar. At expiry the contract will be settled in USD at a rate determined by a pre-agreed fixing level.

NDO (non-deliverable option)   See NDF. An option that is settled in a hard currency rather than the underlying currency.

Notional/Notional amount   The amount that is used to calculate payments made under an option or forward contract. The notional does not change hands, but specifies, for example, the amount of currency that may be exchanged at a pre-determined option strike rate.

Option buyer   Pays an option seller for the right but not the obligation to buy/sell an asset at a pre-determined price at some date in the future.

Option replication   Reproducing the payoff structure of an option contract by actively trading related instruments such as forward contracts.

Option seller   Receives payment from an option buyer and in exchange agrees to sell/buy an asset at a pre-determined price at some date in the future if the buyer so wishes.

OTC (over-the-counter) market   A market in which trading is done directly between two parties rather than via an exchange. Prices may not be publicly available and credit considerations are more relevant. May offer greater flexibility regarding size and expiry dates etc.

OTM (out-of-the-money) option   See also ITM option. An option that has no intrinsic value. For a vanilla option:

Intrinsic value (call) = Max(0, Underlying price – Strike price)

Intrinsic value (put) = Max(0, Strike price – Underlying price)

Outright/outright forward   The rate at which currencies may be exchanged on some future date. The outright forward rate is constructed by adding forward points to the spot rate.

P/L   Profit and loss. The gain or loss accrued on trading assets.

Payoff   The remaining intrinsic value of an option at expiry. Will be paid to the buyer of an option by the seller. May be zero if the option expires out of the money.

Payoff (call) = Max(0, Underlying price – Strike price)

Payoff (put) = Max(0, Strike price – Underlying price)

Peg (currencies)   The management of a currency so that the conversion rate into another currency (or a precious metal such as gold) is controlled; a formal peg keeps the rate constant, a sliding peg allows a slow creep of the exchange rate. Other ways to manage a currency are to insert a floor or a cap on the exchange rate, or to tolerate trading only within a pre-defined band.

Pip   A unit of change in an exchange rate. For EURUSD, for example, prices are quoted to four decimal places and a pip corresponds to a one-digit change in the fourth decimal place.

Position   The amount of a financial asset or currency held by a trader. Assuming no initial holdings, buying an asset results in a 'long' position and selling an asset results in a 'short' position.

Premium   The price of an option contract. A buyer will need to pay a premium to the seller (writer) of an option.

Pricing   The process of discovering the price of a contract using no-arbitrage constraints and valuation models. The price so discovered will be consistent with whatever assumptions about future market movements underlie the models.

Put option   An option to sell a financial variable, like an equity share, an index or a foreign exchange rate.

Quote currency   The second currency listed in a currency exchange rate. For example, USD is the quote currency in the EURUSD exchange rate. The exchange rate states the number of units of the quote currency that can be exchanged for one unit of base currency.

Rho   The sensitivity of an option or option portfolio to changes in interest rates. For currency options there are two exposures relating to the rates for the base and quote currencies.

Risk management   Assessing and protecting against risks to the value of a portfolio of securities. Risks may arise due to sensitivities to market movements and the passage of time, as well as due to concerns over creditworthiness of counterparties etc.

Risk reversal   A long risk reversal strategy comprises long call option and short put option positions. The spread between the implied volatilities of the components can be used as a measure of volatility skew and is often quoted in the market.

Secondary market   The market in previously issued financial instruments.

Settlement   A business process which involves the delivery of a security, usually coinciding with payment. The price at which the security is exchanged is typically determined several days in advance.

Short   To be short of a financial instrument is to have sold it, to owe its value to someone else. Hence the phrases 'go short', 'I want to short that', etc. See also long.

Short squeeze If a currency moves against widely held positions, some speculators may be forced to unwind their bets, adding momentum to the development. If the trend continues, more and more market participants may be 'squeezed' out of positions, usually at a loss.

Skew The volatility skew reflects the difference in implied volatility for options of different strike prices. Several factors contribute to this phenomenon and some may be market specific. For example, in equity markets put options may have higher volatility (be more costly) than comparable call options, but the opposite may be true for electricity markets where price spikes rather than collapsing markets are of the greatest concern. The fact that financial market returns tend to have fatter tails than assumed under the Black-Scholes-Merton pricing model also plays a role in the differing implied volatilities for different strike prices.

Spot premium The option premium is exchanged at the start of the contract term, subject to the usual spot FX settlement convention. See also forward premium.

Stop-loss Usually in relation to an order left in an automated system or with a broker. A stop-loss order will be executed if a pre-defined level is reached and may be used to manage risk relating to market moves.

Straddle option A combination of put and call options with the same strike rate and expiry date.

Strike The fixed price at which the owner of an option can buy (call option) or sell (put option) the underlying asset upon exercise.

Tenor The time period between inception and expiry of a trade. Usually quoted as 1W, 1M, 12M, 2Y etc.

Term structure The structure formed by considering financial variables for instruments of varying tenor. May refer to, for example, implied volatilities for options of different tenors or interest rates for different terms.

Theta The rate of change of an option's value with respect to the passage of time.

Underlying Financial derivatives are so called due to the fact that their values are derived from an underlying rate, index or even another derivative. For FX options, the underlying asset in question is a spot exchange rate between two currencies.

Valuation The process of determining what a financial asset is worth. Various schemes are possible, especially in relation to financial accounting, but for FX options valuation is usually performed by re-pricing an instrument using present market data (marking to market).

Value spot For largely historical reasons, foreign exchange transactions usually involve the exchange of funds happening at the spot date at the earliest. The spot date is typically a couple of business days in the future, but can vary from market to market. Longer periods from trade to exchange of currencies are possible too and these are known as forward contracts (see forward rate).

Vanilla/Vanilla options Vanilla is used in the financial world to convey that an instrument or trade is of the most basic or standard type. For FX options this typically means simple put or call options or combinations thereof. Once sophisticated features such as barriers are introduced, options are often referred to as 'exotics'.

Vega The rate of change of an option's value with respect to changes in implied volatility.

Volatility (market, historical, implied) The standard deviation of changes in market rates. May be calculated for different periods and for different pricing frequencies and is often annualised. Historical volatility is based on actual prices and implied volatility is an expectation of the volatility that will be realised over some future period.

Index